709.24

23.15

Documentary Monographs
in Modern Art

general editor: Paul Cummings

Moholy = Nagy

edited by

Richard Kostelanetz

Allen Lane The Penguin Press

Frontispiece: László Moholy-Nagy, Brighton, 1936. *Photo Serge Chermayeff.*

Copyright © Richard Kostelanetz, 1970

First published in the United States of America in 1970 by
Praeger Publishers, Inc., New York

Published in Great Britain in 1971 by
Allen Lane The Penguin Press
Vigo Street, London W1

ISBN 0 7139 0205 1

Printed in the United States of America

contents

list of illustrations

preface

The knowledge of historical continuity is one of man's most valuable stepping stones in his evolutionary progress. The purposeful accumulation of experiences can protect him from the repetition of mistakes, so that his creative power can gradually be saved for socially productive tasks.—L. Moholy-Nagy, *Vision in Motion* (1947)

I could not find any argument against the wide distribution of works of art, even if turned out by mass production. The collector's naive desire for the unique can hardly be justified. It hampers the cultural potential of mass consumption.—L. Moholy-Nagy, "Abstract of an Artist" (1944)

This is a documentary monograph about László Moholy-Nagy, one of the seminal figures in modern art; and not only because Moholy, as he preferred to be known, was a prolific and effective writer, but because he also was his own best commentator, the book contains numerous excerpts from his own prose, nearly all of which have been unavailable previously between hard covers, in addition to reproductions of his work in various media and, at times, critical remarks by others about this work. No other significant figure in modern art was as versatile as Moholy; and so rather than organize what follows into the conventional chronological structure, it seemed advisable to emphasize the diversity by dividing the pieces into eight standard—and yet, in context, rough—categories: painting, photography, design, sculpture-architecture, light machines, film, education, and social philosophy, although some essays could be put in one group as conveniently as in another. This scheme assumes that the entire book demonstrates Moholy's talent as one of the very best writers on modern art. The essays reprinted here were originally produced at various times, for various audiences, at various lengths, in any of three languages; so despite the inevitable repetitions of a teacher delivering the same lines time and again, the developments in Moholy's thinking on certain issues are clearly documented. The date of authorship accompanies each essay. The book opens with my own introduction to Moholy's life and work and closes with several comprehensive essays on his achievement and prophecies. The customary approximate chronology and a selected bibliography of both Moholy's writings and essays about him are also included. This monograph is less written than put together; but it is designed to be read from start to finish, as well as consulted for occasional reference. Moholy himself, so I like to believe, would have relished this book, which reproduces his work and ideas in a conveniently accessible spine-bound multiple.

Credit goes first of all to Sibyl Moholy-Nagy, the artist's widow, for lending me rare manuscripts and photographs, translating certain material from Moholy's idiomatic German, and granting me blanket permission to use it, and for her sustained and efficient interest in the project. In particular, I should like to thank her for aid in obtaining the following photographs: front cover, frontispiece, 7, 8, 27–33, 36, 39–48, 50–53, 60, 63–67, in addition (except where noted) to photographs of works in her collection. Lloyd C. Engelbrecht of the Library at the University of Illinois–Chicago Circle took me through the Moholy papers; and Jan van der Marck and Karin Rosenberg of the Museum of Contemporary Art in Chicago kindly provided many photographs and allowed me to use their chronology and bibliography as bases for my own lists. Engelbrecht also added several citations originally gathered for his forthcoming doctoral thesis on the School of Design. Carol Iannone generously helped wherever she could, and several writers, editors, and publishers deserve my thanks for permitting me to reprint materials they control. Final gratitude goes to Paul Cummings, as editor of this series, and to John Hochmann, Nancy Reynolds, Regina Cohen, and their associates at Praeger Publishers.

Grateful acknowledgment is made to the individuals and organizations who granted permission to reprint selections appearing in this book. All possible care has been taken to trace the ownership of every excerpt and reproduction included here and to make full acknowledgment of its use.

RICHARD KOSTELANETZ
May 14, 1970

chronology

1895   Born in Bacsbarsod, Hungary, July 20.

1913   Enrolled as law student in University of Budapest. Befriended by writers and musicians. Contributed to avantgarde magazines.

1914   Called into Austro-Hungarian army and sent to Russian war front.

1915   While recovering from shell shock, started to make pencil and crayon sketches.

1917   Severely wounded in hand. During convalescence in Odessa, then in Szeged, began making grease-crayon and watercolor portraits. With four friends from Szeged, including Ludwig Kassak, organized an artists' group that called itself MA, the Hungarian word for "today." Co-founded the literary review *Jelenkor*.

1918   After discharge from the army, returned to Budapest to take bachelor's degree in law. Continued drawing and painting.

1919   Began to acquaint himself with the work and ideas of Kasimir Malevitch and El Lissitzky. Left for Vienna in the fall. Collaborated with the MA group in the publication of the contemporary art quarterly *Horizont*.

1920   Made his first experiments with photograms—photographs without camera. Moved to Berlin where he devoted himself to collages in the spirit of the Berlin Dada group. Met Lucia Schultz, whom he married in 1922.

1921   Met El Lissitzky in Dusseldorf and made first trip to Paris. Contributed prose to *MA, De Stijl, Cahiers d'art,* and other periodicals. Briefly shared a studio with Kurt Schwitters.

1922   With Ludwig Kassak in Vienna edited *Das Buch neuer Künstler,* an anthology of modern art and poetry. Herwarth Walden of Galerie der Sturm in Berlin arranged his first exhibition. Walter Gropius, brought to the gallery by the art writer Adolf Behne, invited Moholy-Nagy to join the faculty of the Staatliche Bauhaus in Weimar. Attended Constructivist Conference in Weimar organized by Theo van Doesburg.

1923   In the spring began teaching at Weimar Bauhaus. Succeeded Paul Klee as head of the metal workshop and Johannes Itten in the foundation course. Collaborated with Oskar Schlemmer and others on murals, ballet and stage designs; engaged in photography, light and color experiments; and worked in typography and layout. With Walter Gropius, planned, edited, and designed the fourteen *Bauhausbücher,* while also collaborating on the periodic *Bauhaushefte.* Described his own paintings as "Constructivist," with emphasis shifting from line to colored form.

1925 Moved with the Bauhaus to Dessau.

1926 Began to paint on unusual surfaces—aluminum, bakelite, etc.

1927 With J. J. P. Oud and Willem Pijper, participated in the founding of the avant-grade monthly *i 10,* edited by A. Müller Lehning in Amsterdam.

1928 Because of rising political pressures, resigned in January from the Bauhaus, following example of Walter Gropius. Returned to Berlin primarily to make successful career as a stage designer for the progressive State Opera (Krollopera) and the Piscator Theater until 1933. (*Tales of Hoffman,* 1929; *The Merchant of Berlin* by Walter Mehring, 1930; *Hin und Züruck* by Paul Hindemith, 1930; *Madame Butterfly,* 1931; and other productions.) Designed exhibitions in Berlin, Brussels, and Paris. Interest continued in photograms and documentary films. As painter, further experiments with new materials: neolith, galalith, trolit, colou, rhodoit. Established himself as layout and typographical designer.

1929 Separated from Lucia Moholy. Extensive experiments with film.

1930 Exhibited *Light-Display Machine* at the Internationale Werkbund Ausstellung in Paris. This sculpture became the subject of his best-known film, *Lichtspiel Schwarz-Weiss-Grau.* Also experimented with "drawn sounds" and other methods for implanting sounds directly on film. Met Sibyl Peech, whom he later married.

1933 Participated in CIAM Congress in Greece, which he also filmed.

1934 Moved to Amsterdam, where a large printing company offered him facilities for experiments with color film and photography. Designed display at the Utrecht "Jaarbeurs" demonstrating the manufacture of artificial silk. Comprehensive retrospective, Stedelijk Museum, Amsterdam.

1935   Moved to London, his immigration sponsored mainly by Herbert Read. Designed the Courtauld exhibit at the Industrial Fair, worked as layout and poster designer for International Textiles, Imperial Airways, and the London Transport. Did interior design and display, Simpson's. Contributed photographs to three books and made documentary films on *Life of the Lobster* and *New Architecture at the London Zoo.* Began to experiment with Plexiglas in three-dimensional paintings, which he called "space modulators." Associated with artists gathered around *The Circle*— Myfawny Evans, Naum Gabo, Barbara Hepworth, Henry Moore—in addition to John Grierson's experimental film group.

1936   Commissioned by Alexander Korda to create the special effects for *Things to Come,* from a novel by H. G. Wells, but the sequences were dropped from the final print, to be shown separately. Resumed two-dimensional painting.

1937   Offered and accepted directorship of the New Bauhaus in Chicago, a school founded by the Association of the Arts and Industries. After a year the sponsoring organization encountered financial difficulties, voiding contractual commitments to the faculty; and the school was forced to close down before the end of the year.

1938   Opened his own School of Design at 247 East Ontario Street, Chicago, with much of the New Bauhaus staff.

1939   Began work as designer and advisor for Spiegel, Inc., the Baltimore & Ohio Railroad, the Parker Pen Co., and others.

1940   Conducted first summer session at a farm in Somonauk, Illinois, donated by the school's primary financial supporter, Walter Paepcke, president of the Container Corporation of America.

1941   Joined American Abstract Artists. Developed his space modulator conception into three-dimensional sculpture. Linked Institute of Design to the war effort.

1943   Co-founder of Council for a Democratic Hungary.

1945   Increased his activity as a painter and produced many paintings, watercolors, and ink drawings in a variety of new approaches. Also constructed Plexiglas stabiles and mobiles, molded to refract light. Moved location of his Chicago school for the third time. Learned soon after his fiftieth birthday that he had leukemia.

1946   Died of leukemia in Chicago on November 24. At the time of his death he was president of the Institute of Design, then having 680 students in its own building at 632 North Dearborn Street.

Moholy-Nagy: The Risk and Necessity of Artistic Adventurism   *Richard Kostelanetz*

László Moholy-Nagy continues to live in contemporary art, although the record tells us that he died over two decades ago; for he is the only artist born before 1900 whose work, ideas, and example remain variously relevant in this era of light shows, sculptural machines, abstract film, nonrepresentational photography, radically diverse book layouts, streamlined industrial design, artistic environments, and mixed-means theater. Not only did Moholy-Nagy's writings and ideas espouse most of these distinctly contemporary forms, he actually worked in most of them—three, four, and five decades ago. In contrast to his peers but like some of his prominent juniors, Moholy-Nagy created in several media and joined collaborative enterprises rather than living and dying a specialist in one. He was the best kind of eclectic, which is to say, someone whose various choices are informed by an underlying purpose, a coherent logic, and a highly selective awareness. His history makes him the outstanding exemplar of a particular kind of artistic career—horizontal across the arts, rather than vertical into only one; and as a prophetic precursor of so much that is present, he seems in retrospect one of the most seminal minds of twentieth-century art, in his own way the equal of Picasso, Duchamp, Mondrian, and Klee. "By now," wrote the critic Brian O'Doherty recently, "we have just about processed all the heroes, anti-heroes, and 'figures' of the age of modernism"; but to judge by how generally unfamiliar is Moholy-Nagy's name and work, even among those who would walk in his footprints, he still belongs among the unprocessed, not to say neglected.

Moholy, as he was known to those friends who did not call him "Holy Mahogany," was the great adventurer of modern art, heroically risking not only steps across boundaries but also lateral movement along several frontiers, and the territories through which he passed include a number of traditional arts, in addition to a few domains partly of his own creation. As he found the taking of next steps as more consequential than aspiring to intrinsic quality—if one dimension can viably be separated from the other in contemporary art—he also realized early in his career that the freedom granted the avant-garde artist includes the right not only to paint

This essay first appeared in issue No. 10–11 of *Salmagundi* and is reprinted with the permission of Robert Boyers, editor. Copyright © 1969 by Richard Kostelanetz.

in any style he wishes but also to work creatively in any art or area he chooses.

Since his travels also took him through several countries and cultures in the decades after World War I, the record of his life is as diverse and incomplete as that of his achievements. He was born in Bacsbarsod, in the Hungarian countryside, on July 20, 1895; by his teens, he was publishing poetry in native little magazines. In 1913, he began to study law at the University of Budapest and eventually turned to writing and painting, co-founding the review *Jelenkor* in 1916 and joining the Hungarian art group known as MA (meaning "today"), which later founded a periodical with the same name. Wounded in World War I, he became more serious about painting during his recuperation but still took a law degree; he went to Berlin in the early 1920's, becoming by 1922 a co-founder of Constructivism, co-editor of an anthology on modern art, co-author of a prophetic manifesto entitled "The Dynamic-Constructive System of Forces," and a contributor to several advanced art magazines. (He began to sign himself "L. Moholy-Nagy" because he regarded "László" or "Ladislaus" as too stuffy; and he sometimes called himself "Laci," which in English is pronounced like "Lotzi.") Of medium height and stocky build, with peasant features, glasses, and a streak of white through his dark hair, by the early 1920's he was a well-known name and presence in European avant-garde circles. His earliest artistic reputation came from his abstract paintings and nonrepresentational photographs, most of them made without a camera and called "photograms."

In 1923, Walter Gropius invited Moholy to join the Bauhaus in Weimar; thereafter, in addition to his own endeavors in several arts, Moholy taught the basic foundation course (*Vorkurs*) and photography, ran the metal workshop, and co-edited, with Gropius, the fourteen Bauhaus books. "He particularly sought," writes the art historian Donald Drew Egbert, "to acquaint students with the revolution in art made possible by modern technology"; and according to Gillian Naylor, in a recent study, *The Bauhaus* (1968), "It was above all Moholy-Nagy's personal interpretation of Constructivist attitudes that contributed to the emergence of a recognizable Bauhaus style [of industrial design]." Five years later, he followed Gropius in resigning from the Bauhaus due to political pressures and returned to Berlin to finish his light machine, to experiment with new materials, to collaborate with Erwin Piscator's theater and the Berlin State Opera, to make films both representational and abstract, and to explore advanced techniques of exhibition display. The threats of fascism drove him to Holland and, that standard classifications are insufficient; beyond that, the historian scarcely knows where to start. First of all, as designer of the Bauhaus publications, he repudiated both conventional "gray, inarticulate machine typesetting" and the highly ornamental "beauxarts" affectations in typography to originate (perhaps with a debt to El Lissitzky, among others) the now familiar geometric "modern" style of illustrated book design, in which relevant pictures and sometimes epigraphs are mixed in two-page spreads with rectangular blocks of uniform, evenly justified sans-serif type that may vary in size and yet always remains considerably narrower than the width of the page and is sometimes prefaced by sub-heads in boldface type. In his first one-man book, *Painting, Photography, Film* (1925), a sequence of seventy-four shrewdly chosen and arranged pictures abetted by minimal captions, successfully retells the argument already elaborated in the preceding text; and the over-all design of this book, as well as *Von Material zu Architektur* (1929), had enormous influence upon Continental publishing design. Moholy's favorite maxim insisted on "a clear message in the most impressive manner"; and not only does the design of Moholy's own final book exemplify this clean and efficient style at its very best, but its revolutionary influence continues in such recent illustrated volumes as the two Quentin Fiore–Marshall McLuhan collaborations, *The Medium Is the Massage* (1967) and *War and Peace in the Global Village* (1968). (However, compared to Andy Warhol's *Index* [1967] or Merce Cunningham and Frances Starr's *Changes: Notes on Choreography* [1969], Fiore's neo-Bauhaus style now seems archaic; and Moholy's own curiously conservative preference for "absolute clarity" and impersonality discouraged more inventive, not to say idiosyncratic, typographical expression.)

Yet, books were not the only applied medium to experience Moholy's penchant for revolutionary designs. In Berlin he did several extremely imaginative stage sets, including one with light and sound projections on a continuous strip and another for *The Merchant of Berlin* (1930) with several levels that antedates the Living Theater's similarly vertical staging in *Frankenstein* (1965); and the extraordinary settings Moholy created for Korda's *Things to Come* set an imaginative standard for that art. (Their absence from the final print is attributable to professional jealousies; but the excised footage has been shown separately.) The asymmetrical but geometric London window displays reproduced in both *The New Vision* and Sibyl Moholy-Nagy's biography would still seem conspicuously abstract and innovative on Fifth Avenue; and incredible as it may seem, while in Chicago he also designed a six-purpose handsaw and other tools for Spiegel's Mail Order House, and a vista dome passenger car for the B. & O. Railroad.

In short, his design esthetics apparently favor the Veblenian persuasion that efficiency and regard for creature comfort in themselves create beauty, in contrast to the position derived from William James that a beautiful object will enhance the lives of those who use it. Moholy characterized his own position as starting with the Louis Sullivan adage of "form follows function," to which he would add the latest "scientific results and technological processes." He once told a reporter from *Time,* "I don't like the word beauty. It's a depressing word. Utility and emotional satisfaction: These are important words. These are the things design should give." More than once his interest in radical design informed an architectural proposal, like the 1922 sketch, also displayed at the Museum of Modern Art "Machine" show (and previously reproduced in *The New Vision*) of a "Kinetic Constructive System," which is a tower with two internal spiral tracks at different angles of incline —"a structure with paths of motion for a sport and recreation." In retrospect, nonetheless, industrial and theatrical design seem the most modest of Moholy's diverse endeavors, and architecture was hardly a sustained ambition for him.

As an artist who assimilated abstractionism from his professional beginnings—he was, after all, just that much younger than, say Kandinsky or Picasso—Moholy applied nonrepresentational syntax to photography by developing the "photogram," or abstract cameraless photography, in 1921, the same year that Man Ray devised a similar process he egotistically christened "Rayographs." In making these pieces, three-dimensional objects were placed directly on light-sensitive paper, which was then exposed for an appropriate duration; and Moholy later learned to complicate the resulting visual field of blacks, whites, and grays by modulating the light and even exploiting such elementary devices of the medium as negative printing. His purpose was, as he wrote in the catalogue to a 1923 exhibition of his work, "the concretization of light phenomena . . . peculiar to the photographic process and to no other technical invention." A few years later he worked with photomontage (or photographic collage), in which some snippets from several prints are placed on a board of fundamentally unrelated images—what he called "a multiple image condensation fixed within a single frame"; and such pictorial collages as *The Structure of the World* (1925) epitomize his masterful exploration of forms and possibilities indigenous to this medium. During the 1940's he envisioned the potentialities of photographic color "understood for its own sake and not as a sign or symbol representing an object," but scarcely realized these aims. Moholy advocated that everyone learn to use a camera or suffer a modern form of illiteracy, and he also emphasized photography in artistic education, because, as his friend Sigfried Giedion wrote, he regarded "the camera as a means of increasing the range and precision of visual perception." In the course of his travels, Moholy also took innumerable documentary photographs, collecting several into books with texts by others on *The Street Market of London* (1936), *Eton Portrait* (1937), and *The Oxford University Chest* (1939), and reportedly appreciating the photos as much for their abstract qualities as their representational accuracy. They bear little resemblance to the precise and harsh realism so fashionable in 1930's American photography. Beaumont Newhall, in *The History of Photography* (1964), reprints a 1928 overhead shot of a Berlin street scene, on the back of which Moholy scribbled, "A bird's-eye view of trees which form a unity with the pattern of the street. The lines running in many directions, placed each behind the other, form a rich spatial network." He was clearly less interested in reproducing reality than in discovering an interesting picture when he developed the print. If the historically earliest photography emulated the realistic aspirations of classical painting, thereby eventually making the medium a vehicle of reportage, Moholy imitated the forms and perceptions of more contemporary art, so that his photographs not only define those expressive languages intrinsic to the medium, they also clearly look like photographs and nothing else.

Painting was the art Moholy originally pursued, and it was the one he continued, with only one extended interruption, throughout his career. Repudiating a brief juvenile flirtation with Van Gogh-like expressionism, as seen in a self-portrait done in 1916, he rapidly defined an abstract position. Such youthful works as the collages of 1920 reveal a debt to Dada and to Moholy's friendship with Kurt Schwitters, not only in their conglomerate visual syntax but also in their imagery of aimless mechanisms; *ZIII* (1922) announces the pervasive influence of Malevitch and Russian Constructivism: several kinds of geometric shapes—rectangles, circles, squares, and, particularly, straight lines—are painted in flat colors and superimposed on a rather spare field in a style already clarified, though, to my mind, undistinguished. In his supremely suggestive *Transparency* (1921), he took several transparent sheets painted with colored forms and put them on top of each other, so that their colors blended at points of overlapping intersection. A true abstractionist who believed his forms had no representational or symbolic resonances, he boasted that a good painting could be hung upside down and still persuade. He also initiated the custom of giving most of his works either descriptive titles or just numbers and letters. His paintings in the middle of the 1920's reveal a decided concern with pure color that, though Moholy was not a distinguished colorist, extended into the second phase of his work with paint. After abandoning the two-dimensional medium around 1928, perhaps because the limited syntax and spare field of Constructivist painting were too minimal for his maximal imagination, he took up paint again in London and Chicago, creating a succession of innovative rectangles in which painted Plexiglas stands an inch or two in front of a plywood back, so that images on the front sheet reflect shadows on the back sheet at angles and shapes variably dependent on the extrinsic light sources and the viewer's changing perspective. These paintings realized an ambition announced in his earliest essays on the medium—to move "from pigment to light." Moholy also cut holes in Plexiglas and painted on sheets with wavelike ridges (the brilliant *Papmac* [1943]); later he curved the material into convex and concave sculptural shapes. Moreover, a 1940 work such as *Space Modulator with Fluctuating Black and White Arcs* approaches optical ambiguity, because the spectator's eye cannot definitively deduce whether the black or the white arc is in front of the other. "This kind of picture," he wrote in *Vision in Motion,* "is most probably the passage between easel painting and light display," or between painting and relief; and perhaps because his senses of material and rhythm (in both time and space), as well as his aptitude for invention, were superior to his painterly eye, these "space modulators," as he collectively called them, stand as his most important "paintings."

In 1922, just before Moholy assumed his position at the Bauhaus (and perhaps because of his precocious appointment), in order to warn/challenge his prospective colleagues, he "ordered" five paintings (two of which have since been lost) of porcelain enamel on steel, identical in pattern but different in size, from a sign manufacturer by telephoning instructions to the factory supervisor—an innovative experiment that at first strikes us as a Cagean procedure designed to produce an unprecedented, "chance" result; however, since both Moholy and the supervisor were working from the same graph paper and the same color chart, the experimental aim was not at all to create aleatory art but to prove the existence of objective visual values and to emphasize the artistic primacy of conception—two points that, together with the procedure, caused considerable controversy. "In comparison with the inventive *mental* process of the genesis of the work," he rationalized in *Painting, Photography, Film* (1928), "the manner—whether personal or by as-

signment of labor, whether manual or mechanical—is irrelevant."
(The idea of an esthetic work untouched by artist's hand, thereby
challenging the convention of "individual touch," has had much
recent currency among the avant-garde.) Moholy was also the
first major modern artist to regard "multiples," or innumerable
copies, as a legitimate form for a serious artist's work.

Though he returned to the flat-surface medium now and then,
particularly for a series of almost hysterical expressionistic drawings and paintings executed just before his death—on them, indicatively, he worked not with the usual straight edge but with free-hand
strokes (and to which he gave such uncharacteristically macabre
titles as *Leu No. 1,* and *Chi-Finis*)—painting always remained too
limited for both his polymathic bent and his developing interests in
unusual materials and light. Back in 1919, as he wrote in his autobiographical essay, "On my walks I found scrap metal parts,
screws, bolts, mechanical devices. I fastened, glued and nailed them
on wooden boards, combined with drawings and paintings. It
seemed to me in this way I could produce real spatial articulation,
frontally and in profile, as well as more intense color effects. . . .
I planned three-dimensional assemblages, constructions executed in
glass and metal. Flooded with light, I thought they would bring to
the fore the most powerful color harmonies. In trying to sketch
this type of 'glass architecture,' I hit upon the idea of transparency."
And much of his subsequent work, in painting as well as sculpture,
pursued these tendencies toward both greater dimensionality and
light modulation.

Moholy's earliest sculptural efforts were more clearly within the
Constructivist stream. His *Nickel Construction* (1921) casts materials rather advanced at the time in simple (or "pure") geometric
forms. On a metal base is placed a turret with two spokes running
through it and an adjacent tower over a foot high; and from the
top of the tower to the edge of the base runs a spiraled strip. This
form seems indebted to the classic of Russian Constructivism,
Vladimir Tatlin's extremely influential *Monument for the Third
International* (1920), where the Industrial Age is evoked as a
spiral ribbon contrasting with vertical columns—a visual form that
Moholy himself subsequently favored. By 1923, he was making
constructions of both opaque and transparent glass in combination
with nickel and fiber matting (none of which have survived); and
continuing to explore materials for their influence upon light, late
in his career he turned again to thermoplastic Plexiglas, this time
as a lightweight sculptural material that could be shaped to modulate changes in the surrounding light, even though the object itself
remained stationary. Such pieces as *Light Modulator* (1943) and

Space Modulator (1945) realize with particular success Constructivist aspirations of volume implied or enclosed rather than amassed, and a spatial presence that does not end at the piece's rim, displaying, in addition, the familiar Moholy manipulations of various hues between darkness and light, his incipient kineticism, and exploiting the translucent object's variable appearance in space; and though Moholy's sculptural syntax is indebted to both Cubism and Constructivism, with a dash here and there of Futurism, his structures by this time had staked a historical position beyond Cubist-Constructivist sculpture. To Herbert Read, in his *Concise History of Modern Sculpture* (1964), a work such as Moholy's *Plexiglas and Chromium-Rod Sculpture* (1946) is thoroughly revolutionary with respect to the tradition of the art, because it lacks "a sensational awareness of the tactile quality of surfaces; a sensational awareness of the volume or (to avoid this ambiguous word) the mass encompassed by an integrated series of plane surfaces; and an acceptable sensation of the ponderability of gravity of the mass, that is, an agreement between the appearance and the weight of the mass." Of course, in being among the first to repudiate all these traditional criteria, Moholy's work became the precursor of much that is radical and interesting—"anti-sculptural"—in recent sculpture. "As a young painter," he wrote in that autobiographical essay, "I often had the feeling, when pasting my collages and painting my 'abstract' pictures, that I was throwing a message, sealed in a bottle, into the sea. It might take decades for someone to find and read it."

"When I think of sculpture, I cannot think of static mass," Moholy once told his wife; and her biography recalls how he sealed their relationship by taking her to see an object he had been sporadically building all through the 1920's. The articulation of light, as noted before, had always been among Moholy's primary concerns; even as a very young man, he wrote a poem that includes such lines as "Learn to know the Light—design of your life." "Light ordering Light, where are you?" "Light, total Light, creates the total man." Although he built *The Light-Display Machine* (1930) as a theatrical prop (to produce by reflection an environmental illumination), rather than as an esthetic object, Moholy's technical collaborator in the project liked the invention more for its intrinsic movement, that is, as a kinetic sculpture. Either way, this light-reflecting machine, four feet high, with vertical spines, a perforated shield, a moving balance ball, and visible gears, belongs among the truly revolutionary exemplars of twentieth-century art. As one of the first machine-driven mobiles, it differs from such nonmechanical kinetic art as the more popular air-stimulated mobiles of Calder and George Rickey (a form Moholy proved rather impractical, it reveals that, long before he employed John Cage, Moholy acknowledged the freedom of unpitched, unstructured, and even aleatory musical sounds. He also envisioned all kinds of advances in the medium's technologies, even publishing in 1924 a scheme for three simultaneous projections on a concave screen—roughly equivalent to "cinerama." In *Vision in Motion* is this characteristic prophecy: "The improvement of the film depends on the perfection of color, three-dimensional projection, and sound; upon simultaneous projection; successions of screens arranged in space and smoke, duplicate and multiple screens; new automatic super-impositions and maskings."

Three years after accepting Gropius's invitation to join the Bauhaus, Moholy co-authored a book entitled *Die Bühne im Bauhaus,* recently reissued as *The Theater of the Bauhaus* (1961), that contains other similarly prophetic visions of possible future theaters. Concerned on one hand with the Bauhaus ideal of radically different, but more humanly congenial, environmental structures and, on the other, with expunging each art of impurities derived from foreign media, he conceived of a theatrical performance devoid of "literary encumbrance," that would emphasize "creative forms peculiar only to the stage," and "total stage action," which he interpreted as a "concentrated activation of sound, light (color), space, form and motion." More specifically, Moholy would, first of all, break down the traditional distances between the communicative stimuli, whether human or mechanical, and the audience; for he thought that these theatrical elements, once freed of their imposed contexts, could be used in unprecedented combinations. He also envisioned certain technological innovations still not achieved, such as mobile loudspeakers suspended on overhead wire tracks, and recognized the availability of all materials, including "film, automobile, elevator, airplane, and other machinery, as well as optical instruments, reflecting equipment, and so on." From these propositions followed visions of two kinds of radical theater. One, which he called "Theater of Totality," is a remarkably direct precursor of the recent Theater of Mixed Means, in which human performers stand, in Moholy's phrase, "on an equal footing with the other formative media." The other vision, called "The Mechanized Eccentric," and characterized as "a concentration of stage action in its purest form," is a humanless environmental field of lights, sounds, films, odors, music, mechanized apparatus (even robots and motorized costumes), and simulated explosions. Both the original German and the recent American edition of the book include a fantastic and suggestive "score" for this multi-media extravaganza. "There will arise an enhanced *control* over all for-

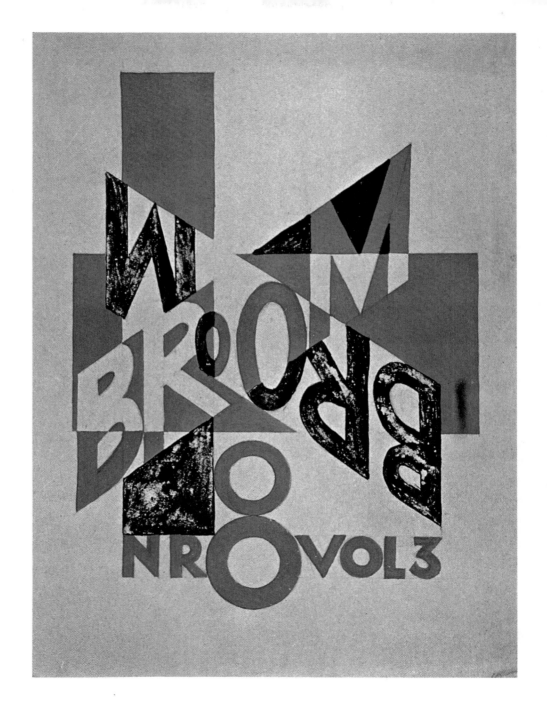

I. Title page for the avant-garde magazine *Broom,* New York, 1923.

II. *C XII, 1924.* Oil on canvas, 36″ x 28″. Collection Mrs. Sibyl Moholy-Nagy, New York.

III. *The Great Aluminum Painting, 1926.* Oil on engraved mat aluminum, 31¾″ x 38¾″. Collection Mrs. Sibyl Moholy-Nagy, New York.

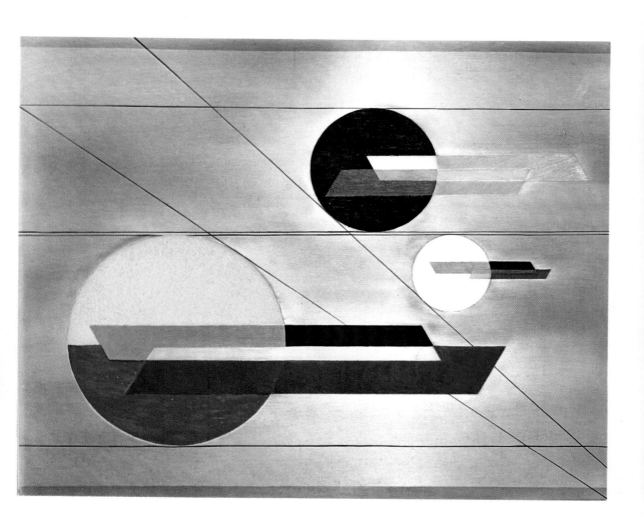

IV. Three-dimensional painting on white background and rear and front
surface of transparent celluloid sheet, 1926. 16″ x 20″. Collection
Mrs. Sibyl Moholy-Nagy, New York.

V. *A 19,* 1927. Oil on canvas, 23½″ x 37½″. Collection Mrs. Sibyl Moholy-Nagy, New York.

VI. *Copper Painting,* 1937. Oil on engraved copper, 20″ x 27″. Collection
Bauhaus-Archiv, Darmstadt. *Photo Galerie Klihm, Munich.*

VII. *Hotel Terrace, Ascona,* 1928. Color photograph.

VIII. *Neon Signs, Chicago,* 1939. Color photograph.

IX. *Billboard, New York,* 1940. Color photograph.

mative media," he declared on behalf of his vision, "unified in a harmonious effect and built into an organism of perfect equilibrium." Unfortunately, Moholy was never able to compile his own theatrical conceptions, though Xanti Schawinsky, a sometime student at the Bauhaus, produced something similar to "Theater of Totality" at Black Mountain College in the late 1930's, and Moholy's own ideas informed nonliterary mixed-means theatrical activities of the past decade.

The German refugees of the 1930's brought to America ideas and examples, often embodied in their own skins; and their presence here crucially shaped the quality and character of post-World War II American culture. Though Moholy had fewer students distinguish themselves in the fine arts than, say, Hans Hofmann or Josef Albers, both of whom lived and taught much longer, his ideas shaped generations of design teachers, who espouse his Chicago curriculum to this day. His example also influenced the creation of both fine and commercial art, as much through the persuasiveness of his writings, teaching, and personal legend as the circumstances of the age. (Of his immediate influence, Lloyd Engelbrecht, who is completing a history of the Institute of Design, judges, "Moholy made a big impact on a small number of people, most of whom went into college teaching.") Historically, Moholy was among the immigrant influences who helped make the key thrust of 1950's American art decidedly abstract rather than as representational as 1930's realism; if nothing else, Moholy wrote some of the most persuasive pages on the social and human relevance of artistic abstraction. Secondly, he exemplified the currently admired idea of the artist as not just a painter or a poet, but someone involved in a creative adventure that may ultimately take him through any medium—where his willingness constantly to explore rather than concentrate on one kind of product becomes the measure of his particular professional integrity. This radical attitude is not without its pitfalls, fostering at times the recently influential but incipiently solipsistic rationale that art is anything (literally anything!) that "artists" do; but the more reasonable benefit is that practitioners today can exploit a lateral freedom practically unknown to their predecessors.

Moholy's own artistic adventurism, along with his characteristically Hungarian capacity for cultural adaptation, may explain his extraordinary ability to keep abreast of the changing historical and artistic situation; for not only did he successfully establish himself in a succession of new cultures and learn at least two new languages, he also stood continually at the frontier of that New World which is twentieth-century art. He died much too soon, missing a contemporary scene characterized by esthetic opportunity and technological access that he would have relished far more than his professional contemporaries. (What other early modern artist would have considered the creative possibilities of television?) He had so thoroughly mastered the processes of an open-ended artistic career and accepted the inevitability of change; unlike most other major figures of his generation, he was not likely to dig his premature grave at some historic position.

Inevitably, the question arises whether Moholy might have been a greater artist had he concentrated on one or another of his enthusiasms; but that is really a useless inquiry, like asking whether steaks should not be pears. It is hard to believe, as I noted before, that Moholy wanted to create "a great painting" or "classic designs," though his commitment to nothing short of the most significant art and activity shines through all his work; for in the diversity of his experience, as well as the courage of his adventure, Moholy's greatness is most clearly revealed. The point is that his highly defined creative sensibility worked through several artistic media, exploring and yet always respecting the particular nature of each, in some cases contributing significant work and affecting the direction of their modern traditions. In incomparable diversity and persevering eclecticism was, paradoxically, both his coherent totality and singular achievement, as well as an accumulated personal experience that, in the literal sum of his perceptions, marked him as one of the great minds of the age. In the end, Moholy was, in his fashion, as fecund an inventor as anybody in modern art; he was certainly a more various innovator, who made the risk of artistic adventurism a contemporary necessity.

In Answer to Your Interview   L. Moholy-Nagy

1. What should you most like to do, to know, to be? (In case you are not satisfied.)
2. Why wouldn't you change places with any other human being?
3. What do you look forward to?
4. What do you fear most from the future?
5. What has been the happiest moment of your life? The unhappiest? (If you care to tell.)
6. What do you consider your weakest characteristics? Your strongest? What do you like most about yourself? Dislike most?
7. What things do you really like? Dislike? (Nature, people, ideas, objects, etc. Answer in a phrase or a page, as you will).

Originally published in *The Little Review*, XII/2 (New York, May, 1929). Reprinted by permission of Mrs. Sibyl Moholy-Nagy.

8. What is your attitude toward art today?
9. What is your world view? (Are you a reasonable being in a reasonable scheme?)
10. Why do you go on living?

When I was a school-boy, in the Latin hour, we used to pass around secretly a "confession-book" . . . in it each one had to answer truthfully certain questions. The most important questions were usually the following:

Do you believe that friendship can exist between man and woman?

Are you in love?

Where did you meet her?

Each chose for this purpose a pseudonym: Apollo, Hephaistos, "Lederstrumpf"—, "Dowegofarther" was chosen by one.

In that confession-book we all lied in chorus.

This memory still makes me happy; the world is a ball; the questions of the confession-book again roll around to me. I shall rise to my heights—a chance to lie. One thing however I know today better than in my school-days; if I now wish to lie, it is because I am still unripe.

1. I am a Hungarian and besides Hungarian I know only German. But I should like to know French, English, Italian, and Spanish. Then I should be at home everywhere.

2. When I was a child I thought that I was a king's son, who had been exchanged for another, but who later would come into his own. Today I know that one is what one is . . . chicken stays chicken . . . I am satisfied with my fate. More, I am happy to be as I am. What could I do if I were better than I am? My failings give me impetus in the fight, they sharpen my effort.

3. What do I expect? That some time I will be able to comprehend society, social relations, the relation of individuals to the mass better than I do today. Till now I have been guided in this largely by my feelings. But this feeling is much duller today than formerly, when I really had pangs of conscience if I took a good drink or rode in an automobile.

4. Subjective! That out of gratitude, out of mistaken kindness, I can be forced to make concessions. I know the feeling of being good out of weakness: to let things drag on, in order not to give pain to another, although that other has long since known that all was ended.

Objective! That men will again make war instead of working on themselves.

5. I was still a small boy when a friend pressed into my hand a paper in which my first printed poem appeared.—I am in general quite happy; but when one wishes really to get at something, has it been that childish ambition or an incident of the war? That is a whole novel, but I will make it short: It was in a retreat, after a never-ending march over soaked ground, mud to the knees, face beaten by wind and hail, half blind, every step more falling than advancing, I could go no farther. I was left behind in the dark, on the open field alone, without strength. Suddenly my horse appeared: I wept and kissed him, overcome with joy.

I have never, strictly speaking, been deeply unhappy. Of course I have been very very sad, once when I was able to overcome my jealousy through the recognition of it.

6. It is difficult for me to make up my mind not to want to please everyone. My strongest characteristic: that I am optimistic. I like most about myself that I can be happy; the least: that I have a tendency to become a fanatic.

7. To be clean inside and out. I like least, people who cannot stand me.

8. I do not believe so much in art as in mankind. Every man reveals himself; much of it is art.

9. I find the actual world scheme, in respect of the social system, most incomprehensible and gruesome. I have slowly formed the opinion that, seen in perspective, everything develops organically. This does not necessarily mean that one can accept the present system without opposition.

10. I live because it makes me enormously happy to live.

Letter to Herbert Read, London   *L. Moholy-Nagy*

Berlin, Jan. 24, 1934

Dear Professor Read:

Last night I clipped this review of your book from the newspaper, and I thought that it is high time to thank you for your lovely tender Christmas greeting. Then came your good letter; and all I can say in reply is that I am full of admiration for the English accomplishment in writing letters. They are always concise, full of communication, and yet never without a personal charm, so that

Reprinted by permission of Mrs. Sibyl Moholy-Nagy, who also translated from the German.

one is inclined to take every compliment seriously. It gave me immediately a positive mood.

Otherwise this sort of mood has totally vanished here. We are more sad than gay, and we have good reasons. The situation of the arts around us is devastating and sterile. One vegetates in total isolation, persuaded by newspaper propaganda that there is no longer any place for any other form of expression than the emptiest phraseology. No wonder that one can barely bring oneself to assert one's influence, even in the smallest circle. One is forced into an insane solipsism.

It is therefore a great joy to know that you exist and that you are a friend; and that you share the opinions of the small group of us who are here in isolation.

I thank you for the return of the photos and your recommendation to the Mayor Gallery. I hope—I hope around Easter to return for a longer stay to London.

Warmest Greetings to you, your dear wife, Ben Nicholson, Barbara Hepworth, and Miss Braunfels.

Yours
M-N.

The Contribution of the Arts to Social Reconstruction *L. Moholy-Nagy*

The meaning of "art" has changed since the industrial revolution and a clarification has to come if we should be able to handle the problem from our own angle.

First of all, the esotery of art must disappear; its limitation to specialists; the mysticism around it; the looking out for geniuses only. It is good to believe that in the future art may be explained in intellectual terms with greater clarity than it is possible today. Psychoanalysis already shows the mechanics of dreams, the role of the unconscious. The hope is justified that the mechanics of creative work and its sources will be unveiled one day as well. This may be the preliminary step to understanding its necessary community function and also its vital importance for the individual. He must be activized by doing instead of being merely a receptive participant. Our mass-produced civilization, the tiresome work at the conveyor belts, the cheap narcotics given in records, books, papers, magazines, cinema, radio and, of course, the disappearance

Transcript of a previously unpublished lecture to a conference of PEA, 1943. Reprinted by permission of Mrs. Sibyl Moholy-Nagy.

of leisure killed folk art. The artist who already started to become a specialist in the craftsman-guilds of the middle ages took over every aspect of its functions. Specialization was forced upon us through hundreds of ungoverned happenings and their mostly unforeseen effects; through hastened decisions in accepting and developing the machine as the only means of production; through a first unexpected but later forced gigantic growth of population, profit motives, etc., all claimed today as providential or "economic" necessities. For the time being, very few people know that the present form of specialization is a terrible weapon against us, against human nature.

I am not speaking against the machine or the machine age. The machine is a splendid invention and will form the new basis for a more developed human society. But after the glorious technomania of the twenties, we know today that man cannot master the machine until he has learned to master himself. But how can he achieve this when he even does not know what he possesses, what his abilities and capacities are?

He has delivered himself to thoughtless specialization which results in the development of certain of his faculties and—as a consequence of this—in a rather unnatural passivity outside of his specialized work.

People are taught that the best way of living is to buy other people's energy, to use other people's skill. In other words, a dangerous metropolitan dogma developed that the different subject matters are best handled by experts and no one should violate the borders of his specialized work or profession. So through the division of labor and the mechanized methods not only the production of daily necessities and goods has passed into the hands of specialists but almost every outlet for the emotional life as well. Today the artist-specialists have to provide for emotions. They are paid —if they are—for that. The sad consequence is that the biological interest in everything within the spheres of human existence becomes suffocated by the tinsel of a seemingly easygoing life. Man who has biologically the potential to comprehend the world with the entirety of his abilities, to conceive and express himself through different media, the word, tone, color, etc., agrees voluntarily to the amputation of these most valuable potentialities. Nothing proves better the lost feeling for the fundamentals of human life than the fact that has to be emphasized today: *Feeling and thinking and their expression in any media belong to the normal living standard of man;* to live without them means starvation of the intellectual and emotional side of life as missing food means starvation of the body. The non-verbalized expression of feeling is what we may call

Moholy-Nagy

art, but not art on a pedestal. *Art is a community matter transcending the limitations of specialization.* It is the most intimate language of the senses, indispensable for the individual in society.

Its function is to be a seismograph of the relationships of the individual to the world, intuitive re-creation of the balance between the emotional, intellectual and social existences of the individual.

Everywhere in the world, since about 1910, young artists have tried to understand this. They searched for the best way to express themselves, to solve the problems which painting, sculpture, writing, composition brought to them. They did not search for *"art"* but for *sincere expression.* Intuitively they returned to the fundamentals of their media—the painter to color and light, the sculptor to volume, the architect to space, the composer to tone, the writer to the word. Their work opens the way to the lost emotional sensorial sources and to a kind of socio-biology of the human being. But yet there is a great lag in the people's mind concerning the benefits of this approach.

Nothing more surprising has happened in the life of a nation, except perhaps in Russia, than the establishing of the Federal Art Project in the United States of America. Though it started as a part of the Social Security Act of the WPA it grew in a very short time beyond this relief aspect. The Federal Art Project gave the country a new valuation of the arts, badly needed as the pioneers bringing civilization over a continent with audacity and hard physical work could not see in the arts for a long time anything but luxury. The Federal Art Project broke down this fallacy. It represented a gigantic educational work, not in the sense that it "brought art to the people" or created art for the people, but that it tried to anchor it in, with, among, and of the people.

Since the Federal Art Project is liquidated, a greater responsibility lies with the educators of this country than ever before. It is up to them to see that art should be a part of life. This could be done early, but not as a timetable subject segregated from the other branches of the curriculum, but as an interpenetrating reality with all of them.

If the unity of art can be established with all the subject matters taught and exercised, then a real reconstruction of this world could be hoped for—more balanced and less dangerous.

Moholy-Nagy:
The Chicago Years *Sibyl Moholy-Nagy*

The last nine years of Moholy's life, which he spent in Chicago, were beset by many tragedies and frustrations, but they retain in retrospect the glow of a mission fulfilled. Moholy loved America and had a boundless faith in her future because as a lifelong fugitive from political oppression he had been given here a chance to be all of himself—an artist, a teacher, a highly sociable man. When Le Corbusier was asked why he seemed to love New York despite the devastating criticism he had voiced on practically all its aspects and institutions, he replied: "It's hideous, but it is honest!" It was not the hideousness but this quality of directness which Moholy—a rebel against the hated conventions of the Austrian Empire—loved in America.

The workshop relationship between teacher and student with which Gropius had breached the academic ritual of the German universities remained Moholy's life-long ideal; and he saw it realized in the early years of his school, first called The New Bauhaus and later School of Design. It was part of the great utopian dream which every European born before the Second World War harbors about America. Here everything was to be man to man, free and equal, without conventions. In Moholy this American Dream was sustained by an optimism that would have verged on naïveté if it had not been generated by a profound, deeply serious faith in the perfectability of each human being and in the certainty of his own guiding gifts. Nothing, absolutely nothing, was permitted to come between him and those who were willing to be taught. In a country and a city where, at least in the 1930's, the "prooofessor" was more of a comic figure than a leader, Moholy's limitless willingness to give of his ideas led to curious situations.

The Chicago press had gotten hold of Moholy and his New Bauhaus with single-minded curiosity, and so did every club and civic association in town. Being highly appreciative of beautiful women, he accepted early in his Chicago days an invitation by a Fashion Group to attend a luncheon in his honor at the Drake Hotel. Hardly had the ice cream been served when Moholy got up, unfolded a thick manuscript that had gone over well at Harvard, and started to read with intensity and concentration, ignoring staggering language difficulties in his zeal to win new converts. As time

Transcribed from an address at a retrospective exhibition, Museum of Contemporary Art, Chicago, May, 1969. © 1969 Sibyl Moholy-Nagy. Reprinted with permission.

went by one after another of the fashion ladies took an unobtrusive leave until only three clubleaders and a drowsy waiter were left. When I later tried to point out the incompatibility of lecture and audience, Moholy was annoyed:

"I don't know what you are talking about," he said. "Five people stayed because they got something out of it."

"Three," I said.

"Five," said Moholy. "Why do you assume that neither you nor the waiter have anything to learn?"

Moholy's American Dream went to pieces when the Association of Arts and Industry failed a year after The New Bauhaus opened. The manner of his dismissal and the subsequent false accusations would have sent any other man packing. For Moholy it was the signal for a new beginning of which he had so many in his life. With Plato he believed that a new beginning is like a God, saving all things.

"As long as I have one student I will teach," he said, and founded the School of Design in an abandoned bakery at 247 East Ontario Street with twenty-five hundred dollars and the support of his closest faculty: Gyorgy Kepes, George Fred Keck, Robert Jay Wolff, Andy Schultz and three professors from Robert Maynard Hutchins' "United of Science" group: Charles Morris, Carl Eckart, and Ralph Gerard. They all agreed to work for a full year without any salary and they did. The decisive support, the financial cement that had to go into the foundation, was still missing.

We repainted the abandoned commissary, tried to exterminate cockroaches as touchingly tame as pets, and sewed some eighty yards of black darkroom curtains for the former baking ovens. The school was ready to open in February, 1939. Moholy had to hock his wristwatch with the headwaiter of the Kungsholm Restaurant in order to pay for a smorgasbord dinner to which he had invited his staff the night before the opening, but we were by then so totally attuned to our mission that nothing could blur our faith in Chicago. And that brief period between February, 1939, and Pearl Harbor, less than three years later, justified that faith. We got some eighty to ninety day and nighttime students who have to this day retained contact and conceptual loyalty to Moholy's ideas in such fields as architecture, product design, photography, film and teaching. The most important aspect for the survival of the school was Moholy's extraordinary ability to make lasting and devoted friends among leading industrialists, financiers and simply people willing to work with and for him.

The key figure, however, in the development of that tiny cell of a Bauhaus school in Raklios' Bakery into the Institute of Design was Walter Paepcke. Moholy's obsession to prove the interrelatedness of art, science and industry was fully understood by the President of the Container Corporation of America. He was one of those rare men whose awareness of and respect for creativity was stronger than his material prudence. When he gave us a farmhouse in Somonauk, Illinois, as a summer school, there developed between these two men a friendship which went much beyond Paepcke's function as chairman of a newly formed board of the Institute of Design. They both loved art, good talk, horses and chess. "Walter even lets me win," said Moholy with admiration, recounting his war experience with a major who had sent him on the most dangerous patrol duty, each time Moholy had beaten him in a game of command chess.

The Second World War, of course, was a disaster for our school. Students and teachers were called up, personnel left for factory jobs, and the raw materials needed for instruction vanished from the civilian market. One night Walter Paepcke came to our apartment on Lakeview Avenue to tell Moholy in the gentlest possible terms that he and the board had decided to close the school as no longer viable. Moholy was stunned. I had seen it coming for months, but for him the war was merely a tragic and obstructive interlude. It could not interfere with the perfection of a curriculum that would serve the returning veterans to start a new life.

"Beyond teaching, the school has a mission," Moholy pleaded. "We are invaluable for the war effort—we have a lot to contribute."

"What for instance?" said Paepcke with unconcealed skepticism.

"I have several programs in my mind," Moholy hoisted a pure white lie. "I have been developing some ideas for months. Tell you what, Walter, tomorrow I'll put it all in writing, and day after tomorrow you can present it to the board."

At four the next morning, Moholy got me out of bed and on the typewriter, and by noon we had a "war effort" program that would make the Institute of Design as essential to an American victory as, say, Mrs. Roosevelt's smile. The three-point emergency program of the Institute of Design, which Moholy had conjured up overnight, consisted firstly in a rehabilitation program for wounded veterans which, under the slogan "Better Than Before" and the supervision of Dr. Kurt Sommer, trained nurses and Red Cross workers in a new kind of creative work-therapy. Despite his life in the roaring and libertine twenties, Moholy remained a Puritan in his relationship to women. When he voiced his despair at the unresponsiveness of the therapists, Dr. Sommer explained dryly, "These old maids, they are overworked and underfertilized." Moholy repeated this to me. "Underfertilized? Do you think he really meant . . . ?" He certainly did.

The second war effort was Moholy's appointment to the Mayor's Civil Defense Commission and his project to camouflage the waterfront of Lake Michigan to fool invading aircraft. This meant stormy trips on patrol boats that made him seasick, and precarious flights in small reconnaissance planes that made him airsick. It reminded me of the times in England when he had shot his famous movie on the *Life of the Lobster,* following the fishing fleet with alternate spurts of shooting and being sick, or when the gorillas of Whipsnade Zoo tried to pull his legs through the roof of their cage while Moholy shot their antics from above, all for his film *The New Architecture of the London Zoo.*

The most successful project financially was the replacement of the unobtainable bed-springs of steel by plywood coils developed in the Institute workshop. To prove their resilience Moholy invited our fat janitor to take a nap while he photographed him, only to find that from then onward Gus preferred the role of a sleeping manikin to that of a caretaker.

Gradually the American administration for a successful comeback went into action. A Friends of the Institute of Design Association was formed, and its members were more enthusiastic than knowledgeable. A lady contributor insisted that the school design all her valentines, and another member conditioned a five-thousand dollar contribution on changing the name of the Institute to his own. The real bonus was the Saturday Children's Class, which was one of Moholy's best-loved projects. He invented highly original programs—an underwater zoo of plastic animals; a mechanical ballet in which each child presented a part of a dismantled alarm clock; group poetry sessions. On the couch in his office reposed every day the painting or construction on which he had been working the night before. It had to travel with us to the school and back, although Moholy never painted in his office. The almighty commissioner for gasoline rationing gave me an A card, because his wife had convinced him that Moholy could not be parted from his creative work, nor their own children from the benefit of Moholy's Saturday class. He collected the children's reactions as if they were the eternal judgments of Roger Fry. "It's speed, it's airplane speed!" would delight him, or "Now I know how night looks." His own daughter at age six sternly rejected the realistic painting of a faculty member as "a 'story.' A picture is what my Daddy does!"

As things grew more and more precarious during the war years, Moholy tried to get some more foundation support. But Carnegie turned him down flatly, pointing to the war effort. A day after

Moholy received this refusal he left for New York and returned two days later with a pledge for ten thousand dollars. "I simply stayed in the President's ante-room until he gave in (or up!)."

The end of the Second World War brought deep psychological changes to American society. A feverish desire for bigness and prosperity replaced the long period of economic instability that had started with the Great Depression of 1930 and had been the decisive awakening of America's creative search. Veterans flooded schools, demanding condensed skill courses that would fit them into the postwar boom. Moholy did not understand. To him the symbiosis between teacher and student was fundamental; it was the spring and not the goal. He loved to quote Pestalozzi: "Not knowledge but the ability to acquire knowledge is the task of education." Moholy's relationship with the businessmen on his board grew more strained in this contest between prophecy and expediency; yet it was during this time of bitter personal defeats that he created his most beautiful Plexiglas sculptures and wrote his most important book, *Vision in Motion*. On his last visit to New York, hopelessly ill with leukemia, and a mere ten days before his death in November, 1946, Moholy-Nagy could say to his friend Robert Jay Wolff, "I'm not sure how my paintings will be judged in the future. But I am proud of my life."

Dynamic-Constructive Energy-System
L. Moholy-Nagy and Alfred Kemeny

Vital construction is the embodiment of life and the principle of all human and cosmic development.

Transposed into art it now means the activation of space by dynamic-constructive systems of energy, i.e., the inter-construction of energies actually opposed in physical space, and their construction into space, which likewise functions as energy (tension).

Construction as an organizational principle of human striving has led, in latter-day art, from technology to a static form that has degenerated into either technological naturalism or formal simplifications that vegetate in a confinement to horizontals, verticals, and diagonals. The best example was an open, eccentric (centrifugal) construction, which did indicate the tensions of space and forms, but without resolving them.

We must therefore replace the *static* principle of *classical art* with the *dynamic* principle of universal life. In practice: instead of static *material*-construction (relationships of material and form), we have to organize dynamic construction (vital constructivity, energy relationships), in which the material functions solely as a conveyor of energy.

Carried further, the dynamic single-construction leads to the DYNAMIC-CONSTRUCTIVE ENERGY-SYSTEM, with the beholder, hitherto receptive in his contemplation of art-works, undergoing a greater heightening of his powers than ever before and actually becoming an active factor in the play of forces.

The problems of this system of energy involve the problem of pendent sculpture and of the film as projected spatial movement. The initial projects of a dynamic-constructive energy-system are limited to experimental and demonstrational devices for testing the connections between matter, energy, and space. Next comes the use of the experimental results in the creation of art-works in freer motion (freer of machine and technological motion).

—Translation from the German by Joachim Neugroschel

Originally published by Galerie der Sturm, Berlin, 1922. Reprinted by permission of Mrs. Sibyl Moholy-Nagy.

To Post-Impressionist Painting in
Hungary   *Ernst Kállai*

Moholy-Nagy shows strong cubistic landscapes, calm, even, and deep luminous planes, the thoughtful, serious stasis of a timeless spaceperception. Then again he has lithographs, portraits, and semi-abstract compositions in which a formal totality is crystallized to a feverish, pulsating, yet luminously clear and pure height. One cannot escape a comparison which in this one aspect illuminates the whole unbridgeable difference between two generations: in Moholy-Nagy the artistic expression of an objective, crystalhard lifepositivism based on highest intelligence and willpower; and on the other side Kokoschka, his art a symbol of a decadent, only in nervesubstance and extravagant vibrations living superculture.   (*1920*)

From Pigment to Light   *L. Moholy-Nagy*

The terminology of art "isms" is truly bewildering. Without being exactly certain what the words imply, people talk of impressionism, neo-impressionism, pointillism, expressionism, futurism, cubism, suprematism, neoplasticism, purism, constructivism, dadaism, surrealism—and in addition there are photography, the film, and light displays. Even specialists can no longer keep abreast of this apocalyptic confusion.

It is our task to find the common denominator in all this confusion. Such a common denominator exists. It is only necessary to study the lessons of the work of the last hundred years in order to realize that the consistent development of modern painting has striking analogies in all other spheres of artistic creation.

The Common Denominator

The invention of photography destroyed the canons of representational, imitative art. Ever since the decline of naturalism painting, conceived as "color morphosis," unconsciously or consciously sought to discover the laws and elementary qualities of color. The more this problem emerged as the central issue, the less importance was attached to representation. *The creator of optical images learned to work with elementary, purely optical means.*

Approached from this point of view all the manifold "isms" are

"From Pigment to Light" was written 1923–26 and originally published in *Telehor* (Brno, 1936). Reprinted by permission of Mrs. Sibyl Moholy-Nagy.

merely the more or less individual methods of work of one or more artists, who in each case commenced with the destruction of the old representational image in order to achieve new experiences, a new *wealth of optical expression*.

Signs of the New Optics

The elements of the new imagery existed in embryo in this very act of destruction. Photography with its almost dematerialized light, and especially the use of direct light rays in cameraless photography and in the motion-picture, made clarification an urgent necessity.

Investigations, experiments, theories of color and light, abstract displays of light-images—as yet far too fragmentary and isolated —point toward the future, though they cannot as yet provide a precise picture of anything like the future's scope.

But one result has already emerged from these efforts: the clear recognition that apart from all individual emotion, apart from the purely subjective attitude of the spectator, objective factors determine the effectiveness of an optical work of art: factors conditioned by the material qualities of the optical medium of expression.

Minimum Demands

Our knowledge concerning light, brightness, darkness, color, color harmony—in other words our knowledge of the elementary foundations of optical expression is still very limited (in spite of the tireless work of the numerous artists). Existing theories of harmony are no more than the painters' dictionary. They were elaborated to meet the needs of traditional art. They do not touch our present esthetic sensibilities, our present aims, much less the entire *field of optical expression*. Uncertainty reigns even with regard to the most elementary facts. Innumerable problems of basic importance still confront the painter with the need for careful experimental inquiry:

What is the nature of light and shade?
Of brightness—darkness?
What are light values?
What are time and proportion?
New methods of registering the intensity of light?
The notion of light?
What are refractions of light?
What is color (pigment)?
What are the media infusing life with color?
What is color intensity?

The chemical nature of color and effective light?
Is form conditional on color?—On its position in space?—On the extent of its surface area?
Biological functions?
Physiological reactions?
Statics and dynamics of composition?
Spraying devices, photo and film cameras, screens?
The technique of color application?
The technique of projection?
Specific problems of manual and machine work?
Etc. etc. etc.
Research into the physiological and psychological properties of the media of artistic creation is still in its elementary stages, compared with physical research.
Practical experience in the creative use of artificial color (light) as yet scarcely exists.

The Fear of Petrification

Artists frequently hesitate to apply the results of their experiments to their practical work, for they share the universal fear that mechanization may lead to a petrification of art. They fear that the open revelation of elements of construction, or any artificial stimulation of the intellect or the introduction of mechanical contrivances may sterilize all creative efforts.

This fear is unfounded, since the conscious evocation of *all* the elements of creation must always remain an impossibility. However many optical canons are elaborated in detail, all optical creation will retain the unconscious spontaneity of its experience as its basic element of value.

Despite all canons, all inflexible laws, all technical perfection, this inventive potency, this genetic tension which defies analysis, determines the character of every work of art. It is the outcome of intuitive knowledge both of the present and of the basic tendencies of the future.

Art and Technique

The attempt was made, at least partially, to restore the capacity for spontaneous color experience—which has been lost through the spread of the printed word and the recent predominance of literature—by intellectual means. This was only natural, for in the first phase of industrial advance the artist was overwhelmed by the intellectual achievements of the technician, whose achievements embodied the constructive side of creation.

Given a clear determination of function, the latter could without difficulty (at least in theory) produce objects of rational design. The same was assumed to be true in art, until it became apparent that an exaggerated emphasis on its determinable intellectual aspects merely served as a smoke-screen, once the elements of optical expression as such—quite apart from their "artistic" qualities—had been mastered. It was of course necessary first to develop a standard language of optical expression, before really gifted artists could attempt to raise the elements thus established to the level of "art." That was the basic aim of all recent artistic and pedagogic efforts in the optical sphere. If today the sub-compensated element of feeling revolts against this tendency, we can only wait until the pendulum will react in a less violent manner.

From Painting to the Display of Light

All technical achievements in the sphere of optics must be utilized for the development of this standard language. Among them the *mechanical and technical* requisites of art are of primary importance.

Until recently they were condemned on the grounds that manual skill, the "personal touch," should be regarded as the essential thing in art. Today they already hold their own in the conflict of opinions; tomorrow they will triumph; the day after tomorrow they will yield results accepted without question. Brushwork, the subjective manipulation of a tool is lost, but the clarity of formal relationships is increased to an extent almost transcending the limitations of matter; an extent in which the objective context becomes transparently clear. Maximum precision, the law of the norm, replaces the misinterpreted significance of manual skill.

It is difficult today to predict the formal achievements of the future. For the formal crystallization of a work of art is conditioned not merely by the incalculable factor of talent, but also by the intensity of the struggle for the mastery of its medium (tools, today machines). But it is safe to predict even today that the optical creation of the future will not be a mere translation of our present forms of optical expression, for the new implements and the hitherto neglected medium of light must necessarily yield results in conformity with their own inherent properties.

Purposive Progress of Thought, Circular Advance of Technique

During the intermediary stages, however, we must not overlook a well-known factor retarding the advance of art: individual pioneers invent new instruments, new methods of work, revolutionizing the traditional forms of production, but usually a long time must elapse before the new can be generally applied. The old hampers its advance. The creative potentialities of the new may be clearly felt, but for a certain time it will appear clothed in traditional forms that are rendered obsolete by its emergence.

Thus in the sphere of music we must for the present content ourselves with the noisy triumphs of the mechanical piano and of the cinema organ, instead of hearing the new electro-mechanical music that is entirely independent of all previously existing instruments. In the sphere of painting the same revolutionary significance already applies to the use of spraying devices, of powerful enamel reflectors and of such reliable synthetic materials as galalith, trolit, bakelite, zellon, or aluminum. The situation is similar in the realm of the cinema, where a method of production is regarded as "revolutionary" whose creative achievements are scarcely greater than those that might be obtained could classical paintings be set in motion.

This situation is unsatisfactory and superannuated when judged in terms of a future in which light-displays of any desired quality and magnitude will suddenly blaze up, and multicolored floodlights with transparent sheaths of fire will project a constant flow of immaterial, evanescent images into space by the simple manipulation of switches. And in the film of the future we shall have constant change in the speed and intensity of light; space in motion constantly varied through the medium of light refracted from efflorescent reflectors; flashes of light and black-outs; chiaroscuri, distance and proximity of light; ultra-violet rays, infra-red penetration of darkness rendered visible—a wealth of undreamed-of optical experiences that will be profoundly stirring to our emotions.

—Translation from the German by F. D. Klingender
and P. Morton Shand

Isms or Art   *L. Moholy-Nagy*

The two forms of visual expression, representational and abstract, have been passionately discussed and mutually derided during the last years. If one did not decide for or against one or the other, one was suspected of lack of character. In reality, as far as contemporary means of perception go, the two forms of visual expression have so little in common that they cannot be evaluated on equal

Originally published in *Vivos Voco,* V/8-9 (Leipzig, 1926). Reprinted by permission of Mrs. Sibyl Moholy-Nagy.

terms. The confusion has its origin in muddy realizations and incongruent application of means and terminologies. In the accelerated tempo of our time we cannot afford to be fuzzy about causal relationships and their visualizations. No one today is outside the influence of contemporary values, whether ideas or objects.

The same driving force that incessantly pounds innovations into the consciousness of every newspaper reader, every telephone user, every radio listener, every ordinary consumer, is also behind modern art. It is the purest concentration of the organic-functional element as synthetical experiment of all creative goals. We are witnessing today the pressure of a tremendous increase in intellectual and technological development which is transposed into the first groping attempts at sublimation through contemporary means of form and expression.

The Isms

In the art terminology of our day the "Isms" have become the sole means of classification. But in reality there is no such thing as an Ism but only the work of individual artists who have succeeded in achieving a conformity between their vision and the subconscious aspirations of their times. Despite vast differences in this optical interpretation the common bond—in painting—is the ultimate clarification of the principles of optical communication. Isms are efforts to overcome painting traditions. They are incessant pioneering attempts toward a pure functionality whose elementary means of expression correspond to our sense organism and its tension relationship to the perceptive world. It takes many detours before this pure functionality can be achieved. Instead of building up there is first of all demolishing—demolishing analogies to the historical painting in which elementary means are in the service of literary representation. The development of photography has done much to separate this mix-up of form and means—here the story, there the pure experience of optical chromatic composition. It took almost 100 years till this demonstrative separation of two in themselves fully valid means of visual creation could be made.

The common aim of all the Isms, from Naturalism to Constructivism, is the constant, subconscious struggle to conquer the primary, autonomous, purely painterly means of creation. The elementary optical means: color, point, line, plane in their inexhaustible relationships, manipulated through direction, proportion, volume, texture, have been the endeavor of all painters in all ages. All the well-known optical rules, the Golden Section and other modular canons, aimed at an elementary optical order. Our so-called Isms: Impressionism, Pointillism, Futurism, Expressionism, Cubism, Suprematism and Constructivism, are nothing else but time-conditioned transfigurations of this search for an elementary optical order. All deformation, breaking up, distorted proportions, hazing, discoloring of the natural model, is prompted by a desire to liberate form from its burden as the carrier of interpretive meaning. Every artist, categorized in any of the Isms, had to start anew with the destruction of the "Abbild"—pictorial representation, even if he were totally unconscious of his motivation. There always was in every true painter an *a priori,* a primordial, knowledge how color, plane, line and point will, through his hand, create new sensations of proportion, volume, tension relationships; but there always was the reigning idol of the image. He always had "to start from nature." This monopoly of depicting what meets the eye has been undercut by photography, which is a far superior mechanical process; and has intensified the search for an autonomous optical concept, free of the academic restrictions.

The successive Isms went about this search in different ways. Impressionism used color chemistry to achieve "atmospheric effects"; Cubism deformed the object and dissected space; Futurism depicted simultaneity of actions, an interpenetration of static and kinetic elements; Expressionism projected "the inner image," Neoplasticism discovered the emotional meaning of the plane; Suprematism aimed at a painterly orientation in infinite space; and Constructivism went down to the primordial visual perceptions: the raw materials and structural relationships, singularly optical, including the new element of pigment-free light. All these approaches reached by their specific detours a canon of pure primary means. Few were conscious of the fact that not the destruction of pictorial tradition but the creation of an autonomous art is the ultimate goal. Blind to the achievements of differently oriented concepts, every new school felt the need to start again at the beginning.

Actually the search for means to liquidate the academic tradition has been terminated with Expressionism and Cubism. No matter from how many corners how many painters dared again the jump into the center of the optical problem, the truth had been established that *the optical creator can only think and work in optical means.* This revelation precludes the appearance of new Isms since we know now what painting with pure optical interrelationships is or should be. And with this knowledge that is sinking into the cultural consciousness of a new generation, the old battlecry: here representational, there abstract, has become meaningless. We have two cleanly separated perceptive goals before us: the visualization of elementary optical relationships in painting and the representation of formal and social relationships in photography and film.

—*Translation from the German by Sibyl Moholy-Nagy*

Letter to Fra. Kalivoda   *L. Moholy-Nagy*

You are surprised that I am again arranging a growing number of exhibitions of both my earlier and more recent work. It is true that for a number of years I had ceased to exhibit, or even to paint. I felt that it was senseless to employ means that I could only regard as out of date and insufficient for the new requirements of art at a time when new technical media were still waiting to be explored.

1.

Ever since the invention of photography, painting has advanced by logical stages of development "from pigment to light." We have now reached the stage when it should be possible to discard brush and pigment and to "paint" by means of light itself. We are ready to replace the old two-dimensional color patterns by a monumental architecture of light. I have often dreamed of hand-controlled or automatic systems of powerful light generators enabling the artist to flood the air—vast halls, or reflectors, of unusual substance—such as fog, gaseous materials or clouds, with brilliant visions of multicolored light. I elaborated innumerable projects—but no patron ever commissioned me to create a monumental fresco of light, consisting of flat and curving walls covered with artificial substances, such as galalith, trolit, chromium, nickel—a structure to be transformed into a resplendent symphony of light by the simple manipulation of a series of switches, while the controlled movements of the various reflecting surfaces would express the basic rhythm of the piece. I longed to have at my disposal a bare room containing twelve projectors, the multicolored rays of which would enable me to animate its white emptiness.

Have you ever witnessed a large search-light with its vast cones of light flashing wildly across the sky and searching further and further afield into infinite space? I envisaged similar results. But the flowing chords of my visions formed fully orchestrated symphonies of light that were not confined to the staccato rhythm of the flash-light signal code. That was only one of my plans, one of many similar dreams of light and movement, for the realization of which

Written in 1934 and originally published in *Telehor* (Brno, 1936). Reprinted by permission of Mrs. Sibyl Moholy-Nagy.

all the resources of physical science with its incomparable instruments (e.g. for polarization and spectroscopy) were to be utilized.

Although the chances that these dreams will assume a concrete shape in the near future are remote, it is possible even today to envisage the basic system of the future architecture of light.

The creative manipulation of light can be discussed under two main heads:

I. Light displays in the open air:
   a) *The illuminated advertising displays* of today still generally consist of linear patterns on flat surfaces. It is now our task to enter the *third* dimension and to achieve real spatial differentiation in such displays by the use of special materials and reflectors.
   b) *Gigantic searchlights and sky-writers* already play an increasingly important role in advertising displays (e.g. American firms, Persil), and
   c) *Projections onto clouds* or other gaseous backgrounds through which one can walk, drive, fly, etc., is already possible today.
   d) *Light displays* revealing a vast expanse of light with ever changing planes and angles, an interminable network of multicolored rays, to the spectator seated in an airplane will certainly form an impressive part of future municipal celebrations.

II. Indoor light displays:
   a) *The film* with its unexplored possibilities of projection, with color, plasticity and simultaneous displays, either by means of an increased number of projectors concentrated on a single screen, or in the form of simultaneous image sequences covering all the walls of the room.
   b) *Reflected light displays* of pattern sequences produced by such color projectors as László's color organ. Such displays may be of an open isolated nature or they may be multiplied by means of television.
   c) *The color piano,* whose keyboard is connected with a series of graduated lamp units, illuminates objects of special materials and reflectors.
   d) *The light fresco* that will animate vast architectural units, such as buildings, parts of buildings or single walls, by means of artificial light focused and manipulated according to a definite plan. (In all probability a special place will be reserved in the dwellings of the future for the receiving set of these light frescoes, just as it is today for a wireless set.)

2.

Dear Kalivoda, you are acquainted with my Light-Display Machine and with my "Lightplay Black-White-Gray." It took a great deal of work to assemble all this material, and yet it was only a very modest beginning, an almost negligible step forward. Nor was I able fully to carry out my experiments even within this limited sphere. You have every right to ask, why I gave in, why I am again painting and exhibiting pictures, after once having recognized what were the real tasks confronting the "painter" of today.

3.

This question must be answered, quite apart from any personal considerations, for it is of vital concern for the rising generation of painters.

We have published many programs, issued many manifestos to the world. Youth has every right to know why our claims have failed, why our promises have remained unfulfilled. At the same time youth has the duty of continuing the quest, the search for new forms to advance the cause of art.

4.

It is an irrefutable fact that the material dependence of the artist on capital, industry and working equipment presents an insurmountable obstacle today to the successful creation of a true architecture of light; merely produces emotions of space and color which for the time being are all without any practical value. While the possession of a few brushes and tubes of color enables the painter in his studio to be a sovereign creator, the designer of light displays is only too often the slave of technical and other material factors, a mere pawn in the hands of chance patrons. Moreover, there is a dangerous tendency to regard "technique" as the negation of "art." Many artists fear to display any exact knowledge in and any mastery of skill in technical matters. A cowardly maxim proclaims that intellectual attainments are damaging to the artist, that feeling and intuition alone are required for the task of creation—as if there had never been a Leonardo, as if the creative energies of the cathedral builders Giotto, Raphael and Michelangelo had not been rendered incalculably more fruitful by their universal knowledge and their mastery of technique. For the artist preoccupied with his task the mastery of the technical problems it implies is not, after all, an insurmountable difficulty. But even when he has solved these problems he is left with the paralyzing impossibility of concrete demonstration. Where could he find a hall today in which to demonstrate to the public what he has created? He is forced to put his dreams in cold storage until they evaporate as a result.

It is a superhuman task to fight for the realization of these plans, if, owing to lack of knowledge of the results that could be obtained, there is no public to assist in the struggle.

5.

A further point deserves especial attention: a widely organized and rapid news service today bombards the public with every kind of news, art news included. The virtues of this service are universality of interest and speed, its vices: greed for big "scoops" and blatant superficiality. Without interest in evolution it overwhelms its public with sensations. If there are no sensations, they are freely invented or deliberately improvised. In their hands the public with its mechanized education and lack of ideas of its own succumbs to the influence of the papers and magazines. The passionate desire for participation, the longing for direct contact with the forces of artistic creation become transformed into the average newspaper reader's "interest," an artificial interest leading away from the real sources of experience, because it lulls sensibility by creating what is only a semblance of mental activity. As a result all real contact with the forces and achievements of artistic creation ceases, for cheap interpretation renders this superfluous.

And yet in spite of all obstacles and in spite of the fact that town life, press, photography, films and the rapid and uncontrolled spread of civilization have leveled our color sense to a scale of grays from which most of us will have the greatest difficulty in escaping, we must regain the receptivity for color that we till recently possessed. We must escape from the exuberance of uncontrolled emotion in our handling of color and learn to raise the struggle for the mastery of optical technique to a constructive level.

6.

There are many obstacles to the accomplishment of this task. Above all, the basic discord between man and his technical achievements, the retention of antiquated forms of economic organization in spite of changed conditions of production, the spread of an outlook inimical to biological necessity, which transforms the lives of workers and employers alike into a ceaseless rush. The productive capacity of man is constantly increasing, but while he is fascinated by the ever renewed spectacle of a record output of commodities, he loses all sense of even his most elementary biological needs—and this at a time when a sane use of his new technique would enable him to satisfy them to a far greater extent than has ever before been possible.

7.

It would be purely an evasion of the issue, if one were to search for the causes of this state of affairs in mere matters of detail. The reason for our present condition is to be found in the rapid spread of industrialism and the fact that it has been forced into the wrong channels by our capitalist production. The ruling class alone is interested in maintaining the present form of industrialism. Every attempt to create a planned economy, to reconstruct our uncontrolled, industrialized world on a socialist basis, every attempt at enlightenment even, necessarily encounters the conscious or instinctive resistance of the ruling caste of society. And for the same reason, every creative achievement, every work of art prognosticating a new social order and striving to restore the balance between human existence and industrial technique is categorically condemned. The relatively meager results of new experiments in art are due to the social system that rules our existence, the hidden ramifications of which actually extend to those circles where one would expect to find hostility to it.

8.

Thus the pioneers of these experiments are forced to approach a public which is unprepared for their message either by almost devious means or with but small, carefully selected installments of their creative achievements. According to the temperament of the artist their method of approach usually follows one of two courses. Those who follow the first method apply their creative energies to the problems of the day and to the obvious facts of existence as transmitted by tradition and accepted without question by their contemporaries. Their task is simply the perpetuation of our cultural tradition.

Those following the second method derive their creative inspiration from all that is as yet in an embryonic state, all that points to the future and has never been subjected to the test of experience. As true revolutionaries of art they endeavor to take new forms of experience in their single stride. Although this contrast by no means implies a valuation, it is nevertheless true that the tempo of cultural development depends on the depth to which these revolutionary ideas shall penetrate. Even the manner in which the problems of the day are interpreted is directly influenced by them.

But since time is a limiting factor for all of us, we are often forced to select the method of gradual evolution, if we aspire to be able to pass on at least some fraction of our creative achievements.

9.

Since it is impossible at present to realize our dreams of the fullest development of optical technique (light architecture), we are forced to retain the medium of easel painting for the time being.

Nevertheless, I consider it necessary to continue my experiments with synthetic substances such as galalith, trolit, aluminum, zellon, etc., and to retain them as media for my work, because the use of these materials in art will help to demonstrate their applicability in a wider sphere.

10.

This is the chief, though not the sole reason why—without discontinuing my experiments in the use of light—I still paint pictures.

—*Translation from the German by F. D. Klingender
and P. Morton Shand*

Subject Without Art *L. Moholy-Nagy*

In my opinion there is no opposition of principle between representational and non-representational art, provided either fulfills its formative and educational tasks both for the individual and for the masses. But it is, of course, of importance to note which technique is applied to these tasks in any given historical moment. What, then, is our own historical position?

In our museums, illustrated publications, theaters, cinemas, photographs, we are assailed by a deluge of optical messages and visual entertainments. But where in this dorado of sights is the purposive, organizing element that alone can give aim and direction to our work? True art has also an educational function, and in the midst of the vast social controversies of our age we can no longer afford a "L'art pour l'art," an art of escape. We must take sides and proclaim our stand.

From *The Studio,* XII, No. 259 (November 4, 1936).

Freud's theories and the literary slogans of the Surrealists have concentrated public opinion on the subconscious. Art attains its effects in the main by means of subconscious sensations. (For otherwise any problem or new discovery could be successfully established solely through intellectual arguments.) And I am convinced that the subconscious can similarly absorb the revolutionary social ideas only by means of congenial conceptions expressed in a specific medium. The non-political approach of art is thus transformed, by means of the subconscious, into a weapon of an active attitude to reality, pressing for the solution of the urgent social and economic problems of today. But at the same time there can be no doubt that the utter ignorance of the great majority regarding the problems of *technique* is the greatest handicap for those wishing to establish a planned economy by socializing the means of production. There are many ways of removing that ignorance. Abstract art is one of them. It achieves this end, not through any fetishistic regard for technique, but through its subtle, scarcely notable influence on the subconscious. Thus in abstract painting—to mention only one of its many spheres—the regulative principles of color configuration, the discovery of the specific psycho-physical role of each color value, the combination of manual skill with mechanical devices, the conception of montage and the introduction of direct light, all provide a subconscious parallel to modern industry. I am not afraid to state this fact. Even a complete mechanization of art might not, it seems to me, imply a menace to its essential creativeness. For compared with the process of creation the problems of execution are only important in so far as the technique adopted—whether manual or mechanical—must be completely mastered. This raises the interesting problem of mechanized representation: photography, photo-montage, the film, which are transforming the traditional role of the representational painting by their revolutionary technique. Camera work has all the attributes of reality. The easel painting must capitulate in the face of this radical, mechanized conquest of kinetic reality. From the intellectual point of view, painting may preserve its historical significance; but sooner or later it will lose its subconscious potency as a means of representation. Here again we find that the former distinction between art and non-art, between craftsmanship and mechanical technique is no longer in any sense an absolute one. Painting, photography, film and light display no longer have any exclusive sphere of activity jealously isolated from one another. They are all weapons in the struggle for a new and more purposive human reality.

In Defense of "Abstract" Art   *L. Moholy-Nagy*

Because he is not informed about the historic sequence of the artist's efforts, the layman is often unable to find the main direction, the "sense" in the art-isms of his contemporaries. There may be too many names: impressionism, pointillism, neo-impressionism, fauvism, expressionism, cubism, futurism, suprematism, neoplasticism, dadaism, surrealism, constructivism, nonobjectivism. But in analyzing the paintings of these various groups one soon finds a common denominator, the supremacy of color over "story"; the directness of perceptional, sensorial values against the illusionistic rendering of nature; the emphasis on visual fundamentals to express a particular concept. Contemporary art generally tends more toward the direct and sensuous than the literary conceptual values. It emphasizes more the general, the universal than the special. It is based more upon biological than symbolic function.

It is a favorite saying that an artist has to start from nature, that no painting or sculpture exists which hadn't been stimulated by direct visual experience. Such statements are often quoted to disparage the efforts of the younger generation. "There is no abstract art. You must always start with something. Afterwards you can remove all traces of reality."—Picasso.

It is time to make a counter-suggestion, and show that such statements are erroneous because it is only the relationship between visual elements, and not the subject matter, which produces visual structure with an intrinsic meaning.

Like the semanticist, who strives for logical cleanliness, a clearing away of loosely trailing connotative associations in the verbal sphere, the abstract artist seeks to disengage the visual fundamentals from the welter of traditional symbolism and inherited illusionistic expectations. We should exult in this puritanic task and not merely be frightened or stumble into a possible richness which the old connotations may yet yield. We must leave the arts with a clean surface that only permanent and vital meaning, native to the age yet to come, may adhere.

The intrinsic meaning of an abstract painting, as a peculiar form of visual articulation, lies mainly in the integration of the visual elements, in its *freedom from the imitation* of nature and the philosophy connected with it. In the past, nature—observance and contemplation of it—has been a mighty stimulus because of its balanced, organic performance. But the naïve idea of identity taken over from late Greek culture led only to a servile imitation. The

From *Journal of Aesthetics and Art Criticism,* IV (1945).

first powerful lever of liberation was concomitantly developed with the empirical technique of scientific research, that is, the "laboratory aspect" of science where the conditions of observation can be produced and varied at will. Impressionism and Cubism brought a re-evaluation of nature in terms of visual research still intermingled with naturalistic elements. The art of the postcubist period derived its first abstraction from nature, but later it freed itself from that departure and articulated the basic means of visual impact—shape, size, position, direction, point, line, plane, color, rhythm—and built with them a completely new structure of vision. This was their attempt to grasp emotionally the problems of space-time. One function of abstract art was and is the experimental demonstration of the forceful possibility of such an approach and to extend it also to the problems of the inner vision and the inner vision in motion.

This fundamental concept and concern of the abstract painter does not seem to be involved in the details of "social reality." Consequently, abstract art is often interpreted by the social revolutionaries as the art of the escapists. But the artist's duty is not to be always in opposition. He sometimes can better concentrate his forces on the central problem of visually constituting this world *in statu nascendi* and only treat the shortcomings of society as transitory facts on the periphery of his efforts. In a deeper sense, the interpretation of space-time with light and color is a truly revolutionary act.

Color and light are the prime movers of abstract, nonobjective painting; the basis of a research which serves with its pure structural values, not only as a measuring rod for a new esthetics, but in their symbolic values for a desirable new social order. On another level, abstract painting can be understood as an arrested, frozen phase of a kinetic light display leading back to the original emotional, sensuous meaning of color.

In the Renaissance, the function of color was auxiliary to the perfect illusion of objects in space. Monocular perspective was devised to produce that illusion with the help of color. It is important to observe that these paintings had to be viewed from one certain point whence the scene would appear undistorted. We find unbearable this fixed relationship of the spectator to the painting in which his observation is permanently bound. (In fact, we find unbearable all other fixed and rigid relationships in this world today.) Renaissance painting wiped out the pre-Renaissance directness of visual experience and became not only static but also strongly illustrative. Pre-Renaissance painting did not try to imitate reality. It admitted that it had been painted to express moods, devotion, wonder, and ecstasy with the sensuous and emotional power of color. It emphasized less the "story" and more the vital performance of color to which the spectator could react directly without reasoning and conscious analysis. The decay started with the vanishing-point perspective which seemed to be a dazzling performance, since the painter could render scenes as the eyes perceived them. Suddenly every effort was concentrated on the perfection of imitation, with the result that three hundred years of practice by the "perspectivists" taught everybody to evaluate painting by its illusionistic potency. Their method of rendering became the automatic possession of generations who did not even have to learn the original rules of geometric construction; who knew by heart "how to do it."

When photography appeared, the excitement of this manually produced space and object illusion diminished; it could not stand the competition of the mechanically perfect execution of most complicated, though also monocular, photographic perspectives. Contemporary painters, confronted with the static, restricted vision of a fixed perspective, countermarched to color and produced on the flat surface a new *kinetic* concept of spatial articulation, vision in motion.

●

Vision in motion is seeing while moving.

Vision in motion is seeing moving objects either in reality or in forms of visual representation as in cubism and futurism. In the latter case the spectator, stimulated by the specific means of rendering, re-creates mentally and emotionally the original motion.

Vision in motion is simultaneous grasp. Simultaneous grasp is creative performance—seeing, feeling and thinking in relationship and not as a series of isolated phenomena. It instantaneously integrates and transmutes single elements into a coherent whole. This is valid for physical vision as well as for the abstract.

Vision in motion is a synonym for simultaneity and space-time; a means to comprehend the new dimension.

Vision in motion also signifies planning, the projective dynamics of our visionary faculties.

1. *Landscape with Houses,* 1919. Oil on cardboard, 26″ x 34″. Kunst Kabinett Klihm, Munich. *Photo Landesbildstelle Rheinland.*

2. *Composition No. 19,* 1919. Oil on canvas, 44″ x 36½″. Courtesy Busch-Reisinger Museum, Harvard University, Cambridge, Mass. (Gift of Mrs. Sibyl Moholy-Nagy).

3. *Large Emotion Meter,* 1920. Oil on canvas, 37½″ x 29½″. Stedelijk van Abbemuseum, Eindhoven. Photo courtesy Museum of Contemporary Art, Chicago.

4. *E IV Construction VII,* 1922. Oil on canvas, 40″ x 32″. Galerie Klihm, Munich. Copyright Mrs. Sibyl Moholy-Nagy, New York.

5. *A X 1,* 1923. Oil on canvas, 53″ x 46″. Collection Mrs. Sibyl Moholy-Nagy, New York. Photo courtesy Museum of Contemporary Art, Chicago.

6. *A X L II,* 1927. Oil on canvas, 37⅛″ x 29⅛″. The Solomon R. Guggenheim Museum, New York (Gift of Mr. and Mrs. Andrew Fuller).

7. *Chicago Space 7,* 1941. Oil on canvas, 47" x 47". The Solomon R. Guggenheim Museum, New York.

8. *Ch. Feb. II,* 1943. Oil on canvas. Collection Zug, Zurich.

9. *Leu 3,* 1944. Oil on canvas, 3″ x 3″. Collection Mrs. Elizabeth Paepcke, Chicago.

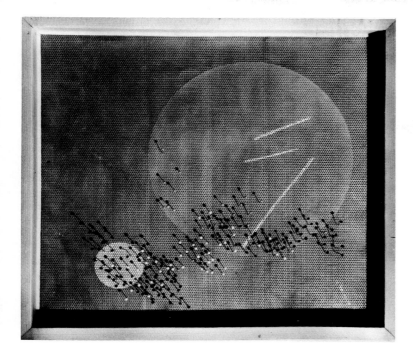

10. *Construction with Pins on Perforated Zinc,*
    1935. 4″ x 6″. Collection Mrs. Sibyl Moholy-
    Nagy, New York.

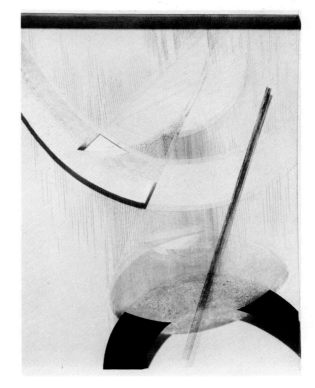

11. *Mills No. 2,* 1940. Oil on Plexiglas, 35″ x
    26″. The Solomon R. Guggenheim Museum,
    New York.

12. *Space Modulator (The Ovals),* 1943–45. Oil on Plexiglas, 36″ x 24″. The Solomon R. Guggenheim Museum, New York.

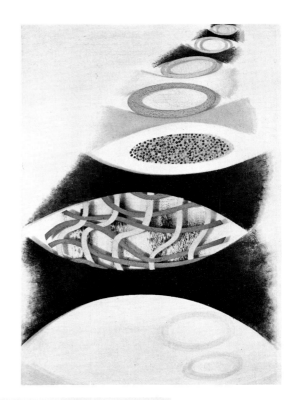

13. *Space Modulator—Red Over Black,* 1946. Oil on Plexiglas with screening, 18⅛″ x 25½″. The Detroit Institute of Arts. Photo courtesy Museum of Contemporary Art, Chicago.

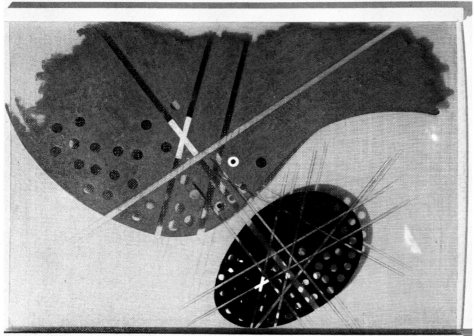

14. Photogram, 1922. Collection George Eastman House, Rochester, N.Y.

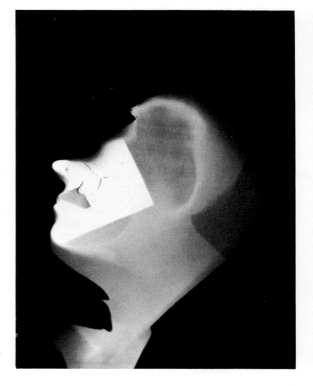

15. *Self-Portrait,* 1924. Photogram with torn paper. Collection George Eastman House, Rochester, N.Y.

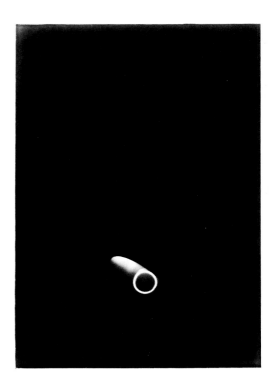

16. Photographic triptych, 1922. Collection Mrs. Sibyl Moholy-Nagy, New York.

17. *The Law of Series*, 1925. Photomontage, 8½″ x 6⅜″. Collection The Museum of Modern Art, New York (Anonymous gift, 1940).

18. *The Shooting Gallery,* 1925. Photomontage. Collection Mrs. Sibyl Moholy-Nagy, New York.

19. *Jealousy,* 1927. Photocollage, 24″ x 18″.
Galerie Klihm, Munich.

20. *Structure of the World,* 1927. Photomontage. Collection
George Eastman House, Rochester, N.Y.

21. *Marseilles,* 1928. Collection George Eastman House, Rochester, N.Y.

22. *Boats in the Old Harbor, Marseilles,* 1929. Collection
George Eastman House, Rochester, N.Y.

23. *Portrait in Negative* (Maria Werefkim, Ascona), 1929. Collection George Eastman House, Rochester, N.Y.

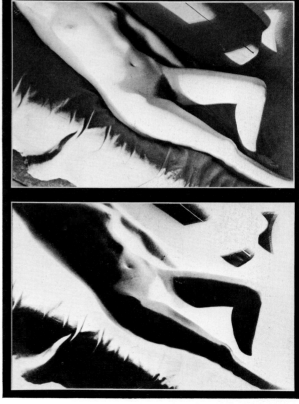

24. *Two Nudes, Positive-Negative,* 1932. Photos Robert E. Mates and Paul Katz, Collection George Eastman House, Rochester, N.Y.

25. *Chairs at Margate,* 1935. Collection George Eastman House, Rochester, N.Y.

26. Photogram, 1940. Collection George Eastman House, Rochester, N.Y.

On 60 Fotos by Moholy-Nagy *Franz R...*

Moholy has been productive in all branches of photograp... whereas the majority of modern photographers confine to a single one. Hitherto his endeavor was to gather and master all possibilities of photography. Moholy has been concerned with the *reality-photo* which primarily aims at nothing but holding fast a bit of immediate reality. Yet he has drawn *new* objects into this sphere of fixation, and this is progress, for in the jog-trot of man's sensible life the selection of objects he enjoys offers but a conventional and limited number of things. The *old,* Moholy has *seen* in a new way: by bolder plasticity, new shades of light and dark, a different distribution in the degrees of distinctness, and above all by a change of perspective. We usually focus sections of reality in a horizontal view-line. The daring sight from above and from below by sudden change of level which new technical achievements have brought about (lift, airplane) had not been made use of very much in pictures. Moholy was one of the first to take delight in these ups and downs. The slanting pictures of a vertical line thus offered (of a house, mast or chimney) are significant, for in a way they open *astronomic* perspectives: vertical in this broader sense is radial position corresponding to an imaginary center of the earth.

Very early Moholy interested himself in the *negative print*. Magical effects lie hidden in this inversion of light and dark.

And also in the *photogram,* which, as is known, is taken without a camera. The objects are put on sensitive paper. They are left a short or long space of time, held close or at a distance, exposed to intense or subdued light, to a mobile or a fixed light: the results attained appear like weird spheres of light, often of marvelous transparency, that seem to penetrate space. Sublime gradations, from gleaming white through a thousand shades of gray down to deepest black, can be produced thus. And by intersection either extreme nearness or the most distant distance is suggested. One must not judge results of photography by the cliché-productions in books. One must have had the original pictures in hand (as in art), for the best reproduction loses some of the preciseness which is decisive.

The photogram is as old as the photograph. But Man Ray's (Paris) and Moholy's (Berlin) is the merit of having applied it in modern form, of having perfected and sublimated the photogram. The "constructivist" Moholy appears most strongly in the photogram. Photography has by no means ousted abstract painting or

From *Moholy-Nagy: 60 Fotos* (Berlin: Klinkhardt & Biermann, 1930).

ɔ Moholy photography is but *one* form of dealing with
vhich other forms remain, and new forms arise.
ɔtomontage" Moholy belongs to the pioneers, who
ɔrgotten by an ungrateful world which has seized
have achieved by labor. Though photomontage also
ɔome generations ago, it yet has only in the present
ɔecome a deliberately forming process. Moholy's photomontage
contains usually some fanciful and gay innuendoes, and yet there
are depths. The satire of the future (comic papers &c.) will make
use of this style. In phototypography as a form of advertisement
such suggestive possibilities are employed to a great extent. However photomontage is not merely *applied photography* in the sense
of literary reference to certain matters or to propaganda: it contains a complete forming principle in itself when well done.

A New Instrument of Vision   *L. Moholy-Nagy*

In photography we possess an extraordinary instrument for reproduction. But photography is much more than that. Today it is in a
fair way to bringing (optically) something entirely new into the
world. The specific elements of photography can be isolated from
their attendant complications, not only theoretically, but tangibly,
and in their manifest reality.

The Unique Quality of Photography

The photogram, or camera-less record of forms produced by
light, which embodies the unique nature of the photographic process, is the real key to photography. It allows us to capture the
patterned interplay of light on a sheet of sensitized paper without
recourse to any apparatus. The photogram opens up perspectives
of a hitherto wholly unknown morphosis governed by optical laws
peculiar to itself. It is the most completely dematerialized medium
which the new vision commands.

What Is Optical Quality?

Through the development of black-and-white photography, light
and shadow were for the first time fully revealed; and thanks to it,
too, they first began to be employed with something more than a
purely theoretical knowledge. (Impressionism in painting may be

Written in 1932 and originally published in *Telehor* (Brno, 1936). Reprinted
by permission of Mrs. Sibyl Moholy-Nagy.

regarded as a parallel achievement.) Through the development of reliable artificial illumination (more particularly electricity), and the power of regulating it, an increasing adoption of flowing light and richly graduated shadows ensued; and through these again a greater animation of surfaces, and a more delicate optical intensification. This manifolding of graduations is one of the fundamental "materials" of optical formalism: a fact which holds equally good if we pass beyond the immediate sphere of black-white-gray values and learn to think and work in terms of colored ones.

When pure color is placed against pure color, tone against tone, a hard, poster-like decorative effect generally results. On the other hand the same colors used in conjunction with their intermediate tones will dispel this poster-like effect, and create a more delicate and melting impression. Through its black-white-gray reproductions of all colored appearances photography has enabled us to recognize the most subtle differentiations of values in both the gray and chromatic scales: differentiations that represent a new and (judged by previous standards) hitherto unattainable quality in optical expression. This is, of course, only one point among many. But it is the point where we have to begin to master photography's inward properties, and that at which we have to deal more with the artistic function of expression than with the reproductive function of portrayal.

Sublimated Technique

In reproduction—considered as the objective fixation of the semblance of an object—we find just as radical advances and transmogrifications, compared with prevailing optical representation, as in direct records of forms produced by light (photograms). These particular developments are well known: bird's-eye views, simultaneous interceptions, reflections, elliptical penetrations, etc. Their systematic co-ordination opens up a new field of visual presentation in which still further progress becomes possible. It is, for instance, an immense extension of the optical possibilities of reproduction that we are able to register precise fixations of objects, even in the most difficult circumstances, in a hundredth or thousandth of a second. Indeed, this advance in technique almost amounts to a psychological transformation of our eyesight,* since the sharpness of the lens and the unerring accuracy of its delineation have now trained our powers of observation up to a standard of visual perception

* Helmholtz used to tell his pupils that if an optician were to succeed in making a human eye, and brought it to him for his approval, he would be bound to say: "This is a clumsy job of work."

which embraces ultra-rapid snapshots and the millionfold magnification of dimensions employed in microscopic photography.

Improved Performance

Photography, then, imparts a heightened, or (in so far as our eyes are concerned) increased, power of sight in terms of time and space. A plain, matter-of-fact enumeration of the specific photographic elements—purely technical, not artistic, elements—will be enough to enable us to divine the power latent in them, and prognosticate to what they lead.

The Eight Varieties of Photographic Vision

1. Abstract seeing by means of direct records of forms produced by light: the photogram which captures the most delicate gradations of light values, both chiaroscuro and colored.
2. Exact seeing by means of the normal fixation of the appearance of things: reportage.
3. Rapid seeing by means of the fixation of movements in the shortest possible time: snapshots.
4. Slow seeing by means of the fixation of movements spread over a period of time: e.g. the luminous tracks made by the headlights of motor-cars passing along a road at night: prolonged time exposures.
5. Intensified seeing by means of
   a) Micro-photography;
   b) Filter-photography, which, by variation of the chemical composition of the sensitized surface, permits photographic potentialities to be augmented in various ways—ranging from the revelation of far-distant landscapes veiled in haze or fog to exposures in complete darkness: infra-red photography.
6. Penetrative seeing by means of X-rays: radiography.
7. Simultaneous seeing by means of transparent superimposition: the future process of automatic photomontage.
8. Distorted seeing: optical jokes that can be automatically produced by
   a) Exposure through a lens fitted with prisms, and the device of reflecting mirrors; or
   b) Mechanical and chemical manipulation of the negative after exposure.

What Is the Purpose of the Enumeration?

What is to be gleaned from this list? that the most astonishing possibilities remain to be discovered in the raw material of photography, since a detailed analysis of each of these aspects furnishes us with a number of valuable indications in regard to their application, adjustment, etc. Our investigations will lead us in another direction, however. We want to discover what is the essence and significance of photography.

The New Vision

All interpretations of photography have hitherto been influenced by the esthetic-philosophic concepts that circumscribed painting. These were for long held to be equally applicable to photographic practice. Up to now photography has remained in rather rigid dependence on the traditional forms of painting; and like painting it has passed through the successive stages of all the various art "isms": in no sense to its advantage, though. Fundamentally new discoveries cannot for long be confined to the mentality and practice of bygone periods with impunity. When that happens all productive activity is arrested. This was plainly evinced in photography, which has yielded no results of any value except in those fields where, as in scientific work, it has been employed without artistic ambitions. Here alone did it prove the pioneer of an original development, or of one peculiar to itself.

In this connection it cannot be too plainly stated that it is quite unimportant whether photography produces "art" or not. Its own basic laws, not the opinions of art critics, will provide the only valid measure of its future worth. It is sufficiently unprecedented that such a "mechanical" thing as photography, and one regarded so contemptuously in an artistic and creative sense, should have acquired the power it has, and become one of the primary objective visual forms, in barely a century of evolution. Formerly the painter impressed his own perspective outlook on his age. We have only to recall the manner in which we used to look at landscapes, and compare it with the way we perceive them now! Think, too, of the incisive sharpness of those camera portraits of our contemporaries, pitted with pores and furrowed by lines. Or an air-view of a ship at sea moving through waves that seem frozen in light. Or the enlargement of a woven tissue, or the chiseled delicacy of an ordinary sawn block of wood. Or, in fact, any of the whole gamut of splendid details of structure, texture and "factor" of whatever objects we care to choose.

The New Experience of Space

Through photography, too, we can participate in new experiences of space, and in even greater measure through the film. With their help, and that of the new school of architects, we have attained an enlargement and sublimation of our appreciation of space, the comprehension of a new spatial culture. Thanks to the photographer humanity has acquired the power of perceiving its surroundings, and its very existence, with new eyes.

The Height of Attainment

But all these are isolated characteristics, separate achievements, not altogether dissimilar to those of painting. In photography we must learn to seek, not the "picture," not the esthetic of tradition, but the ideal instrument of expression, the self-sufficient vehicle for education.

Series (Photographic Image Sequences of the Same Object)

There is no more surprising, yet, in its naturalness and organic sequence, simpler form than the photographic series. This is the logical culmination of photography. The series is no longer a "picture," and none of the canons of pictorial esthetics can be applied to it. Here the separate picture loses its identity as such and becomes a detail of assembly, an essential structural element of the whole which is the thing itself. In this concatenation of its separate but inseparable parts a photographic series inspired by a definite purpose can become at once the most potent weapon and the tenderest lyric. The true significance of the film will only appear in a much later, a less confused and groping age than ours. The prerequisite for this revelation is, of course, the realization that a knowledge of photography is just as important as that of the alphabet. The illiterates of the future will be ignorant of the use of camera and pen alike.

—Translation from the German by F. D. Klingender
and P. Morton Shand

Photography in a Flash   *L. Moholy-Nagy*

I.

The discussion, which is still going on, as to whether photographs should be sharp or soft has its roots in the very beginnings of photography. Daguerre made his pictures on metal plates which

From Industrial Arts, I/4 (London, Winter, 1936).

could be neither retouched nor copied. They were therefore exceedingly sharp, penetrating, documentary.

II.

The Talbotype, discovered at the same time, was a paper negative which could therefore be used to take positive copies, but as the structure of the paper had to be copied also, the Talbotype could never achieve the exactness and sharpness of line, resembling an engraving, which distinguished the Daguerreotype.

III.

Talbot himself, Hill the Scottish painter, and some excellent photographers, such as Salzman, achieved such admirably picturesque results by means of the Talbot process that people became accustomed to confuse the creative intensity of the photographer with the traditional conception of the creative work of the painter. Thus faults were sanctioned which arose only from the inadequacy of the technical process.

IV.

New inventions, such as the glass plate, the dry plate, and the film, made it easier to learn the photographic craft, and as photographers grew more numerous dilettantism increased.

V.

The real promoters of photography in those pioneer days were not so much the small professional photographers as the amateurs and the scientists. The amateurs worked in order to master the methods of photography. The scientists toiled without any artistic ambitions, out of purely documentary interest. Even police record photographs, which were necessarily made as sharp and exact as possible, collaborated without intent in the building up of photographic knowledge.

VI.

Technical improvements were evolved to meet the needs of documentary photography. The possibility of fixing the quickest movement came to the help of the photography of inanimate objects in time exposure, while the snapshot with an increasingly closer approach to instantaneous exposure, was used by the reporter and the sports photographer.

VII.

Again, the discovery of sources of electric light, the possibility of directing intense floods of artificial light upon the object, the high sensitivity of the photographic plate, were all bridges to a direct light-picture.

VIII.

There has, however, grown up a danger that, through the general knowledge of photographic methods, an undesirable state of affairs may appear in photographic work. The idea may become prevalent that it is possible to make "beautiful" pictures without any difficulty by following a given list of directions.

IX.

But the aim of the present should not be to make photography an "art" in the old sense of the word. On the contrary, the real photographer has a great social responsibility. He has work to do with these given technical means which cannot be accomplished by any other method. This work is the exact reproduction of everyday facts, without distortion or adulteration. This means that he must work for sharpness and accuracy. The standard of value in photography must be measured, not merely by photographic esthetics, but by the human-social intensity of the optical representation.

There is no more surprising, yet—in its naturalness and organic sequences—simpler form than the photographic series; that is photographic sequences of the same object.

This is the logical culmination of photography. The series is no longer a "picture," and none of the canons of pictorial esthetics can be applied to it. Here the separate picture loses its identity as such, and becomes a detail of assembly, an essential structural element of the whole, which is the thing itself. In this harmony of its separate but inseparable parts, a photographic series inspired by a definite purpose can become a most potent weapon, or the tenderest lyric.

The pre-requisite for this revelation is, of course, the realization that a knowledge of photography is just as important as a knowledge of the alphabet. The illiterates of the future will be ignorant of the use of camera and pen alike.

Letter to Beaumont Newhall   *L. Moholy-Nagy*

7, Farm Walk
London N. W.11
7 April, 1937

Dear Beaumont Newhall,

Thanks and congratulations for your excellent book *Photography 1839–1937*. I think it is one of the best publications about this matter which I ever saw.

I would think that photogram is a better name than "shadowgraph" because—at least in my experiments—I used or tried to use not alone shadows of solid transparent and translucent objects but really light effects themselves, e.g., lenses, liquids, crystals & so on. A second point: I made my first photograms in 1922 and I gave some of them in the same year to the editors of *Broom,* Mr. [Harold] Loeb and Mr. [Matthew] Josephson who visited me because they heard from [Tristan] Tzara that I made photograms. I did not know in this time neither about [William Henry Fox] Talbot's and other's shadowgraphs nor about [Man Ray's] Rayographs.

Yours, sincerely,
(Signed) L. Moholy-Nagy

Reprinted by permission of Mrs. Sibyl Moholy-Nagy.

Space-Time and the Photographer   *L. Moholy-Nagy*

One of the great surprises for the students of photography must be the discovery that photography follows exactly the same trends as other creative forms of expression. It is dependent on present technical, scientific, sociological trends and their relationships. As these relationships are not obvious to everyone it will be necessary to make an analysis of this statement and show by examples what its meaning is. It may become clear then, that events and actions which form the pattern of our life are more interrelated than is usually taken for granted, and that it is misleading to see photog-

From *American Annual of Photography* (1942).

raphy in its mechanical aspect and for its technological miracle alone. Such an analysis may also eliminate the rather passionate discussion whether photography is art or not. Namely, if photography shows the genuine formulation of the time-bound elements with its own means, then it is doing something-plus besides its mechanical aspect. Secondly, if the thesis of interrelation is valid, then photography is not only capable of being influenced by other elements, but also has the potentiality to influence them. Thirdly, it may be proved that one can produce with photography the same content as with the other means of expression. Fourth, the range of rendering is dependent upon the human grasp, will, and skill.

The mechanical aspects of photography have already changed our technique of encompassing an object, its structure, texture and surface, and have brought us into a new relationship with light and space. But what can we do with these new experiences, how order and fit them into our life? This could be accomplished only through human initiative, thinking, and feeling built upon the new principle: integration. Integration is the attempt today to escape from the irresponsibilities of a strictly specialized existence. An early specialization leads to a mechanical perfection without the vitalizing experience of other fundamentals. Our specialist age is built upon a multiplicity of information pounded relentlessly into the individual by the daily press, magazine, radio and cinema. But tragically, the more he knows in this superficial way, the less he is able to understand, because he has not been taught to relate and integrate his casual and scattered information. Photography too, without coordination with other fields, is nothing but one of these isolated information services.

Photography, as we usually speak of it, is taking photographs with the camera. One of the obvious results is the projection of space on a plane expressed with values of black and white and gray. But what is space? The answer to this question may show the potential value of photography toward integration with many other activities. One of the methods to explain space is to show how to articulate it. Every period in human culture has developed a spatial conception. Such space conceptions were utilized not only for shelter but also for play, dancing, fighting, in fact, for the domination of life in every detail. A new space conception originated mainly through new materials and constructions introduced by the industrial revolution. However, as the technology was derived from new scientific findings, physics, chemistry, biology, physiology, sociology, etc.—all these elements have to be considered in our new space conception too. We can say that this new space conception is the legitimate successor of a space tradition giving such poor results at present. In this way architecture (mentioned here as the most easily recognizable spatial expression) became more a juxta-position of rooms than an articulation of space.

The history of articulated space is dependent on the grasp of the dimensions: one, two, three, and more.

The magnificence of the Egyptian temple could be compre-hended by walking through a one-dimensional straight line, the Sphinx alley, toward its façade. Later, the Greek architect of the Parthenon designed the approach to the temple so that the visitors had to move around the colonnades toward the main entrance. In this way a two-dimensional approach was created. The Gothic cathedral articulated the inside most intriguingly. The spectator was set in the midst of related space cells of the naves, the choir, etc., and so was capable of a quick comprehension of their values. The Renaissance and the Baroque brought man in closer contact with the inside and the outside of the building. Architecture became a part of the landscape and the landscape was handled in relationship to the architecture. Photography can record these changes with reasonable accuracy and can help to reconstruct the spatial spirit of the past. In the last one hundred years one can find any number of photographs with congenial renderings and in the last two decades the spatial records gained much in consciousness of ap-proach. Besides straight records, one can observe the attempt to show delicate space articulations which are often built up with elements in a vanishing point perspective; or with linear elements, as building structures, leafless trees; or with unsharp foreground and distinctly organized subdivisions toward the background.

In the age of balloons and airplanes, architecture can be viewed not only in front and from the sides, but also from above. So the bird's-eye view, and its opposites, the worm's- and fish's-eye views become a daily experience. This fact introduces something extraor-dinary, almost indescribable, into our life. Architecture appears no longer as a static structure, but, if we think of it in terms of airplanes and motor cars, architecture must be linked with move-ment. This changes its entire aspect so that a new formal and struc-tural congruence with the new element, *time,* becomes manifest. This brings a clearly recognizable difference between the experience of a pedestrian and a driver in viewing objects. For the motorcar driver, for example, distant objects are brought into relationship for which the pedestrian has yet no eye.

We all know that the appearance of any object changes when we move past it with speed. High speed makes it impossible to grasp insignificant details. So a new language of spatial orientation and communication is arising in which also photography takes an active part. Something similar can be observed in the advertising field, too, especially in poster making. In 1937 Jean Carlu, one of the best French poster designers, made an experiment. He mounted two posters on two conveyor belts which moved with different speeds. The one poster by Toulouse-Lautrec, from around 1900, moved at eight miles per hour, approximately the speed of a horse and buggy. The other, a contemporary poster, moved at fifty miles per hour, the speed of an automobile. Both posters could be read easily. After this, Carlu accelerated the speed of the Toulouse-Lautrec poster up to fifty miles per hour, and at this speed the poster could be seen only as a blur. It is easy to realize the implications. A new viewpoint in the graphic arts is a natural consequence of this age of speed.

Speed itself can become the subject of a visual analysis. And here again the camera enters the field. We know of innumerable shots of quick motion, sport scenes, jumps, etc.; on the other hand we can observe unfolding buds, moving clouds taken at intervals; similarly the effect of long exposures of moving objects, streets and merry-go-rounds. Professor Harold Edgerton, of the Massachusetts Institute of Technology, made a new form of speed photographs with the help of a stroboscope. The relationship between the velocity of part movements gave him the clue to improvements on the actions of golfers, turbines, spinning wheels and various kinds of machinery. These pictures are the unusual records of juxtaposition of frozen part movements analyzable in each space-time unit. These speed photographs are of more recent date, but they are astonishingly similar to the Futuristic paintings, in fact, they are their exact repetition; e.g., the *Speed* by Balla, 1913. Marcel Duchamp's well-known picture of 1912, *Nude Descending the Stairway,* shows also the same juxtaposition of frozen movement parts.

In 1900 the Futurists had already begun to emphasize movement, saying, "The world's splendor has been enriched by a new beauty—the beauty of speed. We shall sing," they continued, "of the man at the steering wheel." The Futurists' aim was to represent movement, and some of their old statements from 1912 still sound fresh and enlightening. For example, "Who can still believe in the opacity of bodies, since our sharpened and multiplied sensitiveness has already penetrated the obscure manifestations of the medium? Why should we forget in our creations the doubled power of our sight, capable of giving results analogous to those of the X-rays?" Boccioni in *Power of the Street* projected such a double power of sight, such a fusion of the manifold elements of a street into one expressive representation.

The X-ray pictures, about which the Futurists spoke, are among the most outstanding space-time examples on the static plane. They give a transparent view of an opaque solid, the outside and inside of the structure. The passion for transparencies is one of the most spectacular features of our time. We might say, with pardonable enthusiasm, that structure becomes transparency and transparency manifests structure.

Cameraless pictures are also direct light diagrams recording the actions of light over a period of time, that is, the motion of light in space. Cameraless pictures, photograms, however, bring a completely new form of space articulation. It no longer has anything to do with the record of an existing space (or space-time) structure. This is usually created in the form of architecture from elements clearly circumscribed by their masses, lengths, widths, heights. Certainly these elements' masses and weights could be greatly simplified, the span of the openings enormously enlarged. Nevertheless they must be there to serve as the point of departure for the photographic record. The photogram for the first time produces space without existing space structure only by articulation on the plane with the advancing and receding values of half-tones in black and gray and with the radiating power of their contrasts and their sublime gradations. One suddenly becomes aware that here starts an invigorating investigation about the incoherent use of our rich resources. Technological ingenuity provides us with gigantic structures, factories and skyscrapers, but how we use them is shockingly anti-biological—resulting in wild city growth, elimination of vegetation, fresh air, and sunlight. To make bad worse, in the shadow of these modern buildings we thoughtlessly tolerate the slums and every bad condition that goes with them. So it seems that the most abstract experiment of space-time articulation carries a sensible reality, if the right interpretation can be made. Such experiments may signalize a spatial order in which not single structural parts, or large spans of openings will play the important part, but the relationships of neighbor units, buildings and free areas, shelter and leisure, production and recreation; leading toward a biologically right living most probably through a right regional planning; toward a city-land unity. Such an architecture as a new type of space articulation will bring an even more advanced solution than the present pioneers' work. These pioneers already humanized the technological advances even if for a privileged layer. They use the new materials —glass, steel, reinforced concrete, plastics, and plywood—for dwelling purposes in the interest of a more functional and biological living. That this type of contemporary architecture is not yet accepted to a great extent, shows more the missing orientation of a tradition-bound public about their own requirements and benefits than a negative criticism of the new direction. The public accepts technical processes and new inventions more easily when they concern only details of the living standard. The acceptance becomes difficult if it seems to bring radical changes in traditional life habits. Of course many things, appearing first as gadgets or appliances, gain an enormous influence during one generation. Then it is usually too late to call for their elimination.

Our automobiles, trains, and airplanes, for example, can be viewed as mobile buildings and the fact is that this country has today 400,000 families living on wheels in trailers. These vehicles, mobile "houses," will influence the coming architecture. We know already projects of moving houses, sanitariums for example, turning with the sun. The architecture of Frank Lloyd Wright, especially the strongly cantilevered house of Kaufmann's at Bear Run, shows more similarity to an airplane than to traditional buildings. Another American architect, Paul Nelson, designed a "suspended house" where the baths, bedrooms, and library were hanging down from the ceiling. With this kind of arrangement, Nelson gained an enormous free, columnless space inside the fenestration which he designated as the living room. To live in such a house would create the sensation of being in an airplane with an intensified relationship to one's surroundings.

These suggestions may be disturbing to a few people, who probably would be more aghast at the Utopian plan of Professor Bernal of Cambridge, England, to construct houses the walls of which are produced by compressed air, by rotating air streams. The walls would insulate perfectly. The question arises why one should live between stone walls when one could live under the blue sky between green trees with all the advantages of perfect insulation? There is already a house with glass walls by Marcel Breuer in Zurich where the garden grows right into the house through the wall. The trend in new architecture goes more and more in this direction. The buildings of contemporary architects with their undivided gigantic windows allow nature really to enter the house. Every Gropius, Van der Rohe, Neutra or Keck house clearly demonstrates this principle. Of course even the most modern, yet still static architecture is only a transitory step toward a future architecture of a kinetic character. Space-time is now the new basis on which the edifice of future thoughts and work should be built. Contemporary arts, rapid changes in our surroundings through inventions, motorization, radio, and television, electronic action, records of light phenomena, and speed, are helping us to sense its existence and significance.

Binding different space and time levels together, we shall find that reflections and transparent mirrorings of the passing traffic in the windows of motor cars or shops belong in the same category. In photographic rendering they usually appear as superimpositions. Mirroring means in this sense the changing aspects of vision, the sharpened identification of the inside and outside penetrations.

With this instrument of thought many other phenomena (dreams, for example) can be explained as space-time articulations. In dreams there is a characteristic blending of independent events into a coherent whole.

Super-imposition of photographs, as frequently seen in motion pictures, can be used as the visual representational form of dreams, and in this way, as a space-time synonym.

The photomontage, a device often used in advertising, has a very similar technique. The cutting and assemblage of the parts is applied here on a static plane. The effect is that of a real scene, a synopsis of actions, produced by originally unrelated space and time elements juxtaposed and fused into a unity.

The acquaintance with these few attempts of a space-time visualization of which there are many more, may help to clarify the art of the motion picture. Motion pictures, more than anything else, fulfill the requirements of a space-time visual art. We can say that motion pictures can be used today even for very subtle articulation of space-time concepts.

A motion picture is the assemblage of numerous shots. In other words a film scene is "cut"—glued together from different shots. Any film sequence may serve as an example. For instance:

1. A person enters Rockefeller Center, New York.
2. He speaks to an audience.
3. A hand throws a bottle (close up).
4. Bottle flies through the air and misses speaker.
5. Hand slaps face (close up).
6. Hand pounds head (close up).

This scene suggests that one person speaking in Rockefeller Center was attacked by a man throwing a bottle. This man was then slapped and counter-attacked. Well, the peculiarity of this film scene is that all the six shots belonging to it have been photographed at six different places—some even in Europe—at six separate times.

The power of assemblage, the quick fluidity of the action structure, which seems logically to perform this incident, creates the scene as a coherent space-time reality. This, however, never existed.

It takes considerable time to grasp this miracle of illusion when so exactly analyzed. But the fact is that everyone experiences it daily in the cinema and appreciates it as normal stimulus for the senses.

Something similar may happen when one travels. Movements can be perceived on different layers: e.g., Train A is moving from the station and meets Train B slowly moving from the opposite direction. Through the windows of Train A one is watching Train B moving away and when occasionally the windows of the two crossing trains are in direct line one can glimpse beyond a street with cars and pedestrians moving in different directions. With these types of relationships we are constantly heading toward dynamic, kinetic representations of time-spatial existences. The time problem today is connected with the space problem, and it is presented to us with all the elements of knowledge of our period. It involves all our faculties in a re-orientation of kinetics, motion, light, speed. Constant changes of light, materials, energies, tensions, and positions, are here related in an understandable form. It stands for many things: integration; simultaneous penetration of inside and outside; conquest of the structure instead of the façade.

It is in our power to use this conception, and the photographer can be one of the main participants in this task. But he has to focus his attention on the facts which give an adequate record of the actions and ideas of his time. As he cannot do this without participating fully in life, consciously or intuitively his specialized field must be integrated with social reality. So naturally his visual selections will be colored by his attitude toward life. This relationship to society may have the power of rising to objective heights expressing the constructive framework of our civilization instead of drowning in the chaos of a million details. Then the photographer will bring to the masses a new and creative vision. This will be his social significance. For culture is not the work of a few outstanding people. To benefit society their theories have to penetrate into everybody's daily routine.

The reader may be interested in the following descriptions of the illustrations which accompany this article.*

Fig. 1. FROM A RADIO TOWER. BIRD'S-EYE VIEW, 1928. The re-

* Only some of which are reprinted here. *Ed.*

ceding and advancing values of the black and white, grays, and textures, are here very similar to the photogram.

Fig. 2. MIRRORING. *J. H. Brown, School of Design in Chicago.* The black, white and grays, the spatial divisions, size, difference, and distortions create a new type of space articulation.

Fig. 3. BAUHAUS BALCONIES, 1926. A frog's- or worm's-eye view. A new experience in rendering, as the photographer of the old school used artificial means to straighten out the strong converging lines.

Fig. 4. SPRING, 1928. A bird's-eye view of trees which form a unity with the pattern of the street. The lines running in many directions, placed each behind the other, from a very rich spatial network.

Fig. 5. STAIRWAY IN BEXHILL PAVILION, 1936. In this picture the spatial articulation is expressed mostly through the pattern of linear divisions, creating through it a feeling of great spatial richness. However, the light pattern in the form of little planes is more pronounced than the linear divisions.

Fig. 6. RUE CANNEBIERE, MARSEILLES, 1929. A street is seen through a balcony railing. The unfocused railing separates the scene into individual cells through which their spatial quality is more emphasized. These divisions appear also as if they were parts of a broken mirror, where the broken parts are lying on different levels.

Fig. 7. LEDA AND THE SWAN (*photomontage*), 1925. Linear elements, structural pattern, close-up, and isolated figures are here the elements for a space articulation. Pasted on a white surface these elements seem to be embedded in infinite space, with clear articulation of nearness and distance. The best description of their effect would be perhaps to say that each element is pasted on vertical glass panes, which are set up in an endless series each behind the other.

Fig. 8. PHOTOGRAM, 1941. This photogram is really a counterpart of the picture rue Cannebiere, Marseilles, produced without a camera. The only difference is that here the spatial units are more fused together.

Fig. 9. PHOTOGRAM, 1939. The photogram is a picture produced without the camera, only through exposure of the light-sensitive medium to light. The fine gray values between the white and black pole and the receding and advancing values of these gradations may create a spatial articulation unknown to any other medium.

Fig. 10. SPACE MODULATOR IN PLEXIGLAS, 1941. Transparency

and mirroring of transparency forms here a consciously organized spatial pattern.

Paths to the Unleashed
Color Camera   *L. Moholy-Nagy*

1. COLOR PHOTOGRAPHY is still grappling, as it has been for forty years, with the problem of providing a colored reproduction of nature which should be satisfactory in every respect. Emulsions, color filters, and screen plate transparencies, because of the physical formation of their employed pigments, give only an approximate translation of the object's natural coloring. For instance, it is well known that by means of a subtractive process we can obtain from the three colors, yellow, red, and blue, either an intense blue or an intense green, but not both simultaneously, unless we employ a second blue. This insufficiency undoubtedly sets the color-photographer a very important task; he can deliberately choose the nature and degree of his transmutation of nature and lead it to a harmonious result.

This is no unusual statement, only the destruction of an illusion which besets the average spectator of color photography, who is apt to base his criticism upon the assumption that the results must be in full accordance with the reality of the object portrayed.

2. But there is another common illusion which must be dispelled. Most people imagine that the mere existence of color photography means a great advance for photography as a whole. To be sure, it is a step forward in technique, but not in photography. Color photography still sets itself the same tasks which the best photographers of the pioneer period were already solving a century ago. The time is gradually approaching when the color photographer should apply the same practical and theoretical principles which the good modern black-and-white photographer, whether amateur or professional, naturally accepts as a standard.

The impulse to achieve this comes from the new single-exposure camera systems of Bernpohl, Reckmeyer, Taylor-Hobson, Klein and others, which enable three colored sectional pictures to be taken at the same time; also from the improved Finlay process and from the increased sensibility of the new auto-chromatic photographic materials (Agfacolor, Dufaycolor, etc.). They are the first steps toward the unleashing of the color camera, since, aided by these accessories, it is possible to take colored instantaneous snaps, thereby opening up in color the whole series of angles and points of view which have already been taught to us by the unleashed black-and-white camera.

3. Thus, intensified possibilities of reproduction may be anticipated for color photography, transcending what is possible in painting or appreciable to the naked eye. But this does not mean that this technique has as yet created its own problems. All we know at present is that it is a translation of black-and-white photography into color. In order to penetrate into the individual laws of color photography, we should do well to recall an occurrence of fifteen to twenty years ago, namely the way in which the black-and-white film reacted upon static black-and-white photography. We may with certainty assume that the general introduction of color films will give a new impetus to color photography and provide it with an unmistakable range of problems of its own. Today—previous to this introduction—we can only record our own observations, uncertain as yet and feeling our way.

4. It seems to me that the first and most important element of the color film is the artificial source of light. During projection, light penetrates the transparent film, or the layer of color, as the case may be. This gives rise to coincidence between light and color. This coincidence had been lost to color composition since the decay of the art of the stained-glass window.

It has always been one of the aims of painting to reproduce manifestations of colors with the same intensity with which they appear in Nature. This is nothing new to connoisseurs of Impressionist painting, but few are aware that in many points the development of Impressionism has contributed to the clarifying of the problem of the *color film*. It is not only that the Pointillists anticipated the additive method of color photography—Seurat, for example, when he set points of red and green adjacent to one another so as to produce, at a sufficient distance, the illusion of a broad field of yellow, just as in the auto-chromatic Lumière photographic plate or the Dufaycolor film. But in the main it is seen in a healthier attitude to color composition itself, which has not only created a new feeling for color but also laid the foundation of a new confidence in the treatment of *space*. The Impressionists dared to take the first step toward objectivity in optical problems; they were the first to suppress the narrative, story-telling element in painting in favor of the cult of color, and they were the basis of the art of Cézanne, the father of all new forms of expression in painting.

5. It is my conviction that Cézanne's artistic development will for a long time to come remain the practical foundation of color

photography and the color film, so that it seems in place here to determine the course of this development.

We can trace three distinct periods in the art of Cézanne, namely; (*a*) a narrative, psychological stage; (*b*) a naturalistic period; and (*c*) an abstract period.

Since, during the first period, we can speak only of Cézanne the man, it has no relation to our special optical problems. These pictures relate sublimated stories, very susceptible of psychoanalysis (*Temptation of St. Anthony, Murder,* etc.). Cézanne's real development as a painter begins with the second period. He had then recognized that his task was to reproduce the colored phenomena of light playing on the surface of things—that is, the most intense effect of light that color in nature can produce. In order to reproduce these effects in paint, the Impressionists invented an extensive scale of new technical artifices, and Cézanne developed the technique still further. Observed close at hand, the pictures belonging to this second period are seen to consist of opalescent shimmering single strokes, points, tracts of color which, seen at a proper distance, resolve themselves into a wonderful unity, glowing with light, the natural reproduction of a scene, usually a landscape.

This analytical, dissective technique permitted a representation of nature and space with an intensity hitherto unknown. Once this step had been taken, Cézanne could direct his interest to the objective problems of the relation of colors, the very existence of color.

His third period, the abstract, was the culmination of this attitude. In these late pictures he is only concerned with the composition of stretches of space-composing color and colored tensions. He begins with nature, but he overcomes the initial structure and uses it merely as a framework.

6. We know how painting continued to develop. Cézanne's objective creative work had opened up a path by way of Expressionism and Cubism to abstract painting. Today it is possible for a painter to work directly in color without employing a naturalistic accessory construction of natural phenomena.

I should like to emphasize my belief that color photography will continue to develop Cézanne's principles just as it has already in the art of painting. It is not so much the experimental color film as precisely the commercial color film which I expect will return to Cézanne himself after it has gone through a fruitless period of struggle with useless historic styles.

7. The abstract has now seized upon color as the medium of more objective expression. But it has not yet been possible to create the highest intensity of color, as expressed in nature (through reflection or absorption of light by certain bodies). It is thus once

more a question of the same ancient problem, but no longer upon a naturalistic plane.

I made an experiment on these lines in the transparent picture where the picture is painted on the front and back of a transparent material. Adjacent to the colored surfaces there is a perforation. This admits unfiltered light, so that in addition to the pigmentary effect of the painted spaces we have a direct material effect derived from the light striking through upon the background. Thus a kind of spatial kinetics also begins to play its part. When the picture is secured at a certain distance from its background, we have effects of light and shade which appear to move as the spectator walks past the picture.

Real painting of light which would also have the advantage of movement could of course come into being if the color film were properly handled. This will not, however, be achieved by means of a *mechanical* photographic reproduction of nature, but by the creation of forms which are non-imitative.

8. As I have already mentioned, we have for this purpose the most proper element of created form—light itself, movable, multicolored, amenable to control. This light can become active, not only through the differentiation of reflection or through the power of absorption of any particular material upon which its rays are cast, but in the first instance through the action of a human will to create. It is here that the real conquest of color begins, the spiritualization of the direct effect of light. The true kinetic representation of color values will bring us the first great sensation in this respect, and probably through a new form of montage which will create continuity and composition by optical, not psychological, means. Much time will elapse before film reaches the point when color will be divorced from its naturalistic-illusionist meaning. The creation of colored form in light, free from these elements, will probably lead in the end to the abstract cinematograph.

The static equivalent would be the color photogram, analogous to the black-and-white pictures taken without a camera. I have already made attempts in this direction, but I feel that without apparatus on a larger, perhaps more scientific scale, it would be difficult at this stage to put them into execution.

9. All in all we can therefore say:

Firstly: that today the color-photographer must transpose his representations of nature in colored expression according to the chemical-physical constituents of his photographic material.

Secondly: that he must use the unleashed color-photo camera in accordance with the recognized principles of black-and-white photography.

Thirdly: in the color photograms which have still to be developed, he will find the right color-key to color photography.   (*1939*)

Review of Moholy's
Achievement   *Beaumont Newhall*

When he died in 1946, László Moholy-Nagy was reading the final proofs of *Vision in Motion*. The book has become his testament and his monument, for in it he put down the experience of a lifetime of teaching and thinking about art. Its greatest contribution is the explanation of the pedagogical method of the Institute of Design, of which he was the founder. This occupies the first half of the book, and is liberally illustrated with reproductions of work by students. The second half of the book is devoted to Moholy's views on various types of art production: Painting, sculpture, photography, moving pictures, literature, music, city planning.

Throughout the text Moholy has much to say about photography, in which he has always been intensely interested. As an abstract painter he found photography a stimulating visual tool. He considered it a means of discovery, and was much concerned in changing it from what he considered a reproductive technique to a productive medium. This led him to surprising judgments of the past, as when he wrote "In the official history of art, photography was for a long time considered only a mechanical means of recording." Calling to mind what the painters Delacroix, Delaroche, Millet and Matisse had to say about photography, the truth of this sweeping generalization may, perhaps, be doubted. One immediately thinks of Hill and Adamson, of Mrs. Cameron, and of Stieglitz, and one says, with Lamartine, "Photography is the photographer."

He goes on: "When any interpretation tried to elevate photography to art, it was with the esthetic-philosophic concepts customary in the definition of painting." There have always been, it is true, photographers who have imitated painting, using the camera as a short cut to "art." But pictorialism is not inclusive: photographs of every age abound which we admire, not as substitute paintings, but as fragments of reality seized with insight at the moment of revelation. Thus the finest daguerreotypes, the moving Civil War scenes, the portraits of Stieglitz, the street scenes of Atget. Records, yes. But important not because they are the "narrow rendering of nature" which Moholy criticizes, but because through

From *Photo Notes* (March, 1948).

this magic of the camera we face reality with an immediacy which no other medium can parallel.

Moholy was impatient with the natural camera image, which he distorted by tipping the camera up or pointing it down, and by using the negative itself as an end rather than a means. He seldom previsualized the final print, for he was not interested in capturing on film and paper an already discovered vision. On the contrary, he discovered beauty *after* the photograph had been completed. Once, in Carmel, Edward Weston was showing Moholy some of his prints. I was an onlooker. Moholy kept finding in the photographs hidden and fantastic forms, which were often revealed only when —to Weston's obvious, but politely hidden, annoyance—he turned the print upside down. These after-products of Weston's vision fascinated Moholy: he considered photographs not interpretations of nature, but objects in themselves fascinating. I was reminded of the first time I met Moholy. We looked together at a score or more of his photographs. One of them, a view down from a bridge tower at Marseilles, held his attention as if it were a new thing and the work of another. "What a wonderful pattern!" Moholy exclaimed, pointing to a pile of coiled-up ropes. "I never saw them before!"

But more than the image of the lens, Moholy reveled in the photogram, cameraless photography. Objects laid on sensitive paper modulate the light, creating patterns of black-gray-white. The photogram maker's problem has nothing to do with interpreting the world, but rather with the formation of abstractions. Objects are chosen for their light-modulating characteristic: their reality and significance disappear. The logical end point of the photogram is the reduction of photography to the light-recording property of silver salts. To the cameraman this is what Malevitch's *White on White* is to the painter.

The New Typography   *L. Moholy-Nagy*

Typography is a tool of communication. It must be communication in its most intense form. The emphasis must be on absolute clarity since this distinguishes the character of our own writing from that of ancient pictographic forms. Our intellectual relationship to the world is individual-exact (e.g. this individual-exact relationship is in a state of transition toward a collective-exact orientation). This is in contrast to the ancient individual-amorphous and later collective-amorphous mode of communication. Therefore priority: unequivocal clarity in all typographical compositions. Legibility—communication must never be impaired by an *a priori* esthetics. Letters may never be forced into a preconceived framework, for instance a square.

The printed image corresponds to the contents through its specific optical and psychological laws, demanding their typical form. The essence and the purpose of printing demand an uninhibited use of all linear directions (therefore not only horizontal articulation). We use all typefaces, type sizes, geometric forms, colors, etc. We want to create a new language of typography whose elasticity, variability and freshness of typographical composition is exclusively dictated by the inner law of expression and the optical effect.

The most important aspect of contemporary typography is the use of zincographic techniques, meaning the mechanical production of photoprints in all sizes. What the Egyptians started in their inexact hieroglyphs whose interpretation rested on tradition and personal imagination, has become the most precise expression through the inclusion of photography into the typographic method. Already today we have books (mostly scientific ones) with precise photographic reproductions; but these photographs are only secondary explanations of the text. The latest development supersedes this phase, and small or large photos are placed in the text where formerly we used inexact, individually interpreted concepts and expressions. The objectivity of photography liberates the receptive reader from the crutches of the author's personal idiosyncrasies and forces him into the formation of his own opinion.

It is safe to predict that this increasing documentation through photography will lead in the near future to a replacement of literature by film. The indications of this development are apparent already in the increased use of the telephone which makes letterwriting obsolete. It is no valid objection that the production of films

Originally published in *Staatliches Bauhaus in Weimar, 1919–23* (Munich, 1923). Reprinted by permission of Mrs. Sibyl Moholy-Nagy.

demands too intricate and costly an apparatus. Soon the making of a film will be as simple and available as now printing books.

An equally decisive change in the typographical image will occur in the making of posters, as soon as photography has replaced poster-painting. The effective poster must act with immediate impact on all psychological receptacles. Through an expert use of the camera, and of all photographic techniques, such as retouching, blocking, superimposition, distortion, enlargement, etc. in combination with the liberated typographical line, the effectiveness of posters can be immensely enlarged.

The new poster relies on photography, which is the new story-telling device of civilization, combined with the shockeffect of new typefaces and brilliant color effects, depending on the desired intensity of the message.

The new typography is a simultaneous experience of vision and communication.

—Translation from the German by Sibyl Moholy-Nagy

Bauhaus and Typography *L. Moholy-Nagy*

The utilization of machines is characteristic of the technology of today's production and it is significant in its historical development. As in other areas of production, we must unequivocally design our machines for clarity, conciseness, and precision. Today everybody's time is valuable, just as valuable as materials and labor. Among the many problems with which today's typographical artist is concerned . . . the problem of uniform lettering is one of the most important. This type of lettering can be traced as far back as Jakob Grimm, who wrote all nouns with small initials . . . the well-known architect Loos in his collected essays writes: "for the German there is a wide gap between the written and the spoken word. One cannot speak a capital letter. Everyone speaks without thinking of capital letters. But when a German takes a pen to write something, he no longer is able to write as he thinks or speaks."

The poet Stefan George and his group have also chosen uniform lettering as a basis for their publications. If anyone objects to this, saying that it was poetic license, then it must be pointed out that it was the level-headed "association of German engineers" ("Verein Deutscher Ingenieure") who in 1920 . . . came out in favor of uniform lettering in a book, "Speech and Lettering" written by Dr.

From H. M. Wingler, *The Bauhaus* (Cambridge, Mass.: MIT Press, 1969), pp. 114–15. Originally published in *Anhaltische Rundschau* (September 14, 1925).

Porstmann, with the reasoning that our lettering would lose nothing if written with lower-case initials, but on the other hand would become easily legible, more easily learnable, and would become significantly more economical. They added that it should be unnecessary . . . to double the number of signs for a sound when half are sufficient.

This simplification has consequences in the construction of typewriters and typesetting machines, it saves type and shift keys. . . . The Bauhaus has investigated at great length all problems concerning typography and has found the reasons given in favor of uniform lettering to be convincing.

—Translation from the German by Wolfgang Tabs
and Basil Gilbert

Contemporary Typography   *L. Moholy-Nagy*

Typography is modern in concept if it derives its design from its own laws. . . . The utilization of the possibilities offered by the machine is characteristic and, for the purposes of historical development, essential to the techniques of today's productions. Thus, our modern printing products will, to a large extent, be commensurate with the latest machines; that is, they will have to be based on clarity, conciseness, and precision.

The development of printing methods from setting the type by hand to setting it by machine was long and complicated; and the final and unequivocal adjustment to machine-set type will yet lead to greater tensions. The future form of typographical communication will be to a large extent dependent on the development of machine methods; on the other hand, the development of typographical machines will, in some respect, be determined by a reorientation of typography, which today is still largely influenced by handsetting. The typographical process is based on the effectiveness of visual relationships. Every age possesses its own visual forms and its own corresponding typography. A visual experience that allows itself to be articulated depends on light and dark contrasts or color contrasts. . . . The old incunabula, and also even the first typographical works, made ample use of the contrasting effects of color and form (initials, multicolored lettering, colored illustrations). The widespread application of the printing process, the great demand for printed works, along with the economical and money-

From H. M. Wingler, *The Bauhaus* (Cambridge, Mass.: MIT Press, 1969), pp. 80–81. Originally published in *Offset,* VII (1926).

oriented utilization of paper, of the small format, of cast letters, of the single-color print, etc., have changed the vital, contrast-rich layouts of the old printed works into the generally quite monotonous gray of later books.

This monotone of our books has resulted in disadvantages: first, a visually clear articulation of the text has become more difficult to achieve, despite the significant possibilities for articulation offered by the paragraph indent; second, the reader tires much more easily than he would by looking at a layout built on contrasts of light and dark or contrast of color. Thus, the majority of our books today have come no further in their typographical, visual, synoptical form than the Gutenberg production, despite the technological transformation in their manufacture. . . . The situation is much more favorable with newspapers, posters, and job printing, since typographical progress has been almost entirely devoted to this area.

All of today's known attempts at typographical reform consciously or unconsciously start with these facts. The monotony and the lack of contrast in modern books were . . . grasped intuitively, but the reaction to this was nothing but a retrospective demonstration. [These typographers] by the use of hand-set type . . . have produced curious effects, and have called attention to hitherto unknown charms of typographical material—such as lines, rules, circles, squares, crosses, etc. With these structures they "stuccoed" —with a purely craftlike mentality—illustrations, objects, figures, all very interesting because of their uniqueness. But on the whole they were far from influencing significantly any possible future development of typography. This will be left to those typographers who can not only grasp the developmental possibilities and the flexibility of typographical machines and materials, but who can also understand the larger horizon of today's visual experiences. Innovations (such as the wider distribution of photography, of film, and of photoengraving and electroplating techniques) have yielded a new, constantly developing creative basis also for typography. The invention of photogravure, its further development, the photographic typesetting machine, the use of advertising with light, the experience of the visual continuity of the cinema, the simultaneous effects of perceptual events (the city), all these make possible and call for an entirely new level in the field of the visual-typographical. The gray text will change into a colored picture book and will be understood as a continuous visual design (a coherent sequence of many individual pages). With the expansion of the reproduction technique . . . all, possibly even philosophical works, will be printed using the same means for illustrations. . . .

Whereas typography, from Gutenberg up to the first posters, was

27. Poster for automobile tires, Germany, 1926.

28. Book jacket design for *Von Material zu Architectur*, 1929.

29. Labels for the SS Clothing Company, Berlin, 1931. Mat aluminum foil.

30. Detail of rayon exhibit, Utrecht, 1934.

31. Advertisements for vitamin pills, Chicago, 1939.

32. Publicity cover for the Chicago newspaper *PM*, 1939.

33. United States Gypsum exhibition, Chicago, 1941. *Photo Hedrich-Blessing Studio.*

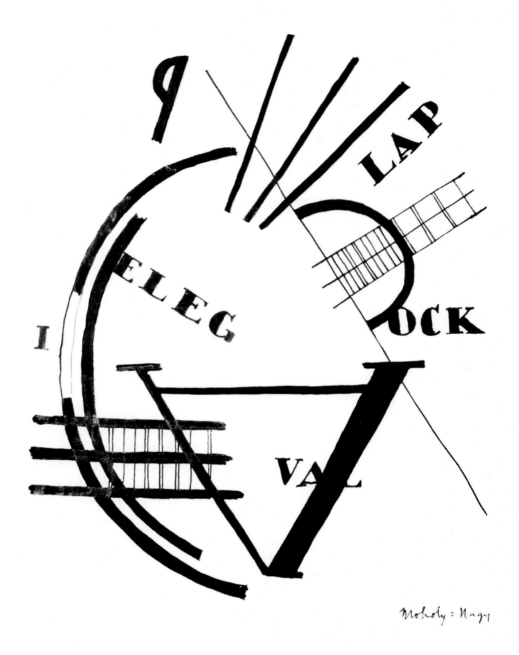

34. *Dada—Collage,* 1920. Collage. India ink on paper, 12⅝″ x 10″. Photo courtesy Marlborough Fine Art (London), Ltd. Copyright Hellmuth Kolbe, Wallisellen, Switzerland.

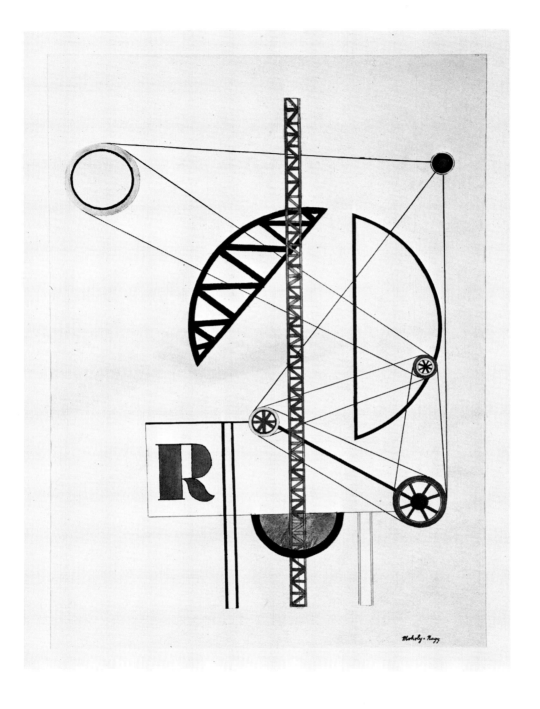

35. *Collage R,* 1920. Watercolor and collage on paper, 24¾″ x 18¼″.
Collection George M. Irwin, Quincy, Ill. Photo courtesy Museum of
Contemporary Art, Chicago.

36. *The Peace Machine Devouring Itself,* 1920
(originally published in *MA*). India ink on paper.

37. *Malevitch* cover design, *ca.* 1923. Watercolor and collage on paper, 20″ x 13½″.
Collection Mrs. Sibyl Moholy-Nagy, New
York. Photo courtesy Museum of Contemporary Art, Chicago.

38. Engraving on steel plate, 1923. Collection Mrs. Sibyl Moholy-Nagy,
    New York.

39, 40. Stage settings for *Tales of Hoffmann,* Berlin State Opera, 1929.
Above: Act I; *below:* Act III.

41–44. Transformation through light projection, *Madame Butterfly,* Berlin, 1930.

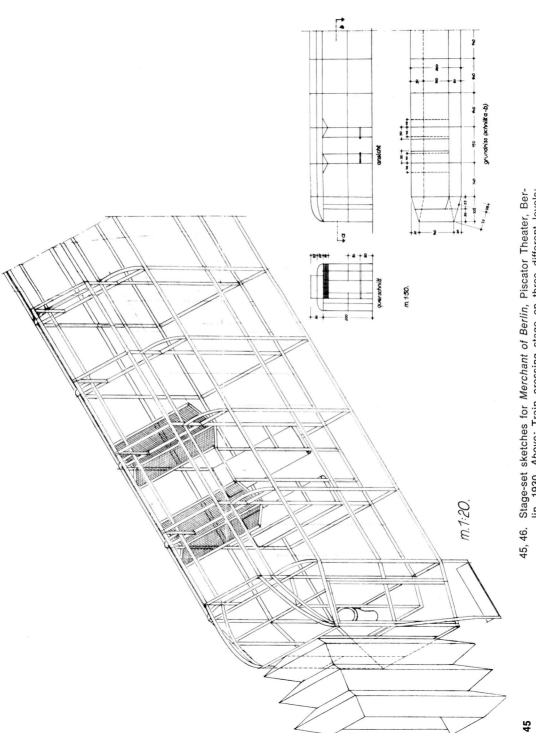

m.1:20.

ansicht

querschnitt

m.1:50.

grundriss (schnitt a–b)

45, 46. Stage-set sketches for *Merchant of Berlin*, Piscator Theater, Berlin, 1930. *Above:* Train crossing stage on three different levels; *below:* Horizontally rotating stage platform; vertically built-up three-story scaffolding with train tracks at three levels (I, II, III).

45

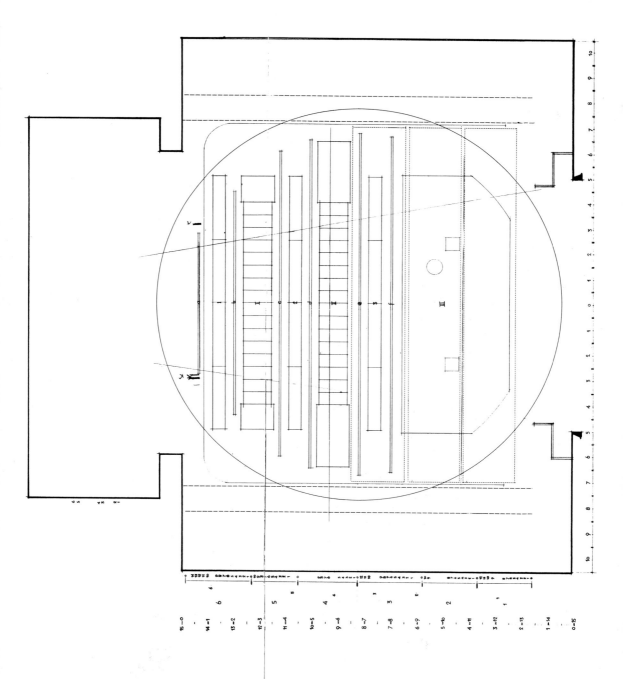

46

47. Stage set for *Merchant of Berlin,* with dedication by the Russian theater director W. Meyerhold.

48. Special effects for the H. G. Wells/Alexander Korda film *Things to Come,* London, 1936.

merely a (necessary) intermediary link between the content of a message and the recipient, a new stage of development began with the first posters. . . . One began to count on the fact that form, size, color, and arrangement of the typographical material (letters and signs) contain a strong visual impact. The organization of these possible visual effects gives a visual validity to the content of the message as well; this means that by means of printing the content is also being defined pictorially. . . . This . . . is the essential task of visual-typographical design.

What is necessary, for example, is a unitary type of lettering, without small and capital letters; letters unified not only in size but also in form. . . . Of course here one could also put up ideal demands which would go far beyond a modernization of our present-day type forms. Our lettering, aside from the very few phonetically derived symbols, is based on a time-honored convention. The origin of these signs is hard to ascertain today. They are very often no more than formal stylistic (or practical) modifications of traditional forms which are no longer recognizable. So, one will be able to speak of an actual reorganization of (printed) lettering only when this reorganization has been carried out in an objective, scientific manner. Perhaps on the basis of opto-phonetical experiments. . . . The adoption of basic forms—such as the circle, square, and triangle—in the reform of lettering admittedly leads today to interesting formal, and even essential practical results. [Seen] from what is today still a Utopian point of view, they are, however, not to be taken as the correct understanding of the problem. . . . [It] is very likely that this kind of investigation will [lead] at first to the construction of automatic typewriters and typesetting machines working from dictation. But for the time being we do not even have a practical type face of the right size that is clearly legible, has no individual peculiarities, is based on a functional, visual form, and has neither distortions nor curlicues. We have, on the other hand, good fonts of type that are sometimes suitable for labels and title pages . . . but when used in larger quantities they begin to "swim." The tensions that stem from contrasting visual effects are most thoroughly created by opposites: empty—full, light—dark, polychrome—monochrome, vertical—horizontal, upright—oblique, etc. These contrasts are primarily produced by means of the type (letters). Today, we seek to create the "style" for our works—not from borrowed requisites but out of this . . . typographical material. There are [but] a few well-suited forms, [however] there are many ways of using them, a fact which contributes to the precision [and] clarity . . . of the visual image. The whole field of the photoengraving techniques also belongs in this area. In order to bring typographical design into conformity with the purposes of typography, it might possibly be well even to use various line directions and the like (thus not just horizontal arrangements). The nature and the purpose of the communication (leaflet or poster) determine the manner and the use of the typographical material. Typographical signs (like points, lines, and other geometrical forms) can also be used to advantage. . . .

An essential component of typographical order is the harmonious arrangement of the surface spaces, the invisible and yet clearly perceivable tension-laden linear relationships that permit various possibilities of balance apart from symmetrical equilibrium. In contrast to the centuries-old static-concentric equilibrium, one seeks today to produce a dynamic-eccentric equilibrium. In the first case the typographical object is captured at a glance, with all the centrally focused elements—including the peripheral ones; in the second case, the eye is led step by step from point to point, whereby [the awareness of] the mutual relationships of the individual elements must not suffer (posters, job printing, titles of books, etc.).

One could point out many more possibilities for achieving new effects that lie in the same direction as the essential typographical development mentioned here.

—Translation from the German by Wolfgang Tabs
and Basil Gilbert

From Wine Jugs to
Lighting Fixtures   *L. Moholy-Nagy*

When Gropius appointed me to take over the metal workshop he asked me to reorganize it as a workshop for industrial design. Until my arrival the metal workshop had been a gold and silver workshop where wine jugs, samovars, elaborate jewelry, coffee services, etc., were made. Changing the policy of this workshop involved a revolution, for in their pride the gold- and silversmiths avoided the use of ferrous metals, nickel and chromium plating and abhorred the idea of making models for electrical household appliances or lighting fixtures. It took quite a while to get under way the kind of work which later made the Bauhaus a leader in designing for the lighting fixture industry.

I remember the first lighting fixture by K. Jucker, done before 1923, with devices for pushing and pulling, heavy strips and rods

From W. Gropius; H. Bayer; and I. Gropius (eds.), *Bauhaus 1919–1928* (New York: Museum of Modern Art, 1938), pp. 136 and 138.

of iron and brass, looking more like a dinosaur than a functional object. But even this was a great victory, for it meant a new beginning. After this we developed lighting fixtures introducing such useful ideas as: the close-fitting ceiling cap; combinations of opaque and frosted glass in simple forms technically determined by the action of light; securing the globe to the metal chassis; the use of aluminum, particularly for reflectors, etc. All of these were adopted for industrial production. In addition to these innovations may be mentioned one which even today presents a very useful solution of one lighting fixture problem, especially in localities where the quick settling of dust makes ordinary lighting inefficient. This principle involves the use of concentric glass cylinders to avoid a glare. From this originated the louvre system of concentric rings of metal and, recently, of translucent plastics. The metal workshop also handled other problems of industrial design: utensils and household appliances.

The function of the metal workshop was a special one, involving simultaneously education and production. We therefore selected for young apprentices problems from which the use of materials, tools and machinery could be learned and which were at the same time of practical use. During those days there was so conspicuous a lack of simple and functional objects for daily use that even the young apprentices were able to produce models for industrial production (ash trays, tea holders, etc.) which industry bought and for which royalties were paid.

Design Potentialities *L. Moholy-Nagy*

Contemporary design started in this country fifty or sixty years ago with the statement of Louis Sullivan: "Form follows function." This means that the function, which is the work an object is designed to do, is instrumental in shaping its form. Unfortunately Sullivan's words were not appreciated; his principle became dormant except in the work of Frank Lloyd Wright.

However, through the endeavors of the Bauhaus artists and their many colleagues in Europe, the idea of "functionalism" became the keynote of the twenties, vitalizing thought and action. But—as usual—functionalism became a cheap commercial slogan, its original meaning blurred.

Today, it seems to be necessary to re-examine this functionalism

From Paul Zucker (ed.), *New Architecture and City Planning* (New York: Philosophical Library, 1944), pp. 675–87.

in the light of present circumstances. In so doing we find that the statement "form follows function" is profound if we apply it to phenomena occurring in nature where "every process has its necessary form, which always results in functional forms. They follow the law of the shortest distance between two points; cooling occurs only on surfaces exposed to cooling; pressure only on points of pressure; tension on lines of tension; motion creates for itself forms of movement—for each energy there is a form of energy." (Raoul Francé.)

Man has used functional suggestions of nature innumerable times. Many of our utensils, appliances, containers, tools, are based upon observations of nature. Nevertheless, "form follows function" translated into the human technology falls very far short of the optimum, compared to nature's infinite number of applications, long, long tested by the trail and error method. Man tries his "best," but his results depend upon his limited knowledge and practice, his ability to reason and grasp. We often find that though for ages he has designed objects for "function," some of them were bulky, burdened with an excess of material and wasted labor, if compared with later developments. It is enough to look at a log cabin and a colonial house; or a primitive lumber stool and a finely articulated rococo chair. In these models, form did follow function, but the later models incorporated the changed technological processes meanwhile developed. In designing for human consumption we find that function is not only the work to be accomplished for a limited mechanical task, but must also fulfill biological, psychophysical and sociological requirements as well.

Form Follows Function as Well as Scientific and Technological Developments

New discoveries, new theories and the new techniques in scientific research brought industrial applications in all fields of production. Electricity, the gasoline and Diesel motors, motion pictures, color photography, radio, metallurgy, new alloys, chemurgy, plastics, airplane, electronics inevitably press toward change in design.

The history of the chair is a very revealing example. The functional justification of a chair is seating. Its form, however, depends upon the materials, tools and skills available in a certain period. The old craftsman had only one material suitable for a chair, wood. With that and a few hand tools, he did a very fine work. For example, the rococo chair with its carved, slender, curved legs, without elaborate bracing devices was a masterpiece of wood construction. It not only looked light but actually was light in weight.

Moholy-Nagy

Our problem now, is to use present day materials and machines as capably as our ancestors used the limited means and tools at their command.

In addition to discovering new properties and uses of wood, the industrial revolution developed new materials, such as seamless steel tubing, plywood, and plastics, and with them new methods of production that used machines instead of hand tools. Today we can produce new chair forms, such as seats with two legs instead of the usual four, and in place of forty or fifty joints, four or none at all. Tomorrow there may be no legs needed, just a seat on a compressed air jet.*

Scientific research and testing substantiate such a suggestion, and even more daring ones based upon new sciences such as electronics. High frequency short-wave radio heating has already revolutionized the traditional glueing process, cut down assembly time and reduced the number of operations.

The plastic-molding industry inevitably presses toward new applications, too.

Established Paths of Thought

It appears then that the best designer is the person who knows all contemporary resources and can understand their trend most completely. This goal does not seem to be very difficult to attain—one would think that the present scientific and technological information would help to apply the potentialities at hand. This is, however, far from the truth. It took a hundred years, after we had plumbing in the kitchen, for the designer of the water kettle to exchange the small spout for a large one which can be held directly under the faucet without the need of taking off the lid. In spite of the new light source, electricity, most people live with "newly designed" colonial oil lamps and baroque candelabras into which the electric bulbs are inserted. The heat-insulated handle of a flatiron shows a similar development. First the handle was covered with

* There may arise difficulties as far as public acceptance of new design is concerned. The solid and sturdy plywood chairs made in the Institute of Design in Chicago looked so incredibly light that people at first hesitated to use them. A similar reaction retarded the general recognition of the first steel tube chair by Breuer. Of course, when it was accepted, it was often misused. Steel is a heat conductor. Breuer considered this and designed his chairs so that the human body did not touch the metal structure. The imitators copying only the appearance did not consider this important feature.

I recall another story also. In 1916 the police in Rotterdam, Holland, ordered an architect to place two columns under his cantilevered balcony, made from reinforced concrete, "even if they were made from cardboard." "The projection may frighten the public" . . . was the argument.

rags, then it was made from wood, first hand-carved, then turned on the lathe. *This* handle was then literally translated into plastics though it could have been designed without difficulty in accordance with the properties and mass production possibilities of the new material, which allow the design of a better insulating and hand-fitting handle as it was indeed discovered later. The same applies for the handles of tools which are today molded in plastics still imitating the traditional wood handles turned on the lathe.

There are many old forms which have no legitimate existence today, and the obvious conclusion is that it is extremely difficult to leave the established paths of thought, since mass production requirements applied to the fulfillment of the function could bring to the fore better, cheaper and more beautiful products. These goods could be fabricated more economically and quickly if redesigned according to the present production standards. It is tragic to see the helplessness of designers in some traditional fields which remain rather untouched by contemporary thinking.

The reason may be that since the nineties the cultural background and respectability of a family has been expressed by "conspicuous waste," such as period furniture and lighting fixtures which were imported from French and Scottish castles. Mass production followed this trend with cheap imitations. The result was price stagnation because the principles of mass production could not be well applied to design with the character of handicraft.

New Technology: The Age of Assemblage

The finest solutions in design usually came through new inventions where tradition did not hamper the freshness of approach, such as the steam engine, electric motor, telephone, radio and photocell. Their form had to be found through their function plus the technological processes available. The technology of the industrial revolution started out with the division of labor which led from simple assemblage forms to the conveyor belt and other mass production practices.

First, and for a rather long time, the idea of the assemblage prevailed. This was the age of the bolt, the rivet, and the screw. This method allowed the production of the most diversified goods from standard stock such as the angle iron, steel band, brass plate, gauged sheet, rod, tube, screw, bolt, hinge, caster, etc. Materials and semifinished products could be stored in great quantities. The production risk of ready made goods was small, since only as much was produced as sold.

Other Methods

Later, with the opening up of new markets, more goods were needed so quicker mass production methods were introduced. The methods of bolting, riveting, and screwing were followed by welding, casting, molding, shaping, stamping. Instead of the ribands and profiles there came the seamless tube and corrugated and curved slabs. Curving of a flat sheet is a customary strengthening procedure, and curving it, like the eggshell, in all directions, is the most substantial structural manipulation we know. It achieves the advantages of a skeleton structure with the skin only.

Such designs were mainly developed by the motor car industry, especially when, after the dirigible, the airplane appeared, and kinetic studies and wind tunnel experiments were introduced. In mass production this technique could be utilized on a large scale because tooling and retooling, costly dies, new machines, expensive preparations could be amortized through the great number of units sold. The smoothly "streamlined" body of a car is stamped today by one action from flat sheets of steel. It is a kind of steel egg, structurally sound and excellent in performance. The results of these studies were taken over by the designers of all goods from lather and cream mixers to ships, locomotives, cars and highways. Around 1930 a "streamlining" fever swept indiscriminately over the designs of every type of goods. In the first moment this appeared to be exaggerated especially since in nature "streamlining" implies a shape round which the medium streams so smoothly that resistance is at last practically *nil;* there only remains the slight "skin-friction," which can be reduced or minimized in various ways.*

Industrial streamlining was introduced originally for a more economical organization of objects moving with great speed and there was apparently no need to "streamline" ashtrays and other static objects. Nevertheless the new form principle radiated into the production of every type of *goods,* mobile or static. This had its good reason. In streamlining sharp edges had to be smoothed down, consequently, casts, molds, stampings as well as finishes such as nickel and chromeplating, polishing, enameling, laquering and plastic molding could be more easily produced.

* "No creature shows more perfect streamlining than a fur-seal swimming. Every curve is a *continuous* curve, the very ears and eye-slits and whiskers falling into the scheme, and the flippers folding close against the body." (From Sir D'Arcy Wentworth Thompson, "On Growth and Form," [Cambridge, England: Cambridge University Press, 1942].)

New Working Conditions

The social effects of this type of production are great. The new principle of design, creating *one-piece objects,* mass-produced by automatic action of the machine, will one day greatly reduce if not eliminate the assembly line. This would change the present working conditions in which fatigue of the worker, the restricted use of his manifold abilities have to be considered as a serious drawback.

The possible limitation of the division of labor on such an unhealthy scale may act as a fine incentive for the designer. He may see that it is essential to incorporate into his work more than skill and knowledge. To be a designer means not only to be a sensible manipulator of techniques, an analyst of the present production processes, but also to accept the social obligations connected with it. Thus design is dependent not alone on function, science and technological process, but upon social implications as well.

Social Implications

The relationship of employer and employee, unemployment, the requirements of a minimum subsistence, longevity, and dozens of other matters have changed our outlook on the social structure and with it our approach to design.

The higher living standard and the emancipation of women necessitated labor-saving devices, refrigerators, vacuum cleaners, and washing machines.

Research on matters of health preceded the greater hygiene— the bathroom as a standard unit. The intensity and exhausting quality of industrial work, the crowded dusty cities increased the importance of recreation and leisure. Sports, cinema, radio, television, travel, the community center, and the idea of the weekend belong in this category.

Economy of Production

Of course, many other elements have to be added to this analysis in order to see all of the components of a "functional" design.

One of the most important among them is the requirement of distribution. Mass distribution caused changes on an unprecedented scale. The vast increase in the means of transportation, crating, knock-down furniture, tank cars and refrigeration of perishable goods, frozen foods, canning, mail-order houses, catalogs, price lists, advertising, sales agents brought about an incredible growth of the service industries. The considerations of mass production brought price reductions and greater competition. By millions of units the saving even of a fraction of the monetary unit meant a competitive advantage.

Cutting down fourteen drops of solder to thirteen—as did happen in one of the giant industrial plants, resulting in a yearly saving of 30,000 dollars, substantiates the requirements of economy of production. The same is valid for the different types of "recoveries" as, for example, silver from photographic developer, formerly poured down the sink; tin from empty cans; grease from the housewives' pans for glycerine; sawdust for plastics, etc.

All this stimulated simplification of processes, economy or organization, elimination of waste, better packaging, safety measures, even new forms of rehabilitation. Notable achievements in this field were the Taylor System and Gilbreth's Scientific Motion Studies of workers.

They all manifested improvement in production.

The Artist's Role

The detailed analysis of the elements given in these pages seems to produce an unfailing recipe for the new trends in design. Being informed of the scientific discoveries as well as the sociological trends; calculating the necessary requirements for function; knowing the techniques which can be applied to their realization, would imply that a design made on the basis of all this could not fall short of perfection.

The truth is that in spite of the possible definition of elements there remain imponderables which cannot easily be defined.

Of course we may rationalize these imponderables, since after the execution of a design all of its elements can be traced back to facts which are the subjects of conscious reasoning. The difficulty is only before the design is made, *before* the execution takes place. The reason is that sometimes there is a possibility of alternative design solutions.

Certain structural tasks could be solved in one or in another material or in several ways with one material. At present, a reinforced concrete column with a circular, hexagonal, pentagonal as well as square section would suffice for a building structure. Which should be chosen? Is a circular or a square dining table more functional? Electric or gas range? Fluorescent or incandescent light? China dish or glass? Window frames with horizontal or vertical divisions? Spiral stairways or straight ones? Tubular steel chairs with two or four legs? Low wing or high wing airplanes? And so on.

The answer comes from the intuition of the designer. His

choices are not based upon interchangeable considerations of the single elements *per se* but the relationships which are created by the single elements as parts of an entity which produces the new meaning, the "right" solution. The artist accomplishes this by insight, sensitivity. They are his guides for structure, proportion and form. They help him to evaluate, re-use or discard historical forms according to their technical, sociological and biological rightness. Not everything that we know or feel can be verbalized by a language which uses logic and reason as its main characteristics. A number of intuitive assurances may be expressed better by the artist. In this way, his influence is direct because his language infiltrates into the channels of emotion without needing to be consciously analyzed for rational contents. Many discoveries and new forms of the industrial revolution were accepted in their esthetic potential because the artist's interpretation made their use legitimate.* However his abilities are not mystical. His geneology can be traced.

The Avant Garde

Around 1920 the new artists discovered the excitement of a "structure." They looked with great enthusiasm at bridges, oil and radio towers, tunnels, spiral stairways, machinery, etc. It was the first time they were able to see the emotional and esthetic qualities of engineer structures which were the pure carriers of functional requirements. This introduced the period of simplification, later the complete purification, the stripping of decoration, deornamentation of goods, furniture and architecture. Losing its symbolic meaning, the ornament and its application turned a long time ago into empty decoration, producing a pseudo quality. The Impressionists and Cubists discovered the genuinely sensual and emotional quality of textures originating through the ingenious combination of tools

---

* In 1870 Édouard Manet, the head of the French Impressionists, offered to paint frescoes in the city hall depicting the "beauty" of railway stations and market halls in Paris. The official opinion of that time saw in such technological matter only an esthetic nuisance. Manet's offer was *not* accepted. Even fifteen years later the same public opinion fought against the Eiffel Tower as the destroyer of the beautiful city.

S. Giedion reports about the revolutionary foresight of Horta, the Belgian architect, in his book *Space, Time, and Architecture* (Cambridge, Mass.: Harvard University Press, 1941). In 1895 Horta dared to expose to the eye the iron structure inside a private villa, considered then a sacrilege.

The Dadaists, especially Marcel Duchamp the painter, emphasized the beauty of "ready made" objects such as clothing racks and the toilet bowl in the days of 1916, when it was derogatory for an artist to care for objects of daily routine.

and materials. This new generation was largely responsible for today's texture taking the place of ornaments and for the stabilization of the idea that machines can be understood as legitimate "tools" of the artist and designer.

However, this new technology was so far the domain of the specialists. The academic standards of higher education, the humanities, and a misinterpreted art history turned the students away from the machine though they had to be conditioned to its significant forms, uses and potentialities. At the same time they needed information about the general upheaval which followed the quick spread of this new technology.

The work of the last two generations brought new knowledge and shaped constructive attitudes for a new life structure. The next step was to disseminate and put them to use. Education was the given vehicle.

Unfortunately, strictly vocational education aimed at nothing but quick breeding of specialists. There remained mainly, the synthetizing ability of the artist to condense ideologies visually or in other ways of sensorial transfer. Expressing them as emotional content, he could catch the spirit of an epoch in his work. But the artist himself did not know too much about the expediency of such an expression. His synthetizing power was formerly, so to speak, an automatic sequel to his work, the connotations of which ranged from illustrations to recording of events. For centuries what a painter had to express was not questioned. He had the whole realm to document passing events, phenomena, persons, incidents, objects, landscapes. Within the finality of this problem everything else was of secondary importance, namely, the organization of the expressive elements which today we consider as fundamental. But when photography seized upon the formerly primary task of painting, and documentation was taken over by the machine with an unprecedented precision, radically new orientation became necessary: a revision of the artist's task in order for him to hold a well-balanced course of responsible relationships between his abilities and the collective requirements of society; to generate group conscience based upon human potentialities; to find ways to adjust the mechanics of creative impulses and the forms of expression to the present technology. If one looks at the work of the best representatives, one finds in them the embodiment of a splendid knowledge of their metier and a profound will to spread the virtue of discrimination and balance. For the time being, they are only a few, often misunderstood. They are sometimes attacked and compelled to take refuge in catacombs, in order to preserve their pioneer efforts, share the common faith, and serve as a mutual audience.

Training

There must be, naturally, a mental adjustment of the individual toward this changed world and nothing helps better to this adjustment than the understanding of its advantages. Even so the universal acceptance of the new trend in design, may take time as people without clear orientation are often confused by either sentiment or "novelty" propaganda. The sentiment propaganda operates with the obsolete emotional means of the "good old days" and the like. Novelty for the sake of novelty tries to create the illusion of new organic demands without serving real needs. It is usually an artificial stimulation of business. Such stunts can bring only short-lived success as they depend upon the elusiveness of fashion, which merely *simulates* organic changes. One remedy against this is the conscientious training of a new generation of producers, consumers and designers who have grasped the importance of the basic relationship of "form and function." In this spirit the Institute of Design, Chicago, tries to educate its students, by going back to the fundamentals and building up from there a new knowledge of the social and technological implications of design. The new generation of designers, who have gone through such a training, will be invulnerable against the temptations of fads, the easy way out of economic and social responsibilities.

Industrial Design   *L. Moholy-Nagy*

Industrial design is a new profession. So far it has been more of an adventure than based upon exact knowledge of the requirements of industrial production, its technology, sales, and distribution techniques. The successful industrial designers of this country have come from stage design, painting and architecture—people with imagination and fantasy within the new realms of esthetics based upon mass-production potentialities and who were not hampered by the tradition of the handicrafts. The older the craft, the more restraining influence it has upon the imagination of the designer. It is easier to design a new product which is based upon the new sciences and technologies than for example to re-design the ways and shapes of pottery, one of the oldest handicrafts of mankind. It is an old saying that "form follows function." This means that the shape of an object is defined by the work it has to do. After a million years of trial and error, nature has produced well-functioning

From *Parker Pen Shoptalker* (June, 1946).

shapes, but human history is much too short to be able to compete with nature's richness in creating functional forms. However, the ingenuity of man brought forth excellent results in every period of his history depending upon his science, technology, esthetics and other requirements. This means that the simple statement, "form follows function," has to be complemented in the human sphere with another statement, that is, form also follows, or should follow existing scientific technical and art development, including sociology and economy.

Economic considerations influence and direct design. For example, design in this country is essentially different from that of Europe. The economy in the United States is based upon frequent change of models and a quick turn-over, because by this method a country rich in resources, raw materials and human ingenuity can afford to be wasteful by declaring models obsolete long before their technical usefulness has ceased. In contrast to this, the European design, based mainly upon export, tries to produce long lasting goods and to conserve raw materials. In other words, the European export economy had to take the consumers' wishes into consideration because the money they paid out for imports represents a loss in the importing country's economy.

At present a great socio-economical change is taking place in this country—not true for Parker Pen—but true for other industries which must look for export markets in order to utilize their production potential and avoid unemployment. This will sooner or later require a revision of the idea of artificial obsolescence, i.e., the frequent replacement of merchandise by a new "design" before the previous one becomes technically obsolete. That revision is imperative if we desire to compete in the world markets.

Because these ideas are not familiar to the average public, "design" at present is mainly a weapon for sale, missing the inherent qualities of design, planned and organized function. So "design" is at present usually nothing but an exterior cloak around an engineered product and its main characteristic is to be "different" although the function remains the same. The industrial designer today is usually called in to "style" or "fashion" a product and the more often he changes the "design," the more he contributes to the salesman's paradise. It is natural that production and prosperity depend upon sale and that the salesman plays an important role, but his function will not be lessened and degraded if the designer learns to be an artist, planner and organizer who gives the product its organic function rather than its superficial "style." This means striving for "standard," that is the development of products toward their completeness in production, looks and use.

Under the pressure of the salesman, most of the designers succumbed to a superficial "style." This in the last ten years has been "streamlining," as it was previously ornamentation. But streamlining was originally invented for moving objects and there is no reason for an ash tray to be streamlined. However, certain elements of streamlining are exceedingly economic in production, especially since mass-production methods of stamping, pressing, casting and molding have been employed. They assist in easier production, assemblage, and finishing.

We can say that our period is one of speed and motion which justifies "streamlining." But when it becomes only a mechanical application—we have to fight against it, as we did against the mechanical utilization of symmetry with which everything in previous periods could be made "harmonious."

The "51" pen is one of the most successful designs of small utility objects in our period. It is light, handy, extremely well shaped, unobtrusive, and perfectly functional. Now that the cap is changed and simplified, I am only waiting for the acceptance of a more appropriate Parker arrow clip and then my delight will be complete.

When I first came to the Parker Pen Company, it was often thought that my duties were to style and fashion the products which the Research and Development Department considered as well engineered. Slowly, however, they yielded to my curiosity as to the mechanical functions of the product and they were willing to take suggestions if I could offer any for the improvement, not only of the appearance, but of its function. Naturally the designer's task is not to compete with the engineer, nor should the engineer indulge in the idea that he can do a perfect design, but their collaboration must be intimate. The designer has to know about the industrial processes and the basic mechanical principles involved in a certain problem and has to try to add to the specialist's findings his experience in the different fields from which sometimes useful analogies can be derived. This relationship is now established with the firm and I am very happy about it, especially as I often had experiences with firms where this notion of close collaboration was not acknowledged.

There is one more point which should be mentioned because there are so many mistaken ideas about design. In many firms everyone is called upon to judge the merits of a design irrespective of qualification for it. Many good designs have been eliminated from production or marketing because of the votes of personnel who had neither the knowledge nor the feeling about the merits of a design. Nothing is more important for the work of the designer than a customer with farsight, conviction, and the right "hunches" for future developments.

Obituary Note   *Kenneth Parker*

One of the biggest losses this company has suffered in a long time was in the death of Moholy-Nagy on November 24, 1946. No matter how many designers we engage from now on, we shall not have the luck to find another like him. He was not only gifted as a designer, but one of the truest friends this company ever had. His interest in our success and welfare was such you would have thought he was the sole owner of the business.

It is difficult for me to write about Moholy-Nagy because as a rule pieces written in the nature of obituaries are automatically full of high praise, no matter whether really deserved or not, and everybody knows it and discounts it accordingly. I could not over-praise Moholy-Nagy if I tried to.

Some months ago Moholy wrote a short article on Design for *Shoptalker*. I did not like it much but I did not tell him so. I think the reason I thought it somewhat flat was that it failed to convey at all what an extraordinarily valuable set of ideas Moholy continuously applied to our particular business. He had a natural feeling for the correctness of a line or a curve or shape or an embellishment or finish of a surface, a sense for all small things in combination that most of us lack. And that was really the lesser part of his value: he was always very far in the future in his thinking. He was a stimulating mentality if there ever was one.

Moholy-Nagy was born in Hungary. His first recognition as a designer, however, came in an invitation to join the faculty of the famed Bauhaus art and architectural school in Berlin. When the Nazis came into power, Moholy-Nagy and his associates moved to London. From there he went to America and he was one of the founders of the Bauhaus school of design in the old Marshall Field residence in Chicago.

In 1939 Moholy-Nagy opened the Institute of Design on North Dearborn Street, Chicago, which has grown in the span of seven years to be acknowledged as a leader in the realm of industrial design, architecture, photography and sculpture. And it was here that the resultful and personal association between this company and Moholy-Nagy began.

(Signed) Ken Parker

From *Parkergrams* (December, 1946).

Excerpt from Moholy-Nagy and the Theater   *Hans Curjel*

The *Bauhausbuch* "The Stage at the Bauhaus," by O. Schlemmer, L. Moholy-Nagy and F. Molnar, published in 1925, contains two essays: Schlemmer's famous programmatic theses "Man and Marionette" (Kunstfigur) and Moholy's "Theater, Circus, Revue" (Varieté). This is a basic dialogue with the problems of the stage. Moholy contrasts the traditional forms with a "Theater of Surprises of the Futurists, the Dadaists and a Mechanical Excentric." This means a theater "which wants to eliminate all that is logical-intellectual (literature). Nevertheless man must remain the center; but man as a mechanically functioning part of nature. How can such a Total Theater be realized?" asks Moholy. As far as stage optics is concerned, this is his answer: "The Fine Arts have found their pure means of presentation—primary colors, collective, material, etc., correlations. But how can one give human motion and thought sequences equal validity with absolutely controlled sound, light (color), form—and kinetic elements? One can only provide general suggestions for the new theater designer. The repetition of the same thought with the same words in the same and in many-varied tone sequences by a number of actors can be a means of synthetic interpretation (chorus, but not the passive form of the choir of antiquity). Through mirror arrangements, enormously enlarged faces or single gestures of the actors can be accompanied by magnified voices. In the same way can the reproduction of thoughts be made effective through synacoustical (optical or mechanical-phonetical) effects, using projection, gramophone, loudspeaker, or a meshed-gear method of various trains of thought. The literature of the future will, independent of musical-accoustical methods, create specific 'sounds' (associative, ramified) only available to its means. This will not fail to affect the presentation of word and thought flux on the stage."

These are ideas and suggestions that could be offered today by an avant-garde stage director!

Moholy's "Score for a mechanical excentric (synthesis of form, movement, tone, light, color and smell)" proves that he did not merely indulge in high-sounding theories. The sketch, which illustrates his essay from 1924, registers in four columns the sequence of transformations which occur in synchronized form on three stage platforms and a projection screen. His notation method an-

From *Du,* 24 (November, 1964), pp. 11–15.

ticipates the principles which are used today, forty years later, for electronic composition.

It took more than four years until Moholy got his first chance to realize some of his ideas. This chance came at the Berlin Krolloper, which had been founded in 1927. Under the direction of Otto Klemperer, the principal goal was to liquidate through a basic reform the superannuated opera style with its conventional "splendor" and the empty routine acting of the singers. . . . Under these basic premises Moholy was given the commission to create a new stage for *The Tales of Hoffmann* by Offenbach. His assistant for the execution of design was Teo Otto. . . . Offenbach's opera was to be separated from the traditional concept of a gemütliche petty-bourgeois romantic, to reveal, freed from a period-piece atmosphere, its real substance contained in its music: an interpenetration of automaton mechanics and genuine emotions of the soul; the meshing of foreground and background action; the ambiguity of dramatic situations, personalities and their actions. Moholy created imaginary spaces through mere scaffolding which could be set into flowing motion. Light and color effects corresponded to musical-dramatic sequences, and certain actions appeared as double images of realistic acting and simultaneous film projection. For the first time in theater history, steel furniture was used on stage which Moholy's Bauhaus colleague Marcel Breuer had designed and which was considered a most daring innovation. At the sound of the "Barcarole," young girls floated in dreamlike rigid poses on high swings over the heads of the audience. In his own commentary on *The Tales of Hoffmann,* Moholy wrote: "It was an attempt to create spaces out of light and shadow. Among other things, flats and backdrops turn into tools for the interplay of shadow effects. Everything is transparent, and all these transparencies combine into a rich yet still perceivable space articulation."

The second of Moholy's sets for the Krolloper was Paul Hindemith's twelve-minute burlesque *Hin und Zurück* (Thither and Back). It is a short opera persiflage in which the banal action jumps as arbitrarily back and forth as the exuberant, witty, pretensionless polyphonic music. Moholy entered into this spirit. A mechanical dove fluttered across the stage as a prologue, and returned as an optical epilogue. The stage itself was a collage of mechanical props—coffeepot, yarnball, pistol, chair—moving like wind-up toys. But everything was unobtrusive, without emphasis, a minor, but sharply profiled example of a theater of the excentric.

Offenbach and Hindemith were followed in 1931 by Puccini's *Madame Butterfly*. Instead of the usual Western caricature of "genuine Japanese" costumes and knick-knacks, there was a trans-

V sculpture-architecture

Make a Light Modulator   *L. Moholy-Nagy*

Any object may be considered a light modulator, for as it reflects the light it also modulates or changes the rays which strike it. It reflects some rays, absorbs others, possibly permits others to pass through if it is transparent while refracting them to some degree, or if the substance is translucent, it diffuses the rays that are neither reflected nor absorbed.

The human face is the best-known of all light modulators, and certainly it ranks near the top of the list in complexity. Straight lines are few; flat surfaces, if any, are small. Surfaces and lines are nearly all curved and there are very few surfaces of plane curvature —curving in only one direction as on a cylinder, for most are compound curves. Surface texture and color vary with the person's age, for the skin of a baby is vastly different from that of a patriarch, and there are countless degrees of difference between. Add to these natural differences the "war paint" of the cosmetic counter, and you really have a study in surface textures as well as colors.

Then there are the eyes, which present, in addition to their general expression of personality, the specific light-modulating problem of a variation of surface textures, shape, and even of the nature of substance.

The mustache was decried by a famous movie actress as a den of microbes in alarming proximity to the kiss, but to the photographer its presents a problem in light modulation and in such space relationships as depth quite similar to the hair, the eyebrows, the eyelashes, and (if any) the beard. Finally, to add to the problem, there are the lips and the teeth (if they show), and that marvelous study in light and shadow, the ear.

With all this complexity of substance, line, contour, color and texture, the face is a marvelous subject for study of the modulation of light. This accounts in part for the great variety of portraits possible with only one face as the subject. In practice it is frequently difficult or even impossible to have at the photographer's command a face for study purposes, so at the School of Design the student manufactures light modulators out of paper or other materials which can be bent or molded or cut to produce the various shapes, textures, etc., in the photographing of which he must become proficient.

Few detailed directions are necessary for the actual making of the light modulators. Each is the product of the individual's own ingenuity, dexterity and interests. Having seen in the accompanying

From *Minicam,* 3, No. 7 (March, 1940).

MAKE A LIGHT MODULATOR

1. Place a sheet of white paper on a dark background.

2. Bend one corner and notice the shadow cast and the gradual darkening as the paper curves away from the light source.

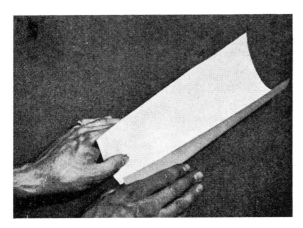

3. Observe the effects of bending up two sides.

4. Fasten the four corners together to see the effect of curvature on light.

5. Cut or tear a hole in the paper and note the effects of this upon the lighting and the number of tones obtained.

6. Watch the effect of adding a second sheet of paper.

7. Add an opaque object or let the light fall across a straight edge before it hits the modulator. Observe how noticeable the curves become, due to the modeling furnished by the tone gradations.

8. Photograph opaque, translucent, and transparent objects with shiny and dull surfaces. Experiment with the light source itself, increasing or diminishing it, focusing it on the object or diffusing it. By William Keck and Robert Tague.

Sculpture-Architecture

9. Light modulator by L. Cuneo. The light modulators shown here were devised and photographed by students at the School of Design.

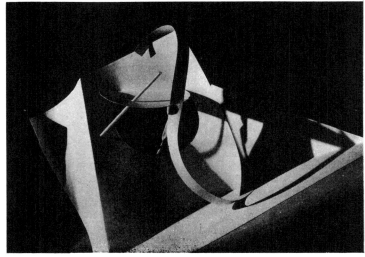

10. Paper light modulators as a product of the imagination are as simple or as intricate as the photographer wishes. By L. Nederkorn.

11. Paper modulator contrasted with a flat panel of grained wood. By Clarence Bielman.

illustrations what some typical light modulators have been, you can imagine what any other modulator might be. If you lay a piece of plain white paper on the top of a table, Figure 1, you will see that even in that form it is one type of light modulator—the simplest possible of all types, for it reflects the light evenly over its entire surface.

Then, if you lift one corner, or one edge, Figure 2, or both edges, Figure 3, or all four corners, you will see for yourself how its light-modulating values change with each slight alteration of position. If you fasten all four corners together as in Figure 4, you can see the reflective effects of various types of curvature on the light, and the space relationships which have been created. If now you cut or tear a small hole near one corner, as in Figure 5, you can observe the changes in light and shadow which have been wrought by this simple act.

Try various bends, cuts and folds of the paper. The variety of modulators possible is endless. Then try adding another factor— perhaps another type of material, more shiny, more nearly opaque, or perhaps more nearly transparent, metal and glass are examples —and observe what this does to the arrangement of light values. Add an opaque object with a straight edge to the assembly or let the light fall across a straight edge before it hits the modulator, and observe how much more noticeable the curves are when contrasted with it. See, too, how much more readily depth and illusions of space are created.

Light the modulator from various angles, and with different combinations of light. Observe what changes are made in each part and in the whole effect.

Photograph the modulator, striving to reveal it to its best advantage—that is, so your photograph will most quickly identify the true shape and nature of your modulator in the mind of another person.

Observe closely. Impress upon your memory the manner in which each feature modulates the light. With some thought and practice you will be able to apply this information to similar surfaces and contours when they appear in the subjects you wish to photograph.

There is an important application of the light modulator in the field of creative photography. As you observe its effects upon *light,* note *your emotional reactions* to each combination of shape, contour, texture, color and lighting. Note how the light was integrated with the other factors to produce that reaction and you have a basis for deliberately producing a similar instinctive response from other persons. Photography, which is painting with light, can achieve this as surely as can painting with oil and pigment, or the shaping of words into sentences. That is the new frontier of photography.

After learning how to photograph a series of light modulators made in this manner, graduate to the photographing of a more difficult object, perhaps a face, which will include all the properties and problems of your whole series of light modulators. Having studied each problem separately, you will know what each type of modulation will mean in the finished photograph. You will need less time to achieve good results.

Obviously this principle can be applied to pictures other than portraits. In making an industrial photograph for advertising purposes, for example, it may be necessary to stop the machinery while the picture is being made. There will be no time for experiments while the machinery is stopped, for each minute costs the manufacturer money. You must know beforehand which view will make a dramatic picture and how to translate the available light into a dramatic picture. There will be many shapes and types of surfaces, and definite space relationships—depth, height, comparative dimensions, interpenetrating objects, surfaces that meet and cut one another, transparencies, mirrorings, etc. If you are familiar with the uses and effects of each individually and in relation to one another in a picture, you will be able to move surely, swiftly and efficiently about your work. Such complete familiarity with these elements can be acquired by study of light modulators of your own manufacture.

The camera and finishing equipment, together, constitute merely the "typewriter" of picture-making mechanically. The quality and power of the finished product depends mainly on the operator, not the mechanism itself. Instead of words, he works with light values —highlights and shadows—and if he modulates and uses them properly he can produce the desired optical impressions of space relationships.

The New Bauhaus and Space Relationships   *L. Moholy-Nagy*

The key to workshop training, which is the real Bauhaus idea, is the very deep, spiritual connection it has with craftsmanship. In the old Bauhaus it was the idea of the founder, Professor Walter Gropius, to have, in spite of a technically and socially advanced

From *American Architect and Architecture,* CLI (December, 1937).

world, the same excellence of production that was significant of craftsmanship in the Middle Ages. This implied a training closely related to architecture, an architecture which integrated all designers' shopwork. Separate laboratories were devoted to the study of wood, metal, glass, clay, stone, textile, plastics, etc., affording the student a possible means of livelihood and certain security. This community of teachers and students was able, day after day and year after year, to produce useful inventions as a result of their studies. This was not due to their knowledge alone, but to their imagination and ability to see the goal of their own lives. The source of their ingenuity was their vision of life and their freedom to utilize the means and knowledge of the time in a new and unrestricted manner.

Raoul Francé's bio-technique, which we shall teach in the New Bauhaus, is an attempt at a new science which shows how natural forms and designs can be translated without great difficulty into human production. This means that nature's ingenious forms can be reduced to technical ones. Every bush, every tree, can instruct us and show us inventions, apparatus, technical appliances without number. I visited the east coast this summer and I was most amazed to see a little animal until then unknown to me—the horseshoe crab. This very thin prehistoric animal shell is constructed in such a wonderful and economical way that we could immediately adapt it to a fine bakelite or other molded plastic form. It is said that Edison, who was one of the greatest of your countrymen, had never invented anything without getting an order for it. His conscious approach to inventions is a great example for our students because whatever was done in human history as an outstanding achievement can be repeated or can be developed to a standard ability. This approach of function and industry is today no longer a revolutionary principle but an absolute standard for every designer. For this reason alone we could not build in the New Bauhaus a creative community again, but could produce only a rigid teaching system.

A fresh outlook can come only through satisfactory designs for our biological needs. Our aims today go far ahead of those of yesterday, of the labor-saving devices built into our architecture. When we design we must relate them on a much greater scale with our psychological, psycho-physical needs beyond those of our physical comfort. This, I confess, cannot be done easily because we do not know enough about ourselves. We must work hard for such a knowledge since our biologists and physiologists, etc. have not supplied as yet sufficient data to enable us to understand the human being and his most important needs. When a clear statement, clear function and clear means are given, the design will not be difficult to execute. A factory, hospital, school or office building is rather definable and we have in each up to now really the most satisfactory designs. The difficulty today lies in the architectural design for dwelling purposes. We are told that we can kill a human being with housing just as surely as with an axe, but we do not yet know how to make him happy. The problem is clearly stated. To help bring about a right solution is the goal which the New Bauhaus has set for itself. But all have to cooperate, the scientists, the technicians and the artists, in order to find which course our designs should take; how they should be controlled, simplified, or enriched in accordance with the needs of the individual today and for future generations.

We must be far-sighted enough to visualize the effect of our actions on mankind and to have sufficient intuition to relate our suggestions to his work and also to his recreation. We must know, among other things, his reaction to material, to color, to form and to space.

We attempt to teach today the understanding and use of spatial relationships much as we are teaching in the grade schools the ABC's which can be put together in words, the words into sentences, and the sentences into expression.

In our definition of space considerable uncertainty prevails at present. This uncertainty is evident in the words we employ, and it is precisely these words which increase the confusion. What we know of space in general is of little help in assisting us to grasp it as an actual entity. The different kinds of space are rather surprising, and you will be amused when you hear the manifold terms which we daily use without exact knowledge of what they convey. We speak today of:

mathematical	crystalline	projective	finite
physical	cubic	metric	infinite
geometric	hyperbolic	isotropic	limitless
Euclidian	parabolic	topographic	universal
non-Euclidian	elliptical	homogeneous	etheric
architectural	bodily	absolute	inner
dance	surface	relative	outer
pictorial	lineal	fictive	movement
scenic	one-dimensional	abstract	hollow
cinema	two-dimensional	actual	vacuum
spheric	three-dimensional	imaginary	formal, etc.

Space

Notwithstanding this bewildering array, we must recognize all the time that space is a reality in our sensory experience; a human experience like others, a means to expression like others; like other realities, other materials. Space is a reality that can be grasped according to its own laws. As a matter of fact, man has constantly tried to use this reality (this material) in the service of his urge for expression, no less than the other realities which he has encountered.

A definition of space which, even if it is not exhaustive, may at least be taken as a point of departure for further consideration, is found in physics—"Space is the relation between the positions of bodies."

An explanation for that may be this: Two bodies exist, say the earth and the moon. The relationship between their positions means space. We can now change earth and moon into other bodies, e.g., to two chairs or two houses or two walls. We can change it into telegraph posts, into wires, into two fingers of our two hands. We must test this simply by sensory experience through our eyes in order to be able to understand it correctly. This experience of the visible relationships of position may be checked by movement—alteration of position—and by touch, and it may be verified by other senses.

We know, for example, through experiments, that it is possible to distinguish forms and space through hearing, too. We know of substitutes for the eyes of the blind which mean that the photo cell is used to translate the visual existence into an acoustical one. We know the localization and function of the organ for balance called the labyrinth through experiments with the swirling porpoise. We know through our own experiences that when we ascend or descend a spiral staircase or land in an oblique airplane, our own balance sense, the labyrinth, records clearly the relationship between our consecutive positions.

According to this, man perceives space

1. Through his sense of sight in such things as wide perspectives, surfaces meeting and cutting one another, corners, moving objects with intervals between them.
2. Through his sense of hearing, by acoustic phenomena.
3. Through means of locomotion, horizontal, vertical, diagonal, jumps, etc.
4. Through his sense of equilibrium; by circles, curves, windings (spiral stairways).

All this sounds very complicated, but once we begin practical work with small models the goal becomes more clear. We must certainly know that a real space experience is a summary of experiences from many categories. If we analyze this we observe that every sense is able to record space relationships, but the highest form of space comprehension means the synthesis of all sensory experiences. Thus our students work first with the simplest perception formulas and slowly reach the peak.

In the near future I hope to construct a spatial kaleidoscope which should be an example for small constructions by the students themselves. I will assemble on a horizontal disc some perpendicular sticks which will revolve. Over the middle of the disc I will place a small elevator containing slats and rods, horizontal and oblique, and spiral forms, and transparent bodies, and then I will move it, too, in a vertical direction.

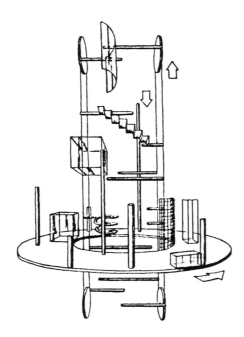

As the disc and the elevator move simultaneously we will have every kind of intersection and every kind of relationship between the "positions of bodies." The movement may be stopped at any time so that an interesting space relationship can thus be easily fixed, and by drawing or other means of representation may be recorded.

To this type of spatial exercise we add the study of perspective and stereoscopic drawing which helps to obtain a spatial vision. I find very often that the grasping of space seems to be, for most people, a very difficult task. They find it difficult to think in terms of space relationships on different intersecting and penetrating levels and heights. Even excellent architects, knowing every part of their subject, everything about technique and function, sometimes have difficulty in visualizing a rich space formula. This is actually the reason why contemporary architecture appears sometimes rather simple in comparison with the Gothic or Baroque.

According to my belief, space experience is not a privilege of the architectural genius. It is a biological function, and we must try to approach it in a conscious way. The biological bases of space experience are everyone's endowment, just like the experience of colors or of tones. By practice and suitable exercises this capacity can be developed. To be sure, there will be many degrees of difference in the maximum capacity, exactly as is the case in other fields of experience, but basically space experience is accessible to everyone, even in its rich, complicated form.

I am convinced that sooner or later we shall have a genuine space system, a dictionary for space relationships, as we have today our color system or as we have our sound system for musical composition. This has another significance, too; it is not enough that the architects will be clear about spatial relationship and spatial composition but, if their work is to be appreciated, the layman, the client, must know about space, too. Of course, in the planning of a modern building the most varied problems come up; social, economic, technical, hygienic. It is probable that upon their correct solution the fate of our generation and the next, in an essential aspect, depends. But in addition to the fulfillment of these elementary requirements, man should have opportunity in his dwelling to experience the fact of space. This means that a dwelling should be decided upon not only on the basis of price and the time it takes to build, not only upon the usual considerations of its suitability for use, its material, construction and economy, but the experience of space also belongs in the list, as essential to the people who are to live in the house. This requirement is not to be taken as a vague phrase of a mystical approach to the subject; it will not be long before it is generally recognized as a necessary element in the architectonic conception, and one capable of being exactly circumscribed. That is, architecture will be understood, not as a complex of inner spaces, not merely as a shelter from cold and from danger, not as a fixed enclosure, as an unalterable arrangement of room, but as a governable creation for mastery of life, as an organic component of living.

The future conception of architecture must consider and realize the whole. Individuals, who are a part of a biological whole, should find in the home not only relaxation and recuperation, but also a heightening and harmonious development of their powers. The standard for architects will then no longer be the specific needs in the housing of the individual, or of a profession, or of a certain economic class, but it will revolve around the general basis, that of the biologically evolved manner of living which man requires.

Architecture will be brought to its fullest realization only when the deepest knowledge of human life in the biological whole is available. One of its most important components is the ordering of man in space, making space comprehensible.

The root of architecture lies in the mastery of the problem of space; the practical development lies in the problem of construction.

On Moholy's Sculpture *Jack W. Burnham*

László Moholy-Nagy's contribution to nonobjective art has been often deprecated since his death in 1946. However, as a teacher and thinker Moholy was responsible for a good share of the methodology which survived the closing of the Bauhaus. He had a genius for understanding the potential of collective visual phenomena (not to be confused with the creation of startling icons— private images were not Moholy's forte) and, in particular, the phenomenology of motion. While a creator of ambitious kinetic devices, his real talent lay in showing young people, with brilliant clarity, the promise of kineticism.

It would be fitting in a historical review of kinetic art to begin with Moholy's famous *Light-Space Modulator,* a device perfected between 1922 and 1931. However, this will be saved for a later examination of light as an art form. As a theorist, though, Moholy's ideas on kinetic art deserve to be examined more fully than they have been up to now.

In 1932 his *The New Vision: From Material to Architecture* was translated into English from German and published in New York. The book offers two things: a description of the *Vorkurs,* the

From *Beyond Modern Sculpture* (New York: George Braziller; London: Allen Lane The Penguin Press, 1968), pp. 235–38.

Moholy-Nagy

Bauhaus basic design course which Moholy along with Joha[...] Itten and Josef Albers helped form, and an outline of the v[...] potentials of materials and structures then available. Significan[...] Moholy's method of categorizing sculpture into evolutionary stages. These five developments of sculpture are: the blocked-out form, the modeled (hollowed-out) form, the perforated form (also assembled constructions are in this category), the form in equipoise, and kinetic sculpture. He lists these steps of sculptural development—"not in the individual, but in the history of culture as a whole"—implying, one assumes, that the stages cover more than just the modern Western tradition. If this is true, then it has been only in this century that his evolutionary theory of sculpture has realized its potential. Previously, kinetic devices may have reflected technical, religious, or recreational values, but hardly ever artistic. His list is more an artistic imperative for this century than a historical survey. Moholy's analysis is essentially a technical morphology. He says, in effect, that the sensual apprehension of form has been overtaken by an intellectual grasp of form, that cultural stylistics are giving way to a burgeoning technology.

Interestingly enough, Moholy inserts *equipoised* sculpture between *perforated* (also called *open*) sculpture and *kinetic* sculpture. Ten years before Calder realized his first mobiles Moholy's students constructed works based on the principle of equilibrium. These student efforts, or at least those photos of them published, never achieved the flexibility or grace of Calder's mobiles. Most of the Bauhaus solutions were rigid Constructivist attempts to balance unequal weights on uneven arms. Moholy recognized that the great obstacle to equipoise sculpture lay in finding a power source not obviously visible. He considered magnetic force and remote electrical control as possible solutions. It was left to Calder to harness random currents of air.

While rest remained the natural state for equipoise sculpture, Moholy felt that motion belonged primarily to kinetics. The intellectual conception of kinetics in the 1920's very much revolved around his idea of *virtual volumes*—the outline or trajectory presented by an object in motion. With this in mind, he sought to represent the transformation of sculptural qualities with the following equation: "sculpture = material + mass relationships, changes to the dematerialized and highly intellectualized formula: sculpture = volume relationships. . . ."

As with Gabo's planar constructions, mass was transformed into volume, weight was reduced, thus the space-filling capacity of sculpture was maintained. *Thingness* continued to be an important consideration to the kineticists of the 1920's. It still is for the present generation of kinetic artists, though their *theoretical* concerns are less a space-object duality. The emphasis presently seems to be on the *qualities of motion* and on *time sequences*. As a result, the immateriality or de-emphasis of form which has taken place seems extreme compared to Moholy's equation, though not far from a later concern of his with musical time.

In his book Moholy includes a thumbnail sketch entitled "The History of Kinetic Sculpture." It is a tribute to Moholy's intellect and visionary powers that the outlines of kinetic histories to date have pretty much followed his pattern. He quotes from Gabo's "Realist Manifesto" and refers to it as a model for the manifesto which he published with Alfred Kemény in 1922, "The Kinetic-Constructive System of Force." In an excerpt from his own manifesto he quotes the usual doctrinaire ambitions of constructive art about exchanging static for dynamic values. The last paragraph quoted, though, contains a singularly important and speculative statement about the future of kinetic art: "The first projects looking toward the dynamic-constructive system of forces can only be experimental, demonstrating devices for the testing of the relations between man, material, power and space. Next comes the *utilization of the experimental results for the creation of freely moving (free from mechanical and technical movement) works of art.*" (Italics added.)

This paragraph implies two things. As a later, expanded version of his *New Vision* would indicate (*Vision in Motion,* 1947), Moholy was well aware that the artistic deficiencies of mechanical motion made it less than a perfect medium, even in its most realized form. Nevertheless, he spoke of the need by artists to continue the kinetic investigation—even with failure as a strong possibility. He surmised that experience in the kinetic medium plus a new acclimatization to time-motion perceptual patterns would be indispensable for the ultimate success of the kinetic cause.

Moholy spoke from experience. He produced one work, *Kinetic Sculpture* (1930–1936), that could well have emerged from the kinetic vanguard studios of Milan, Paris or Düsseldorf during the 1960's. This construction consists of two square forms rotatable from gyroscopic axes, and extended from a plate of polished steel. Inside the two kernel forms are networks of glass tubing partially filled with mercury. It appears that these mercury receptacles are set in motion by hand. The total effect, one would guess, is not overpowering—the movement of the mercury and the turning of the kernel forms do not seem to justify the complexity of the apparatus. Consequently, it is prophetic that in 1922 Moholy saw the necessity of a "freely moving" sculpture (free from mechanical and technical movement), a form of locomotion without the cumbersomeness of classical machines.

Precisely what form this could take he does not specify. Yet he spoke of there being more to the evolution of sculpture than technological development, and insisted that all the experimentation of artists must have "significance for the biological 'nourishment' of man." Moholy had been one of the few artists to recognize the biological relevance of motion phenomena. He perceptively saw that much of the motion produced by technology, while perhaps outwardly impressive, was injurious to the human nervous system. It was not Moholy's purpose, nor that of Gabo, simply to reproduce the environmental chaos of urban technology.

What is the alternative? Certainly Moholy never strove to parody the machine. He was at once too optimistic and temperamentally attuned to the future to be caught in such a dead end. He sensed a greater truth than lamentation for the decline of age-old perceptual sensibilities. He understood that kineticism would be viewed as more than another stylistic innovation. It would mean probing a concern which sat at the very apex of Western desire: breaking the bounds of Classical tradition.

Light—A Medium of Plastic Expression *L. Moholy-Nagy*

Since the discovery of photography virtually nothing new has been found as far as the principles and technique of the process are concerned. All innovations are based on the esthetic representative conceptions existing in Daguerre's time (about 1830), although these conceptions, i.e., the copying of nature by means of the photographic camera and the mechanical reproduction of perspective, have been rendered obsolete by the work of modern artists.

Despite the obvious fact that the *sensitivity to light* of a chemically prepared surface (of glass, metal, paper, etc.) was the most important element in the photographic process, i.e., containing its own laws, the sensitized surface was always subjected to the demands of a *camera obscura* adjusted to the traditional laws of perspective while the full possibilities of this combination were never sufficiently tested.

The proper utilization of the plate itself would have brought to light phenomena imperceptible to the human eye and made visible only by means of the photographic apparatus, thus perfecting the eye by means of photography. True, this principle has already been applied in certain scientific experiments, as in the study of motion (walking, leaping, galloping) and zoological and mineral forms, but these have always been isolated efforts whose results could not be compared or related.

It must be noted here that our intellectual experience complements spatially and formally the optical phenomena perceived by the eye and renders them into a comprehensible whole, whereas the photographic apparatus reproduces the purely optical picture (distortion, bad drawing, foreshortening).

One way of exploring this field is to investigate and apply various chemical mixtures which produce light effects imperceptible to the eye (such as electro-magnetic rays, X-rays).

Another way is by the construction of new apparatus, first by the use of the *camera obscura;* second by the elimination of perspective. In the first case using apparatus with lenses and mirror-arrangements which can cover their environment from all sides; in the second case, using an apparatus which is based on new optical laws. This last leads to the possibility of "light-composition," whereby light would be controlled as a new plastic medium, just as color in painting and tone in music.

This signifies a perfectly new medium of expression whose nov-

From *Broom,* IV (1923).

elty offers an undreamed of scope. The possibilities of this medium of composition become greater as we proceed from static representation to the motion pictures of the cinematograph.

I have made a few primitive attempts in this direction, whose initial results, however, point to the most positive discoveries (and as soon as these attempts can be tested experimentally in a laboratory especially devised for the purpose, the results are certain to be far more impressive).

Instead of having a plate which is sensitive to light react mechanically to its environment through the reflection or absorption of light, I have attempted to *control* its action by means of lenses and mirrors, by light passed through fluids like water, oil, acids, crystal, metal, glass, tissue, etc. This means that the filtered, reflected or refracted light is directed upon a screen and then photographed. Or again, the light-effect can be thrown directly on the sensitive plate itself, instead of upon a screen. (Photography without apparatus.) Since these light effects almost always show themselves in motion, it is clear that the process reaches its highest development in the film.

Dynamics of a Metropolis:
A Film Sketch   *L. Moholy-Nagy*

Building construction with an iron crane (Use of special trick effects—line drawings—melting slowly into the filming of nature) Crane for construction:
>   shot from below
>   diagonally
>   from above
>   elevator for bricks
>   revolving crane

This movement is continued by an automobile racing
>   to the left. The same house is always seen
>   in the center of the picture.

(The house should always be re-photographed to place it in the center.)
>   Another automobile appears which tears along at the same
speed, but in the opposite direction.
>   Tempo, tempo!

From Istvan Nemeskurty, *Word and Image* (London: Clematis Press, 1968), pp. 62–67. This book is a translation of *A mozgokeptol a filmmuveszetig* (Budapest: Corvina, 1961). The scenario was originally drafted in Berlin, 1921–22.

One row of houses rushes by in the same direction, always allowing the house in the middle to be seen. The row of houses runs past and comes back.

Rows of houses race transparently in opposite directions, and so do the automobiles. Faster and faster, so that the spectators are made dizzy.

A tiger, TIGER walks about in his cage
walks back and forth angrily.

High up, clearly visible traffic signals.

Moving automatically
a-u-t-o-m-a-t-i-c-a-l-l-y
(Close up)

up   up

    down   down

up up up down down

1   2   3   4   5

Goods-station.

Shunting yard.

Warehouses and cellars   Dark   Dark

                            DARKNESS

Railway

Highway with vehicles. Bridge. Viaduct. Ships passing below. Above an overhead railway. (Elberfeld)

View of a train from a high embankment, shot diagonally.

A track-watchman salutes standing at attention.

Eyes become fixed. (Close up)

Train seen from a bridge, from above.

From below: from the ditch between the rails the belly of the train as it rushes along. The turning wheels—so fast as to be an indistinct vibration.

TEMPO

TEMPO

TEM

TEM   PO

TEM

      TEEEM

        M

       M POOOOO

                 DOWN

In a department store glass-enclosed lift with Negro children.

Obliquely.   UP

                  UP

Distorted perspective.

Longshot.   A CROWD

At the entrance tethered dogs
Beside the glass lifts glass telephone boxes with callers
Filming from the ground floor through the glass
The FACE of a caller, painted with phosphorescent paint (so as to produce no shadow) turns slowly to the right, directly beside the lift.
Over his head a distant airplane spirals in the air.
View from a slight altitude: a square where
many streets converge.

Masses of vehicles. Tramways, motor-cars, lorries, carts, bicycles, buses drive fast from the square.
Suddenly all of them go backwards.

They pile up in the center of the square.
The square opens in the middle and swallows them up.

(The camera is at an angle to create the impression of falling.)
                                        underground
                                        cables
TEMPO
                            Gas-tank
                            Sewers. (deep beneath the town)

Light reflected on water.
Arc lamp.
Sparks *spraying*.
Highway at night, gleaming city streets.
Gliding automobiles from above, diagonally.

For five seconds only a black screen
Electric advertising with flashing letters:

                MOHOLY   MOHOLY

Fireworks in the amusement park.
Riding on the roller-coaster.
SPEEDing.
Ferris-wheel.
Fun-house.
Distorting mirrors.
Other jokes.
Picture of exhibition in a railway station.
The camera moves in a horizontal circle,
then in a vertical circle

Taut

telephone wires and telegraph cables
between houses.

> Towers of porcelain insulators.
> Radio-aerials on roofs.

Factory.

> Wheels turning.
> An acrobat twirls and turns somersaults.

> Pole-vaulting. A fall shown 10 times in succession.

Variety show. Frantic activity.
Football match. Rough. Fast tempo.
Women wrestling. Kitsch!
Jazz-band instruments. (in Close-up.)

POINTED AT THE PUBLIC

A hollow, shining metal funnel is fixed on the lens of the camera.
Immediately:
a man jerks away his head in a flash. (Close-up)

A glass of WATER.
(only the surface of the water, in Close-up.)
Gushing like a fountain.
Jazz-band, *with its sound*.

FORTISSIMOOOO

Wild dance caricature.
Prostitutes.
Boxing, Close-up.

> ONLY gloves.
> With slow-motion (Zeitlupe) camera

A cloud of smoke. (Coming through a bridge, as a train runs under it)
Chimney-stack, aslant.
A diver plunges down into water.
Propeller turning under the water.
Opening of drain above and under water.
Filming from motor boat along the canal to

RUBBISH dump.
Utilization of rubbish.

> Hills of scrap iron.
> Mounds of old shoes.
> Stacks of tin cans.

Perpetual motion lift, with view. All around.

From here the whole section, back to the JAZZ BAND
(also reversed), should go from
fortissimo to PIANISSIMO

Mortuary. From above.
Military parade.
March-march.

Women riding horses
The two shots are superimposed, so that both are visible.

Slaughter-house. Oxen.
Machinery of a cold-storage plant.
Sausage machine. Thousands of sausages.
A LION's HEAD snarling (Close-up.)
Audience.
A LION'S HEAD snarling (Close-up.)
Policeman with a rubber truncheon in the middle of a crowded
square.
The TRUNCHEON (Close-up.)
Audience in a theater.
Snarling LION'S HEAD (Close-up.)
For a few seconds total darkness.

CIRCLE
Circus.
TEMPO
Trapeze.
LION,   Lion
CLOWN.
LION,   Lion
Clowns
clowns   LION
clowns
Slowly. WATERFALL: with sound.
A body floats on the water.
Soldiers.
March—march.
A glass of WATER
with moving surface.
a brief,
rapid jet of water upwards.

THE END

Remarks for those who refuse to understand the film immediately.

This film mostly flowed from the possibilities offered by the camera.

My aim was for a film to produce an effect by its own action, its own tempo and rhythm, instead of the still fashionable plots that force cinema to ape literature or theater.

The speeding autos are necessary for a shocking introduction. To show the breathless rush, the turmoil of a city. The tiger is used for contrast. And so that the audience would get used to such surprises and inconsistency from the start.

The purpose of this film is not to teach, nor to moralize, nor to tell a story. Its acting is purely visual.

Bridges, trains, ships, etc. are here to illustrate the services and conveniences of an urban civilization.

The belly of the train: this is a visual experience that we would not normally encounter.

The phosphorescent face that slowly turns away: reminding us of fatiguing telephone conversations. A dream-like state. (Glass, glass, glass)—the direction of the movement prepares us for the spiral course of the pilot.

The rushing of a roller-coaster: many things escape your attention. Many things pass unnoticed, because the senses are unable to perceive everything, rapid motion, moments of danger, etc. On the roller-coaster almost all passengers close their eyes at the great downward drop. But the camera does not close its eye. We rarely watch objectively babies or animals because our attention is taken by the apprehension of numerous other circumstances.

The metal funnel: is to frighten so terribly that it should almost hurt.

The surface of the glass of water: should be brilliant.

The frequent recurrence of the lion's head is a nightmare. (Again, again, again.)

The audience of the theater is gay, but we are still conscious of the lion's head.

In general one should understand more from a rapid reading of the manuscript than can ever be expressed by explanations.

Once a Chicken, Always a Chicken   *L. Moholy-Nagy*

A film script on a motif from Kurt Schwitters'
"Auguste Bolte"

1.

A network of lines covers the screen.

A number of eggs roll down an inclined plane—toward the spectator—, those in front are very large, those following diminish in size, single eggs jump into the air.

A hand catches the jumping eggs.

A masked man juggles with eggs.

The man catches eggs out of the air, throws them away again, they vanish. More and more eggs in ever more rapid sequence.

The man can no longer save himself from the deluge of eggs that rains down upon him.

He runs away.

The eggs again run down the inclined plane as before.

The eggs are at first small, then increase in size. Some jump, fall, jump again. Some break. The inclined plane is transformed into the side of a roof, down which the eggs are rolling and leaping.

Another egg. It jumps high into the air and runs with lightning speed down the front of the house onto the street.

Down in the street the egg makes a few more leaps. More and more eggs join it, some break, but the majority roll and leap on.

A street crowded with walking people.

Legs in rapid walking motion, eggs rolling and leaping on the ground between them.

The legs move rapidly, but the eggs even faster.

The legs lag behind, and finally fail to reach the screen.

The eggs roll between the wheels of cars and trams, across tram lines, leap over water courses.

Drops of water and eggs leap into the air. Their whiteness is offset against a dark background.

Now the man is walking along the street. He is moving in the opposite direction to that of the eggs. (Thus if the eggs are moving from the right to the left, the man is walking from the left to the right of the screen. In order to draw the audience's attention to the

Written 1925–30 and originally published in *Telehor* (Brno, 1936). Reprinted by permission of Mrs. Sibyl Moholy-Nagy.

fact that they change their course and follow the man, some eggs begin to leap in the opposite direction.)

Many eggs roll after the man: small ones, large ones, along a fairly crowded street.

Shops with perambulators. The eggs leap through the open doors of shops. They jump into prams.

Ten women, one after the other, push perambulators through the door of a shop.

Again walking people and eggs rolling between their legs.

In the foreground the man is running. He turns a corner.

Ten pupils of a girls' finishing school, with eggs rolling between their legs.

At the corner eggs leap about in distress—they have lost trace of the man.

One egg rolls away from the others and rolls on and on.

It finally reaches the door of a house.

Slowly the door closes behind it.

The porter's lodge. The staring face of a fat woman doorkeeper. Mouth gaping in surprise.

The door again opens—very slowly—a young woman—fresh and bright—steps out of the doorway. In rythmic motion she flicks the broken shells of an egg from her dress. The fat doorkeeper runs after the girl, hands her an enormous baby's milk bottle.

With an ironic and superior smile the girl refuses the bottle. She enters a café.

2.

Short montage sequence showing the interior of the café: a waiter balancing a tray, a man who has accumulated all the available newspapers; dogs under the tables.

The young woman enters the garden in front of the café.

She takes a seat and looks about attentively with a bright expression.

Outside idlers, hurrying, though they have nothing to do.

The girl looks at her cup.

She raises it to her mouth—it contains chocolate with cream.

Small white flowers—myrtles—from a wreath.

The head of the girl with bridal veil and wreath.

Shortly afterward the man with the mask appears.

The girl puts down the cup, looks up.

At this moment ten men with similar masks pass outside.

Nine of them are relatively blurred.

The girl jumps from her seat.

Runs forward and looks after the men oblivious to her surroundings.

Hesitatingly she returns, looks around in a disturbed manner, sits
down. Again jumps up.

Runs a few paces, then slows down, thinking.

Slowly she returns.

Halfway she resolutely turns and rushes along between the rows
of tables.

The waiter carrying vast quantities of trays and crockery rushes
after her wildly shouting and gesticulating in spite of his heavy load.
The man with the newspapers appears with an annoyed expression
from behind mountains of newspapers and furiously looks after the
disappearing girl.

The waiter with his trays bumps into the table of the man.

The man is buried under a deluge of newspapers, which completely engulf him.

The waiter stumbles, but manages to retain his foothold.

Trays, crockery, food—he balances all of it, not a drop of coffee
is spilled from the cups. Eggs leap in their glasses.

The girl is standing outside, looks to the right and left.

Then she walks to the left, where the ten men are strolling along
the street.

The girl rushes after the men.

Breathless she approaches them, she stops abruptly, in order
slowly to overtake them—

but

The men have just reached a street corner. Five turn to the left,
five to the right. The girl now also reaches the corner.

For a long time she remains standing in despair without knowing
what to do. Which way shall she take?

She decides to follow the right group of five men.

She stops half way, hesitates.

She runs back and follows the left group instead.

Halfway she is again beset with doubts. At top speed she rushes
after the right group.

The five men increase their pace.

Breathless the girl again approaches them, stops abruptly, in order to pass them slowly,

but

The five men have reached another corner, three turn to the
right, two to the left.

The girl has also reached the corner, she stops, thinks, and decides to take the right-hand course.

Halfway she stops and turns to the left, stops, thinks and turns to the right again.

The girl quickly follows the right group of men.

Three men walk along the street.

Openmouthed, breathing heavily, hatless and with disheveled hair the girl rushes after them.

Close to the men she stops abruptly, brushes her hair back, quickly puts on her hat, prepares to overtake the men—when the men have again reached the corner, one turning to the left, two to the right.

The girl reaches the corner. Without stopping to think she mechanically turns to the right.

But the men have again reached the corner, when the girl approaches them.

They separate: one turns to the right, the other to the left.

For a fraction of a second the mask of the man walking to the right is sharply defined.

Exhausted the girl reaches the corner.

In stupor she runs a few paces to the right.

The girl suddenly stops and turns to look after the man who went to the left.

But the man has already vanished.

The girl then turns to the right again.

For down the street the man is just entering a house.

The girl rushes after him.

Completely out of breath the girl is standing in a gateway. It is of an immense size, the girl in front of it very small. In the background there are many other gateways, bearing down upon the girl as in a nightmare. With a tired gesture the girl wipes her forehead.

She is climbing steps. Halfway up the stairs a charwoman washing the steps empties her bucket, and a deluge of water sweeps the girl down the whole flight of stairs again. In vain she struggles against the floods: the hand of a woman pulls a doorbell. (This scene is repeated several times.)

Every time the girl is thrown out of a housedoor, her clothes are more damaged: first her hat is missing, then she appears without her coat.

At last her handbag is snatched by some one from inside a doorway.

The bag opens with a sudden jerk: coins and notes fall out, but into the floor inside the door. The door is banged, the money gone. In vain the girl belabors the door with both her fists. Thoroughly worn out she turns away.

She knocks at the door of a flat.

A woman opens it—shakes her head.

Inside a shadow appears in the background. The man with the mask?

The girl pushes the woman aside and rushes toward the man.

A lay figure!

The woman occupying the flat runs after the girl who has begun to demolish the lamp, chairs, table, etc., in a blind rage.

The women fight.

Finally a mighty blow sends the girl flying through the door.

After adjusting her clothes as best she can, the girl continues her search.

Completely at the end of her strength she meets a postman.

Frantically she commences to search the contents of his enormous bag.

The postman lifts up the girl and flings her aside.

The girl is thrown against a notice-board containing marriage bans.

Struggling violently she at once attempts to escape from behind the fence.

At last she succeeds in disentangling herself and slips through the meshes of the fence.

In the background fencing superimposed upon the window of a landing. The girl is standing at the bottom of the topmost flight of stairs.

Half a story higher up is the last door.

Summoning all her courage the girl climbs the few steps.

She rings the bell.

The door is opened by the masked young man.

The girl wants to rush in at once, but the door is slammed in her face.

Dumfounded she rings again.

In vain—she waits for a long time.

Slowly she descends a few steps.

She stops on the landing. Hesitates, returns to the door and rings again.

Again she waits in vain.

She returns to the landing.

She stops in thought, looks at the door and finally returns to it hesitatingly and without hope.

She rings, waits, no result.

Slowly the girl descends two flights of stairs and three steps more.

She turns abruptly, dashes upstairs and throws herself with all her strength against the door, which is shattered by the impact.

Inside is the man with the mask. He takes no notice whatever of the girl.

He is catching eggs out of the air and throwing them away again. The eggs leap and dance all around him, some break.

The girl who has just entered the room with a mighty bounce after having smashed the door, stops and greets him.

Entirely unconcerned the man continues his game with the eggs.

The girl hesitates, then bows again.

The man still ignores her.

The girl then resolutely approaches and grabs his arm.

The man turns his back on the girl and continues his game.

The girl takes hold of both his shoulders and shakes him furiously.

Suddenly the gigantic figure of the marriage registrar looms up in the room; he is wearing a top-hat and morning coat. His hand clasps a flaming sword.

The man and girl in front of him click their heels in military fashion and join hands. The registrar's sword is transformed into a sash.

He walks round them in a circle and encloses them in a flaming ring.

The registrar vanishes as suddenly as he appeared, by walking through the wall.

The man and the girl sit down at two tables facing each other.

They talk, each listening in a detached manner to the other. They almost soliloquize. They make grimaces at each other. Suddenly the girl jumps from her seat.

The man takes his hat, kisses the woman on her forehead and leaves the room.

The woman goes to the window.

Outside children are playing with balls in a park and digging in the sand of a building-plot; laughing faces of children. (Springtime.) The man is going to the registry office.

The registry officer enters the birth of a child, just notified by the man, in a large book.

The household of the young couple is poverty-stricken: dirty children, tiny ones and larger ones. Among them the woman, in despair.

The man is standing at the window and looking out at the street below.

Trees in full blossom, young girls, cars dashing along bright roads.

The man takes his hat.

He goes to the registry office.

The registrar enters another birth in his book.

The woman is standing at the window.

Below children: they play with snowballs in the park and with sledges on the building-plot. Laughing faces of children.

The man again goes to the registry office, etc.

Nine masked men pass the house.

The woman runs out of the door of the flat onto the staircase, as if intending to follow the men.

But doubts beset her, she slows down her pace and finally returns to the room.

Again the poor household, the neglected children.

The man returns. Without a word of greeting he throws his hat furiously onto the bed.

The smallest children cry.

The law-court in which the divorce is being pleaded.

The judge, the two, very small, in front of him, they are encircled by a ring and make desperate attempts to get away from one another. After a number of unsuccessful efforts they turn against each other and commence to fight.

The judge places his hands between them and separates them.

The ring is broken.

The girl hastily retreats, carrying one half of the broken ring.

Holding half the ring the girl quickly passes down a street.

A masked man turns and looks after the girl.

He follows her.

At the corner the girl meets another man, also masked.

He joins the first man.

The girl accelerates her steps.

More and more men are following her.

Finally the girl throws away her half of the ring. It is transformed into egg-shells.

The egg-shells roll after the girl, overtake her.

The egg-shells enclose the girl.

An egg rolls on with ever increasing speed.

Many masked men are running and running.

The egg rolls down a hill.

It comes to rest under a china hen.

The men also roll down the hill. They turn somersaults and stumble, some remain lying on the ground, others rise again.

The men stand round the china hen.

The head of the hen. Its plaster eyelids twinkle.

Problems of the Modern Film   *L. Moholy-Nagy*

The Present Situation

Of late years the principle, that all artistic creation should be appropriate to the specific technical potentialities of its medium, has been generally accepted at least in theory, if not always in practice.

Like other artists, film producers have for the last decade endeavored to apply this principle to their craft. Nevertheless the film today is still to an overwhelming extent governed by conceptions derived from traditional studio painting; and there is little in the current practice of film production to show that the essential medium of the film is *light* not pigment. Moreover the film today is exclusively confined to the projection of a sequence of "stills" on a screen and it is apparently not generally realized that mobile spatial projection is the form of expression most appropriate to this medium. The same conservatism is found in the use of the acoustically amplified film, the sound film, in which the theater chosen for the first model is still meticulously copied. Even theoretical attempts to discover independent forms peculiar to this technique are still exceedingly rare.

The Responsibility

The more the technical equipment of the film and of other related forms of communication and expression (wireless and television with all their manifold possibilities) is perfected, the greater will be the responsibility for elaborating a rational program of work.

The problem is still generally perceived and approached—in a traditional sense. The technician unquestioningly accepts the conventions of the present form of the film, i.e. recording the visual and acoustic reality and reproducing it in two-dimensional projection.

Different aims would certainly lead to different results, and the whole direction of technical inquiry would be changed. A new program of research would lead to the discovery of an entirely new, so far unprecedented form of expression and entirely new possibilities of artistic creation.*

* The distinguished scientist Theremin, inventor of ether-wave music, provided a good example of a false method of approach, when he aimed at imitating the old orchestral music with his new ether-wave instrument.

Written 1928–30 and originally published in *Cahiers d'Art*, VII/6-7 (Paris, 1932).

The Problem

In order to grasp the problem in its full complexity, it is necessary to examine the most important aspects of the film: the optical sphere (vision), the kinetic sphere (motion), the acoustic sphere (sound), one by one. The psychological (psycho-physical) problem—e.g. as it appears, in superrealist films—can only be hinted at in this paper.

The Optical Sphere:
Picture Production, or the "Morphosis of Light"?

It is quite conceivable that painting, as an exclusively manual craft, will continue to exist for some decades to come and that it will be retained for pedagogic reasons and as a means of preparing the way for the new culture of color and light. But this preparatory phase can well be shortened, if the problem is correctly postulated and systematic optical research is organized on these lines.

Symptoms of the commencing decline of traditional painting—I am not referring to the terrible economic plight of the artists at the present time—are already apparent in a number of directions. The development of the suprematist Malevitch may serve as an example. His last picture: a white square on a square white canvas is clearly symbolic of the film screen, symbolic of the transition from painting in terms of pigment to painting in terms of light. *The white surface can serve as a reflector for the direct projection of light, and what is more, of light in motion.*

Malevitch's work is a remarkable example of the new cultural outlook. It might be regarded as an intuitive victory over the misguided efforts of the present-day film, which is more or less successfully imitating the out-dated technique of easel painting in its pictorial composition, its not infrequent lack of movement and its picturesque settings. Suprematism superannuated a clean slate of manual craftsmanship in painting. How can the film revert to the esthetics of the easel picture, when even painters are venturing on new courses? *We must make a fresh start,* taking the new medium and its specific possibilities as our only basis instead of the fundamentally alien technique of pictorial art. That is why the victory of the so-called abstract movements in painting is the victory of a new esthetic of light, which will not merely transcend the old easel picture, but even the most advanced experiments and achievements of modern painting, and their culmination in the picture of Malevitch.

These considerations alone do not, however, enable us to formulate all the basic principles of optical creation. Direct light morphosis and kinetic and refractory light displays both require systematic investigation. The problems of painting, photography, the film are parts of one single problem.

The Light Studio of the Future

The indispensable elements for a new culture of controlled light are: reliable sources of artificial light of variable intensity, reflectors, projectors, instruments for the polarization, integration and refraction of light, improved optical equipment for the reception of images, and above all increased sensitiveness of the receptive medium (including the technical perfection of the three-dimensional and color film.*

Significance and Future of the Film Studio

In our politically and economically disrupted epoch the film as a record of facts, as film reportage, has become an educational and propaganda medium of the very first importance. Nevertheless, it is essential to remember that—like all other means of expression—the film with its characteristic elements of light, motion, psychological montage, has also a purely biological appeal, independent of any social factor (e.g. abstract films). It is for this reason that the studio will continue to play an important role in future film production, for it provides more suitable conditions for the conscious control of this appeal. I do not, of course, deny that even such films will be definitely related in some way to their particular period. On the contrary, I believe that this relation is far more profound than the obviously time-conditioned factor of topicality and that it is predominantly rooted in the subconscious mind and thus constitutes one of the most effective means of ideological preparation for the society of the future.

The studio for the manipulation of light will not, of course, be imitative like the film studios of today. It will not be its ambition to

* If such a provisional laboratory for research into the abstract properties of light could be established anywhere under present conditions it would probably be in Russia. In my opinion, a fair proportion of our present art schools could also without difficulty be transformed into "light academies." But Russia is the only country today in which the production of films is not governed by commercial considerations, optical creation generally, as here conceived, is only in Russia regarded as a cultural activity instead of the manufacture of a commodity. Moreover, no other country provides the same possibility for a radical change in the interpretation of the tasks of art. In Russia the old conception of the "artist" is definitely exploded—the old craft mentality is being superseded by a new conception of mental and cultural organization—invention is no longer exclusively confined to the manual sphere. Instead of thinking in terms of detail the Russian artists attempt to think synthetically (in terms of mutual relationship).

transform plywood into forests or Jupiter lamps into sunshine. Work in that studio will proceed from the basic elements of the medium employed and the development of its inherent potentialities.

The film architect will naturally conform to this new orientation. Apart from its acoustic function, the scenic background of the future will be conceived as a mechanism for the production of light and shade (trellis and skeleton construction) and as a complex of planes for the differential absorption and reflection of light (walls constructed for the organized distribution of light).

Cameraless photography, the so-called photogram, gives us the key to the morphosis of light. Its wide scale of black-white values and of innumerable shades of gray (in the future certainly also of color values) is of profound significance for the film. The same is true of the superimposition of different images.

It is the nonimitative studio alone which will enable us to create these forms of light, whose artistic possibilities have so far remained unexplored. Light morphosis is not, however, the sole problem of the film; problems of motion and sound demand a solution in equal measure. Nor is this all. The film contains a series of aspects which are partly of a photographic nature and in part derived from its new educational function (e.g. the problem of finding an appropriate means for expressing the new concept of space-time).

The Creative Use of Motion

As yet there is no tradition for the use and control of motion in films, for practical experience has been confined to a few decades. Even the first principles of this work remain to be evolved. That is the reason why motion is still so primitively handled in the majority of films.

Our eyes are still untrained to the reception of a number of simultaneous sequences. In the majority of cases the multiplicity of phases in a system of interrelated movements, however well controlled, would still produce an impression, not of organic unity, but of chaos.

For that reason experiments of this kind—however important esthetically—will for the time being have little more than technical or pedagogic interest. Though in some respects rather questionable Russian montage is so far the only real advance in this sphere. The simultaneous projection of a number of complementary films has so far not been attempted.*

---

* Montage alone by no means exhausts the possibilities inherent in motion. The Russian directors' sense of motion is impressionistic rather

Reflections on the Sound Film

The sound film is one of the most important inventions of our time. It will enlarge not merely the visual and acoustic capacities of mankind, but also his consciousness. But the sound film I have in mind has nothing whatever to do with the reproduction of the usual dramatic dialogue and sound sequences. Nor will its sole function be to provide a documentary record of acoustic reality. Insofar as it will fulfill this particular function, it will only be in a similar manner to the use of photomontage in the silent film.

Sound would scarcely be able to enrich the scope of the silent film, if it were confined solely to underlining or emphasizing an optic montage, complete in itself. Results already achieved in one medium—optically—would not be rendered more convincing by being paralleled in another. Only the combined use of both as mutually interdependent components of an indivisible whole can result in a qualitative enrichment or lead to an entirely new vehicle of expression. This is also the only proper field for reportage sound films.

The Present Problem in the Sound Film

We must diligently expand our acoustic receptivity, if we hope to make any real progress with the sound film. Contemporary "musicians" have so far not even attempted to develop the potential resources of the gramophone record, not to mention the wireless or ether-waves. They have a great deal of leeway to make up in remolding their mentality in conformity with these developments.

The sound film ought to enrich our aural experience sphere by giving us entirely unknown sound values, just as the silent film has already begun to enrich our vision.

It is our task to achieve a true opto-acoustic synthesis in the sound film, which will immensurably surpass public taste that is still captivated by the novelty of this medium. In the last resort such a synthesis inevitably implies the emergence of the *abstract*

---

than constructive. Russian montage is particularly successful in the use of associative impressions (which are, however, intentional and not accidental). Through rapid cutting often also of spatially and temporally distinct shots it created the necessary links between the individual situation and the whole.

The constructive montage of the future will give more attention to the totality of the film—in light, space, motion, sound—than to the film as a sequence of striking visual effects.

Eisenstein ("General Line"), Werthoff ("The Man with the Movie-Camera") and Turin ("Turksib") have already made concrete advances in this direction.

sound film, which will provide invaluable examples for all other types of films. The "documentary sound film" and the "abstract sound film" will be reinforced by the "montage sound film," by which must be understood not merely montage of the optical and acoustic sections, but a mutually integrated montage of both. We ought to begin with a series of experiments in the sound element. In other words, sound should at first be isolated from the image sequence, experiments in cutting being confined to the sound track. (It is obvious that musical convention is as much out of place here as the traditions of popular anecdotal painting is in the optical sphere of the film.) The next phase, which could also be absolved simultaneously, should proceed somewhat along the following lines:

1. Experiments in the use of acoustic realism: natural sounds, the human voice, or musical instruments.
2. Experiments in the use of sound units, which are not produced by any extraneous agency, but are traced directly onto the sound track and to be translated into actual sound in the process of projection (e. g. the tri-ergon system uses parallel lines of a varying brightness, the alphabet of which must be previously mastered; but since every mark on the sound track is translated into some note of noise in projection, my experiments with drawn profiles, letter sequences, fingerprints, geometrical signs printed on the track also produced surprising acoustic effects). Finally:
3. Experiments in the combination of both.

The first of these three series of experiments raises the following issues:

The talking film need not necessarily embody an uninterrupted sound sequence. The acoustic impression can be doubled in intensity if sound is arranged in phases of varying length, commencing or ceasing abruptly.

Just as it is possible to arrest an object visually in a great many different ways, from above or below, profile or full face, in normal perspective or foreshortened, similar possibilities must exist in regard to the sound. There must be different sound angles, just as there are different angles of sight. Variously graded combinations of music, speech and noise will be the main method of realizing these effects. In addition there are numerous possibilities for acoustic close-ups, slow motion (the slowing down of sound), acceleration (sound contraction), distortion, duplication and the other methods of sound montage. Optical simultaneity must find its counterpart in the realm of sound. In other words there must be no hesitation about amplifying the acoustic flow, even of speech, with additional, simultaneous sound patterns, or interrupting it by other sound values, whether to slow it down, distort or contract it, and only later to continue the original line, etc. Acceleration or deceleration of normal sound sequences produces the most extraordinary metamorphosis of individual notes into higher or lower octaves as the case may be. These can also be combined in a variety of ways; unlimited opportunities for comic effects are provided by such methods.

In regard to the second series it will not be possible to develop the creative possibilities of the talking film to the full until the acoustic alphabet of sound writing will have been mastered. Or in other words, until we can write acoustic sequences on the sound track without having to record any real sound. Once this is achieved the sound film composer will be able to create music from a counterpoint of unheard or even nonexistent sound values, merely by means of opto-acoustic notation.

The first talking film worthy of this name will be made by the artist who succeeds in discovering forms of acoustic expression that are convincingly appropriate both to the different objects and events and which he selects for his composition for their reactions to one another.

That discovery would enable us to produce acoustic sketches of anything and everything (including topical events). We should also be able to take acoustic "close-ups" (which would represent not a differentiation but an emphasis of sound "situations").

Projection

The rectangular canvas or metal screen of our cinemas is really only a mechanized easel painting, our conception of space and of the relations of space and light, still absurdly primitive, being restricted to the everyday phenomenon of light rays entering a room through an aperture in one of its walls.

It is possible to enrich our spatial experience by projecting light onto a succession of semitransparent planes (nets, trellis-work etc.). I did this in my scenic experiments for the *Kaufmann von Berlin* performed at Piscator's theater in 1930. It is also quite possible to replace a single flat screen by concave or convex sections of differing size and shape that would form innumerable patterns by continual change of position. One might also project different films onto all the walls of the cinema simultaneously as has been advocated with films.

Equally astonishing effects might be obtained by simultaneously focusing a number of projectors onto gaseous formations, such as smoke clouds, or by the interplay of multiform luminous cones. Finally, the abstract morphosis of light and objective film reportage will gain by the emergence of plastic projection which is promised by the development of stereoscopic photography. (The object to be recorded might be surrounded by a ring of synchronized lenses and then similarly projected.)

The sound film and its almost entirely neglected acoustic possibilities will almost certainly lead to revolutionary innovations in these as well as in the following directions.

The Tasks of Film Production

The creative use of the three main elements of the film—light, motion and sound—depends on the cooperation of a whole body of specialists and technicians, since it requires the active collaboration of the photographer,* the physicist and chemist, the architect, lighting expert and operator, the director of the film and the author of scenarios. The creative use of the film as dependent upon the technical possibilities of recording; optical equipment; the degree to which the receptive medium is sensitive to light; the use of ultra-violet and infra-red rays; super-sensitization (just as we can train our eyes to see in the dark, we shall one day have cameras able to react even at high speeds in complete obscurity). It depends on the perfection of color film; plastic film; sound film; and upon the problems of three-dimensional projection: successions of screens arranged in space and smoke reflectors; duplicate or multiple screens; automatic super-imposition and masking; and finally on mastery of the problems of sound and acoustics and of the synthetic coordination of every one of these elements in the art of film montage.

—*Translation from the German by F. D. Klingender and P. Morton Shand*

* Inability to use a camera will in the future undoubtedly be regarded as analogous in point of illiteracy as inability in the use of the pen, but up to the present the study of photography has nowhere been pursued systematically in a manner adequate to its importance. Thus—in spite of the proverbial German thoroughness—the Prussian minister of education was unable to indicate any guiding principles for this work, when in 1928 he officially authorized the teaching of photography in schools. But a syllabus for study and experimental research in photography could easily be drafted on the following lines:

1. Arresting the action of light with or without a camera (ordinary photography, photogram, X-ray and night exposure).
2. The factual record as documentary work:
   a) Amateur photography,
   b) Scientific (technical) photography (micro-photography, enlargement).
3. Fixation of movement and high-speed snapshots (reportage).
4. The study of various mechanical, optical, chemical reactions such as distortions of the optical instrument and of the sensitized medium (melting of the emulsion), intentionally "accidental" exposures, etc.
5. Synchronization: superimposition, montage.

Supplementary Remarks on the Sound and Color Film   *L. Moholy-Nagy*

Recent Achievements

A number of ideas discussed in my earlier film articles have in the meantime already begun to be applied. Synthetic sound script (Humphries, Pfenninger, the Russians Avramov, Janovski, Vojnov, Scholpo) is perhaps the most important project so far realized. Other suggestions for sound tricks have been used in films by Harold Lloyd and Walt Disney, in which acceleration of speech and reversed sound sequences are used to underline comic situations. The successful accomplishment of photography in total darkness by means of infra-red rays is an advance of similar importance. New camera sets for panoramic photography recording the full circle of any given prospect have been constructed in England and Germany. The new photographic perspective is also being extensively used to aid the researches of the art historian.

In the sphere of color new facilities have been provided by the simplification of the copying process achieved in the gasparcolor system; technicolor is already producing excellent direct color continuity, and Lumière's experiments with plastic films also give promise of interesting developments in this sphere.

These technical advances make it imperative to investigate the problems arising from the mutual relations of the silent, sound, and color film.

Back to the Silent Film?

The development of the talking picture has unfortunately verified the gloomiest predictions of the defenders of silent films. A deep gulf separates the artistic standard of the two, and it is undoubtedly true that the qualitative level of the average talking picture is still declining (perhaps on account of the increased commercialization due to the greater cost of sound film production). The tentative attempts of a Werthoff ("enthusiasm") have up to the present never been equaled, nor have they been accepted as a standard for present practice.

For many the conclusion to be drawn from these facts is: back to the principles of silent film montage.

Although this slogan is widely accepted, it is never practically applied, since it is impossible for the sound film to return to the methods of silent film production.

Written 1935 and originally published in *Telehor* (Brno, 1936). Reprinted by permission of Mrs. Sibyl Moholy-Nagy.

The Sound Film Has a Technique Peculiar to Itself

The receptive capacity of the human ear is far less rapid than that of the eye. This physiological fact alone prescribes a distinct technique for the sound film, and it is interesting because it enables us to develop principles of work, which, if applied, will take the talking film far beyond the best achievements of its silent forerunner.

The dominant principle of silent montage was to combine the shortest possible shots in rapid succession. The sound film cutter on the other hand is forced to use shots of far greater length. Thus if a given scene could consist of ten separate shots in a silent picture, it is impossible to use more than two or three shots or the same scene in a sound film.

This is the main cause of the indescribable optical dullness of most sound films. And yet there is no inherent reason why the necessity for a slower rhythm should lead to dullness in the visual sphere.

The "Traveling Crane Camera"

A few directors have instinctively adopted the more fruitful method of taking these two shots with a mobile camera. To understand their principle we must imagine a camera mounted on a crane, able to move at will diagonally, vertically, or in a circle or in a combination of these directions. With such a camera it is possible to take continuous shots of any given scene from innumerable angles and constantly changing points of view from long shot to close up. A considerable number of additional methods could be cited to illustrate my point that pictorial dullness is not necessarily inherent in the unavoidable slowness of sound film cutting.

Thus instead of moving the camera it is possible to move the object itself (revolving stage, conveyor, etc.). Again it is possible to move both the object and the camera. Both may move at the same speed and in the same direction, or at varying speeds and in different directions, thus providing the possibility for an infinite number of variations (shots from swings, roundabouts, moving ships, and airplanes provide further opportunities for enriching the field of vision). Many other optical devices can be used to advantage for the same purpose.

The "Rubber Lens"

I am referring in particular to the method of differentiating the various objects of a given scene according to their relative importance by means of a graduated scale of photographic precision. This would imply a certain approach to the optical methods of the human eye, which also sharply defines the object, and can fix it at any one moment, while its background appears relatively blurred. It is now possible to predict with certainty that the cameraman of the future will have at his disposal a whole series of photographic systems—experts are already talking of "rubber lenses"—that will automatically vary the degree of visual definition as the camera approaches, moves away from, or encircles the object, whether it be a whole scene or a detail to be taken as a close-up.

Color Films and Long-Shot Montage

The slower rhythm of sound film montage appears to me to be far *more healthy* from a physiological point of view, since it tires the eye far less than the staccato montage of the silent film. That does not mean that the old "machine-gun montage" will be entirely abandoned in the future. It will be retained as one among many methods available to the cutter, but it will no longer be the cutting principle *par excellence.*

The same considerations apply with even greater force to the color film. If the montage rhythm of the silent film was in a ratio of 10 to 2 to that of the sound film, the ratio of silent to color montage is 10 to 1. In other words, the color film will use an even slower rhythm than the present black and white sound film. Moreover, the speed of the single shots will have to be reduced, since rapid motion produces greater visual uneasiness and more pronounced flickering in color than in black-and-white photography.

The Visual Axis

Generally speaking it is to be expected that the new element of color will face the film director with many unexpected problems, since up to the present time we have had but few opportunities for experiencing the kinetic potentialities of color values in any concentrated form. While dynamic montage in black and white merely implied a careful evaluation of rhythm and a harmonious sequence of black-white-gray values, montage in color will entail far greater responsibilities for the cutter and director. Apart from the fact that color in itself gives greater emotional emphasis to every single scene, it will be necessary to enhance its psycho-physical effectiveness by introducing a definite visual axis that will link all the successive parts of the future color film. In other words there must be a consciously planned sequence of predominantly red, yellow, blue, pink, etc., parts.

The practical results of the immediate future will show, whether it will be possible to adhere to the basic principle discovered by the Impressionists, or whether that principle will have to be abandoned after a few more experiments. It would, however, be truly disastrous, if the visual axis of the color film were to be sought for in the "gallery tone" (yellow-brown coating) of old paintings. For there is a definite temptation either directly or indirectly to submerge all color values in a monochrome mist drawn like a veil over the whole image.*

The principle of a visual axis has already been applied with great success (probably by the consistent use of a filter or of some other optical device) in the black and white films *Jean d'arc* and *Vampyre,* which are photographically the best films I have seen. In *La petite lily* Cavalcanti used rough canvas screening as visual axis.

Superimposition will play a much more important role in the color film than hitherto. Leaving aside the technical aspects of superimposition (I have used it again and again in my paintings), we can state that it facilitates the smooth transition from one scene to the other without any visual shock. By toning down certain color values one can achieve any given color scheme.

Abstract Color Films and a Winter Sports Film

One thing is certain: the psycho-physical response to color— even without any underlying theme—is so elementary a human trait, that it is safe to predict an increasing use of pure color in the sense in which it is used by modern painters—i.e. in an abstract sense—in the color film.

It is a great mistake, moreover, to regard the complete reproduction of natural coloring as the ultimate aim of the color film. This will never be achieved even in the best possible systems, since the transmitting media, filters, emulsion, etc., and the technical process of reproduction will always to some extent change the colors of the given object. The proper approach to color photography, as to black and white photography, will always be to regard it as a means of interpreting nature, which, when it is mastered, will provide a more and more fruitful medium for artistic creation.

---

* Anyone versed in the technique of the painter will readily understand the problem raised here. The postulate for a single predominant color value implied in the conception of a visual axis does not of course mean that a filter should be used in every color shot; and it does not mean that every shot should have a so-called "filter tinge." It merely implies a scale in which some selected color would predominate, while other colors would of course be also used.

The recognition of this fact is essential if we are to find a healthy escape from the deluge of colored period pictures that are certain to overwhelm us. I am convinced that the most beautiful color films of the next few years will be those having a color scale based on white. A skiing or winter sports film, or a color film enacted in bright modern rooms, will provide new and undreamed of visual experiences. It is a great mistake to believe that the life of today is incapable of supplying an effective color scale.

—Translation from the German by F. D. Klingender and
P. Morton Shand

The Light-Display
Machine *Sibyl Moholy-Nagy*

When Moholy next called for me at my office, he took me to the worker's district near Berlin's *Alexanderplatz*. We climbed dark stairs until we reached a dingy office with a roll-top desk and an archaic typewriter. Moholy told me to wait, and while I stared into the light of a bare bulb I wondered why I did not resent this strange companion who, like a magnetic force, constantly changed my direction. In the two weeks I had known him I had edited several articles written in his picturesque but nonliterary German; I had spent many tiresome hours posing for a magazine title-page which was to show only the silhouette of a woman's body against a glaring backdrop of light, and I had broken dates and appointments to be in Moholy's studio at suppertime, loaded down with packages of cold meat, fruit, and pastry.

"You can come in now," said a wispy little man from a door.

In the center of a workshop stood a construction—half sculpture and half machine—a combination of chromium, glass, wire, and rods, in which I recognized the forms of the light-display film. As it turned slowly, invisible lights flared up and turned off, producing gigantic shadows on the walls and the ceiling.

"This is beautiful," I gasped. "It's magnificent. It is—" and suddenly I saw the difference between concept and reality, "it is almost as beautiful as the film."

Moholy smiled. His whole face expanded with happiness.

"There, did you hear?" he said to the little man.

"Hear what?"

"That the reflection is more powerful than the original, that I was right making a film?"

"Film, tsszz," hissed the man, and it was quite obvious that this was the continuation of an old argument. "But the craftsmanship, the precision, where does that show in your blasted film?"

He took me by the arm.

"Here, Lady, just take a look. See how that clears?" A small black ball rolled softly down a slanting rail passing through a rotating sphere.

"And the grills? Have you noticed the grills?" There was a sequence of chromium grills, their mesh formed by a variety of wire patterns.

"The light reflects differently in every one of them. See?"

From *Experiment in Totality* (Cambridge, Mass.: MIT Press, 1969), pp. 64 and 66–67. First published 1950.

He started the machine again and the light played dramatically on the metal.

"Film, my eye!" he repeated. "Craftsmanship—that's what matters!"

"We've been working on the machine for almost ten years," Moholy said as we went down the stairs. "I pay him whenever I've some money, but it has cost him more in time and materials than I'll ever be able to repay. He's a wonderful fellow. He's as obsessed by motion as I am by light."

All during dinner we talked about the light machine, which acquired human importance. Moholy explained its genesis by drawing on a sequence of calling cards his experiments, from the almost archaic wood sculpture he had done in 1921 to the floating glass construction in the center of the light machine, foreshadowing his later work with Plexiglas. The *Lichtrequisit* had been exhibited in the room Moholy designed for the International Building Exhibition in Paris in 1930, and now he planned to synchronize its motions with a musical score.

"I'm so happy you understand," he said. "This is a wonderful day for me. You don't know what it means to me that you saw it."

I did not know yet either. In future years, on our wanderings through Europe and America, I would come to consider the light-display machine the problem child of my household because it refused to pass custom authorities the normal way. When it finally came to rest in Chicago it had been declared a mixing machine, a fountain, a display rack for various metal alloys and a robot, and it had caused me more trouble than a dozen children. But on that first evening of our acquaintance I admired it, without reserve.

Light Display, Black and White and Gray   *L. Moholy-Nagy*

(Only one part of this film synopsis was ever produced: the final scene (Part VI), which starred the Light-Display Machine [Light Prop].)

I.

Large quantities of matches are thrown on a metal sheet, glowing at white heat. They light nearly at once with little explosions.

From *Art in America* (May–June, 1967), p. 29.

Lightning.

Pyre.

Scenes with candle light; with kerosene light; with gas light; with electric light; carbide; incandescent light; magnesium torch.

The manufacture of an electric light bulb.

Spotlights. Fresnel lens distortions.

Light crosses sky. Lightning.

Light in motion. Iris diaphragm closing—opening; spiral moving; large apertures, closing-opening; masks moving, snapping.

Lights at night. Clouds, moving, dissolving, reappearing.

Play of searchlight beams.

Lighted boats at night, fishing with carbide lanterns, fastened to their bows.

Airplanes in the night.

Tracer bullets.

Car drives along a highway in deep snow. The road is lit up by headlights; relief effects of light and shadow; textures.

Snowdrift.

Moonlight, shadow of twigs on hills and mounds.

Street at night with neon signs. Light spots receding and advancing, articulating space. Wet asphalt surfaces; puddles with reflections and mirror effects.

II.

Smelting mill. Glowing molten steel.

Casting; rain of sparks.

Fireworks at a fair. Magnesium balls. Merry-go-round at night.

A lighthouse.

The wings of a windmill lighted up. Gyration.

Waterfalls by night, illuminated. *Grands eaux,* Versailles.

Virtual volumes. Luminous sticks in different colors moving and rotating on various planes producing glowing arabesques. Prisms multiply and a mirror doubles the scenes. The same scenes distorted by concave mirrors, reflected in motion by convex-concave (ferrotype) mirror upon a white wall.

III.

Theater, Opera. The light equipment. Rehearsal; details of backstage.

The bridge.

Film studio. An artist's studio.

The making of a photogram.

IV.

A metal workshop where the different parts of the Light Prop are
   made.
Vise; lathe; sandpaper belt; disk revolving.
Glass blowing workshop. The glass parts of the Light Prop.
A glass spiral is twisted. Glass grinder grinds segments.
The production of parts made of plastic and of wire mesh.
Assembling of the Light Prop.
Motor; electrical contact; cogwheel transmission; colored bulbs.
Flashes.

V.

A play of stencils for the Light Prop; perforated metal sheets, grills,
   grates, etc.
Play of balls (sorting machine). Small ball bearings are thrown on
   a nickel sheet, from there they fall through a small hole drilled
   in the center of a vertical partition.
Mechanical toys with great variety of the mechanism in motion.

VI.

The shadow of the rotating Light Prop.
The superimposition of metal details with the shadows. The shadow
   revolving; slowly the shadow of a ball surrounded by strong
   light, moving up and down over the original shadow.
The Light Prop turns; it is seen from above, below, frontwards,
   backwards; in normal, accelerated, retarded, reversed motion.
Close-up of details.
A big black shiny ball rolls from left to right. From right to left.
   Over again.
Positive, negative pictures, fades, prisms; dissolving.
Movements, queerly shifting grills.
"Drunken" screens, lattices.
Views through small openings; through automatically changing
   diaphragms.
Distortion of reflections. Pendulum.
Blinding moving light flashes. Revolving spiral, reappearing, again
   and again. Rotation increases; all concrete shapes dissolve in
   light.   (*1928–30*)

Light: A New Medium of Expression   *L. Moholy-Nagy*

"Painting With Light" is an old chapter of human activity. We have documents about antique illumination for theatrical performances in which colored glasses, prisms, etc., were used. Centuries later the magic lantern appeared—fireworks, the light effects of the baroque opera; and, later still, different projects for a color organ. Today, in light, from photography to television, we have more sources for a new art form than at any other period of human history. But unless we learn to clear our minds of the old, traditional ideas of painting, not even the work of talented painters will reach the level of a genuine artistic creation.

It is the general opinion that manual painting is the peak of optical creation. Its basic significance is that different pigments reflect and absorb certain parts of the spectrum. So far as pigments possessed these qualities they were used for the creation of an optical illusion which was actually similar to the light effects which solid bodies performed. Such a three dimensional object showed, if normally lighted, a plastic shape through its lighter and darker shading, and the painter had only to imitate the different surfaces of the solid object by mixing different pigments. However, this manual effort never could repeat the same radiant effect because the direct reflection of the object had always a more intensive value. We call the procedure of traditional painting "mixture by subtraction." The term implies that each new mixed color will be darker than the previous color by itself. This can clearly be seen from watercolors. Each layer darkens the previous one; in other words "it subtracts light." However, besides these primary pigments there are three other primaries, the light primaries, and in the new art of painting with light, they are going to play an important part. They are the red, green, and blue of the spectrum. We call the mixture of light primaries "mixture by addition" because, contrary to the case in pigments, the resultant color is lighter than each of the component colors. We can see this when we throw different lights from different filtered projectors on one spot of a screen. A mixture by addition of green and red lights creates yellow. However, the mixture by subtraction of green and red pigments produces not yellow but an olive brown.

As early as the close of the last century the Pointillist painters, Seurat and Signac endeavored to create an impression of radiant

From *Architectural Forum*, LXX (May, 1939). Copyright 1939 by Time, Inc.

yellow sunshine by the use of thickly sprinkled red and green pigment particles on the canvas. They adduced in support of their theory evidence of a discovery made in 1869 by Ducos du Hauron that the human eye splits the colors of the spectrum, red and green, into minutest points producing a yellow to the vision. Aristotle, also, knew that colors in juxtaposition will mix in the retina when seen from a distance. We find this principle applied in painting as early as the Florentine and Venetian pictures of the fourteenth and fifteenth centuries. Fra Angelico and Botticelli used a first layer of thin coloring for the figures of their paintings, for instance green, and then covered this green surface with innumerable fine red lines; the result was an infinitely spiritualized whitish-yellow flesh color.

Rubens used the optical energy of the "turbid" medium in order to obtain flesh colorings and transparent blue shadows which could not be produced by mixtures of pigment. Rubens painted on a white ground thickly sown with black lines—making the outlines and deeply shaded portions of his model in brown and going afterward over the whole with a creamy, translucent, pinkish white. The result was a radiantly transparent orange rose, a perfect flesh color with bluish transparent shadows.

Goethe gave us the physiological explanation for all this in his anti-Newtonism theory of coloring in which he established that black through a "turbid" medium appears as blue and light gives us yellow-orange up to yellow-red. "Turbid" means layers of transparencies or translucencies.

But not only the Old Masters worked in this way, employing subjective results of optical effects; Van Gogh applied color so thickly that the pigment appeared as a relief; the brushstrokes created shadows and the edges of the strokes were touched by light. Thus light and shadow were drawn into the picture as a determinative, qualitative factor and an effect was obtained similar to that aimed at by the Florentine.

Cézanne carried this research work one step further. He was less interested in the representation of radiant surfaces than in the subtle qualities of colors to perform movements forwards and backwards, up and down, centrifugal and centripetal, etc. He created with these a new spatial representation as well as a new painting quality.

A psychological experiment made at the University of Wisconsin gives a clear explanation how color is able to change sizes. Black, white, yellow, green and blue cubes of the same sizes have been shown each beside the other. The white cube appeared to be the largest, black to be the smallest. Yellow was larger than green, and blue was smaller than green. The same phenomenon can be expressed otherwise. The white cube, being the largest, appeared to be the nearest to the spectator, the black, being the smallest, appeared to be the furthest away from him. This means that if a painter would use these colors he would be able to change their experimental characteristics with certain manipulations. The Constructivists' work often offers the example that black for instance stands in front of white, etc. The after images and the subjective changes in the neighbor colors are valuable means to the painters' spiritual craftsmanship. For example, the upper part of a black plane can appear bluish if a yellow plane is placed beside it; the same black below can simultaneously appear reddish if a green plane is placed beside it.

As yet the psychological and physiological experiences of color have not been sufficiently integrated with the physical laws of light by painters, sculptors, architects, commercial artists and publicity men.

In fact, all color harmony systems concerning the pigments differ from one another, all defining a different number of colors and with them the complementary pairs. Newton speaks about seven colors; Goethe, Schopenhauer about six; Ostwald about eight, and Munsell about ten. Goethe defines the primary complementaries as: yellow-redblue. Blue-redyellow, purple-green. Ostwald defines them: yellow-ultramarine, iceblue-orange, red-seagreen, violet-leafgreen. Munsell: yellow-purpleblue, blue-yellowred, red-bluegreen, redpurple-green, purple-greenyellow. Newton mentioned only once a complementary pair: gold-indigo. Still the fundamental laws of perception of color are an inborn attribute of every human being. In other words the appreciation of color depends upon the general psychological fact that man answers every color with its contrast, with its complementary. Our eyes react to red with green, to yellow with blue and so on.

But until today we were not able to define the complementary color pairs with an absolute exactness. The old masters interpreted the complementary colors individually. That is to say, in spite of the fact that almost all classical paintings were made with complementary color contrasts—red-green and blue-yellow—they show slightly different tones of the complementaries. It even seems as if the personal achievement of a painter depends upon this individual modification of the law of the complementary colors. Now we have to reckon with the extensive use of electric light as a source of illumination. Since the spectrum of this light differs from that of sunlight, the well-known effects of color harmony undergo various transformations. We learned from Goethe that objects lit by colored light produce shadows in their complementary color. For instance, if an object is lit with red light, its shadow becomes green.

One may ask now—is it possible to do anything artistic with the purely physical complementaries or do we have to continue with the subjectively interpreted daylight effects alone? I believe it is possible, but the purely automatic harmonies which are no longer created by pigments but by light projection will probably have to undergo a process of step-by-step development of artistic appreciation. We are so accustomed to the old form of manual painting that we are not yet able to see that later painting may become a "machine painting" without lowering its spiritual level. The technique as part of the creative process is only important insofar as it must be controlled at every stage of production. Besides this, it does not matter at all whether the result itself is achieved by manual or machine operation.

Of course the pedagogic value of the manual pigment painting will not be denied. But this painting will be no more the only art expression. Photography is already a proof. We have to observe its form, its creative process, the superimposition and mirroring, the innumerable lens and prism effects, the mechanical and chemical distortion of the surface, the light-flooded planes, the "chiaroscuro" in the finest gray graduation. Then we know that our wish to express ourselves with optical means can only be satisfied by a thorough knowledge about light. We must become familiar with colorimetry, wave lengths, purity, brightness, excitation of light, and with the manifold possibilities of the artificial light sources. Optical illusions, changes in size, automatic complementaries, surrounding effects of negative shapes, of hue, chroma and value are already in use. In addition we experiment with polished surfaces, with transparencies and translucencies which allow a combination of pigment and direct light effects.

The next step will be the conscious use of reflexes, solid and open shadows, mirroring refraction with prism and grating, polarization and interference of light.

Since the eighteenth century many persons were working in this direction: Pater Castel, Hoffman, Rimington, Scriabin, Hirschfeld-Mack, Thomas Wilfred and Alexander Lazzlo. They all have experimented in the color organ. Viking Eggeling has been the pioneer for the abstract film. There should be mentioned also other forerunners of light display: gigantic light parades of battleships, projectors, search-lights, skywriters, changing light-pictures, floodlight, luminescence, phosphorescence, ultra-violet, infrared, cathod, and polarized X-rays.

The work of the future lies with the light engineer who is collecting the elements of a genuine creation. Great technical problems will be solved when the intuition of the artists will direct the research of engineers and technicians.

It is premature to go into details yet. But one thing is clear—that forthcoming experiments, the study of the physiology of the eye, the physical properties of light and the introduction of new technical means with their "automatic" and "mechanical harmony" will play a very important part.

Consequently we must never cease observing the simple or rich phenomena of light and color which are offered by the daily routine at home and on the stage, in the street and in the laboratory—in our physical and chemical apparatus.

Finally—it seems to me that we should direct all our efforts like the Dadaist Raoul Hausmann toward the creation of an optophonetic art which one day will allow us to see music and hear pictures simultaneously.

Light Architecture   *L. Moholy-Nagy*

Some of my friends are surprised to find my pictures, both old and new, at a growing number of exhibitions. Hitherto I have never exhibited my work and I gave up painting years ago. It seemed to me senseless, in this age of new technical and creative possibilities, to work with old media which are inadequate for the tasks of the present day.

Since the invention of photography the direction of development for painting has been "from pigment to light." That is to say that just as one paints with brush and pigment, in recent times one could have "painted" direct with light, transforming two-dimensional painted surfaces into *light architecture*.

I dreamed of light-apparatus, which might be controlled either by hand or by an automatic mechanism by means of which it would be possible to produce visions of light, in the air, in large rooms, on screens of unusual nature, on fog, vapor and clouds. I made numberless projects, but found no architect who was prepared to commission a light-fresco, a light architecture, consisting of straight or arched walls, covered with a material such as galalite, trolite, chromium or nickel, which by turning a switch, could be flooded with radiant light, fluctuating light-symphonies, while the surfaces slowly changed and dissolved into an infinite number of controlled

From *Industrial Arts,* I/1 (London, Spring, 1936).

details. I wanted a bare room with twelve projection devices, so that the white void should come to life and action under crossing sheaves of colored light.

Have you ever seen a searchlight display, flashing grandly and violently, shooting its arrows of light farther and farther? I had been thinking of something similar, but not the cut-up rhythms of the signal code, but a light-symphony which follows exactly the composer's score. This was only a conception, only a possibility. Yet there are thousands of such dreams of light and motion, in which the marvelous apparatus of natural science, such as the apparatus of polarization and spectroscopy, could play an important part. Alas, such dreams cannot be realized yet.

It required a great deal of work to assemble my basic light element and my "black-white-gray play of light." This, however, is merely a modest beginning, an almost unnoticeable step in advance. I could not continue my experiments properly even in this restricted area. Why, then, did I abandon my projects? Why am I painting again if I have already perceived the proper tasks for the modern "painter"? The question goes beyond my personal position and concerns the whole generation of young painters.

We have published programs. We have sent frequent manifestos out into the world. Youth has a right to know why its demands have not been accepted and its promise remains unfulfilled. Youth also has its duty to develop ideas and carry its demands farther.

It would be easy to give an obvious answer and to say that the physical dependence on capital, industry and the workshop is an unmovable hindrance to the development of light architecture, which holds out no immediate promise of practical application, producing only the emotions denied from color in space. While a painter in his studio, possessing only a few tubes of color and a few brushes, can be a sovereign creator, the artist in "light-play" easily becomes the slave of technical considerations as well as of his material. Technical considerations can, indeed, be given too great an emphasis, especially considering the general fear lest scientific knowledge and controlled technique should dominate art.

It is a legend of cowardice that says that intellectual perception does harm to the artist, that he requires nothing but feeling and intuition for his work. As if we knew nothing of Leonardo, Giotto, the cathedral architect, Raphael, or Michelangelo, whose creative power increased with the increase of his knowledge and the development of his technical skill!

However, after these fears have been overcome, as they soon can be in the intense interest and concentrated effort required by the task and the exaltation of spirit which it induces, there still re-

Moholy-Nagy

mains the paralyzing difficulty of presenting what has been done and demonstrating what has been achieved. There scarcely exists a building in which the creation of the "light-artist" could be made accessible to the public. The dream that has been realized is put away into storage and there it remains until it fades away in the insignificance of its own isolation. It is hard to struggle for the realization of these projects if there is no public to help.

This point deserves special attention. The public is bombarded by a widespread and almost instantaneous news service, shouting all kinds of news, even news about art. The advantages of this service are its comprehensive interest and rapid communication; its faults are continual striving to break records and extreme superficiality. Without displaying any interest for current and developing movements, it crams the public with sensational news. If there is nothing sensational to report, something of a sensational character must be deliberately invented. The public, as a result of mechanized education, devoid of individual views, is thus caught in the wake of the daily press, periodicals and magazines. The natural human sympathy with the creative forces, the urge to creative endeavor is sublimated in newspaper readers into "interest," and this artificially generated interest actually lures him away from the real sources of personal experience, because it produces an illusion of activity, which engenders the deception of that feeling of calm inherent in mental occupation.

Consequently, the public never attempts any creative work of its own. It appears to be superfluous when the means for artificial interpretation are so easy.

To take the case of our present subject "light architecture," the primal desire for personal optical experience is deflected by a torrential spate of black-white variations of films and photographs. Also by the universality of present-day fashionable treatments of them which are influenced in form, color and material by abstract painting. The original source is hidden farther and farther away by meteoric displays in all the categories of applied art.

There are many obstacles in the way of remedying this state. The chief are the great gulf which lies between man and his own technical creations, the deeply conservative persistence of outworn forms of economic structure in spite of the fact that production has been revolutionized, and the spreading of an anti-biological mentality, which turns the lives of everybody, workers and employers alike, into a mad speed-race, without a moment for rest. Man increases his ability for production, and while he stands admiring his record figures, he loses to an ever-increasing extent the capacity to recognize his own elementary biological requirements, although he could satisfy them better than ever before in human history by availing himself prudently of this new technique.

To return to our subject. Life in towns, printing, photography, the films, the too rapid, uncontrolled spread of civilization, have leveled out our color culture to a gray state, from which most people living in the present times can only escape by tremendous effort. We must return to a culture of color which mankind once really possessed. We must develop constructively colored optical work dependent on material, in contrast with that which is uncontrolled and emotional.

An Analysis of Light-Architecture in its practical applications from Notes by Moholy-Nagy follows.

The Play of Light in Enclosed Spaces

The Cinema. The developments which are as yet unrevealed in the progress of the Cinema are very great. Before it are new possibilities of projecting colored and plastic effects either with the aid of a number of projectors directed upon one spot or projections on all the walls of the room.

Refraction. The Color Organ has already been seen, and by such devices or similar apparatus it will be possible to project stenciled and other effects of colored light-play, either by a performer in the room or through television, transmitted from a broadcasting station.

The Color Piano. The Color Piano is an instrument which may be either simple and small or elaborate and large. It is fitted with a keyboard and, by striking the keys, lamps are lit up or flickering shadows are projected.

The Light Fresco. The flood-lighting of buildings has given the public the slightest hint of what is possible when frescoes of colored light become an architectural unit of buildings, interior or exterior. It is extremely probable that in the houses of the future some place will be reserved for these light frescoes, just as today the wireless has its own corner.

Play of Light in the Open Air

Illuminative Advertising

LINEAR EFFECTS ON A PLANE. Linear effects of light on a plane surface are already a commonplace in advertising, as, for example, advertising slides projected onto a screen, Neon and other kinds of electric signs. The time has come for someone to make use of the third dimension and, by taking advantage of both materials and reflections, to create actual structures of light in space.

THE SEARCHLIGHT. Some use has already been made of the searchlight in advertising, although it has not been developed very far.

PROJECTIONS ON CLOUDS. Some experiments have already been made in projecting advertising messages by light onto clouds, hindered somewhat by uncertain weather conditions in this country. This means of advertising, however, is not restricted to distant clouds. Advertising could be projected onto gaseous volume which people might even walk through.

Light in Communal Festivals. As a vision of the future we can imagine the play of light in Community Festivals of coming generations. From airplanes and airships they will be able to enjoy the spectacle of gigantic expanses of illumination, movement and transformation of lighted areas, which will provide new experiences and open up new joy in life.

On Moholy's Light-Display Machine   *Jack W. Burnham*

The most important uses of light as an art form were made by another member of the Bauhaus. László Moholy-Nagy was one of the first moderns to regard the cityscape at night as pure pulsating light sculpture. Car headlights could be frozen into paths of luminous tracery and illuminated advertisements would in time become the basis for an environmental art of darkness. It is perhaps well that Moholy-Nagy never lived to see the overripe fulfillment of his prophecies. His visions of turning outdoor advertising into a nighttime art form were truly overoptimistic. In his basic design course he devised several problems for showing how sculpture in the round could be transformed by alterations of its lighting. In the New Bauhaus in Chicago this emphasis on form through light became the impetus for "Light Modulator" problems. Students were taught not only to see form, but form as it could be created by beams of light and the resulting shadows.

Between 1922 and 1930 Moholy-Nagy, with the aid of an expert mechanic, designed and built his famous *Light-Space Modulator,* a

From *Beyond Modern Sculpture* (New York: George Braziller; London: Allen Lane The Penguin Press, 1968), pp. 290–92.

six-foot-high apparatus of moving aluminum and chrome-plated surfaces driven by an electric motor and a series of chain belts. To achieve its full effect the machine must be experienced in a room darkened, with spotlights alternately thrown upon its turning members. The result: a myriad of dissolving shadows passing over walls and ceiling. Shortly after its completion Moholy-Nagy and his future wife, Sibyl, made a film, "Light Display: Black and White and Gray." In her biography of the artist, his wife recreates some of Moholy-Nagy's remarks about the planning of the film:

> I'm not thinking in chronological terms . . . at least not in the accepted sense. The rhythm of this film has to come from the light— it has to have a light-chronology.
>
> Light beams overlap as they cross through dense air; they're blocked, diffracted, condensed. The different angles of the entering light indicate time. The rotation of light from east to west modulates the visible world. Shadows and reflexes register a constantly changing relationship of solids and perforations.

For several reasons the *Light-Space Modulator* (or *Lichtrequisit,* as it was referred to in Germany) was an important prototype for later light sculpture. Its purpose was not to project but to exist as a three-dimensional object appreciated for itself. Through the use of moving shadows, it permeated the surrounding room. It did not use, as so much earlier Light Art had, Wilfred's "focal stage technique" of backlighting a screen. Instead, the modulator created both shadow and substance; it supported Moholy's feeling that light, if rendered into art, must first be *transmitted* and *transformed* through materials—not projected directly at the viewer. The *Modulator* now stands inactive at Harvard's Busch-Reisinger Museum, where on special occasions it can be operated.

Education and the Bauhaus   *L. Moholy-Nagy*

Sectors of Human Development

A human being is developed only by the crystallization of the sum total of his experiences. Our present system of education contradicts this axiom by stressing preponderantly a single field of application.

Instead of extending our milieu, as the primitive man was forced to do, combining as he did in one person hunter, craftsman, builder, physician, etc., we concern ourselves only with one definite occupation—leaving unused other faculties.

Tradition and the voice of authority intimidate man today. He no longer dares to venture into certain fields of experience.

He becomes a man of one calling; he no longer has first-hand experience elsewhere. In constant struggle with his instincts, he is overpowered by outside knowledge. His self-assurance is lost. He no longer dares to be his own physician, not even his own eye. The specialists—like members of a powerful secret society—obscure the road to all-sided individual experiences, the possibility for which exists in his normal functions, and the need for which arises from the center of his being.

Today, the accent lies on the sharpest possible definition of the single vocation, on the building up of specialized faculties; the "market demand" is the guide. Thus a man becomes a locksmith or a lawyer or an architect or the like (working inside a closed sector of his faculties) and is at best a happy exception if, after he has finished his studies, he strives to widen the field of his calling, if he aspires to expand his special sector.

At this point our whole system of education has hitherto been found wanting—notwithstanding all our vocational guidance, psychological testing, measurement of intelligence. Everything functions—and functions alone—on the basis of the present system of production, which recognizes only motives of material gain.

A "calling" means today something quite different from following one's own bent, quite different from solidarity with the aims and requirements of a community. One's personal life goes along outside the "calling," which is often a matter of compulsion and is regarded with aversion.

The Future Needs the Whole Man

Our specialized training cannot yet be abandoned at this time when all production is being put on a scientific basis. However, it

From *Focus*, II (London, Winter, 1938).

should not start too soon, and it should not be carried so far that the individual becomes stunted—in spite of all his highly prized professional knowledge. A specialized education becomes full of meaning only if a man of integration is developed along the lines of his biological functions, so that he will achieve a natural balance of his intellectual and emotional power, and not along those of an outmoded educational aim of learning unrelated details. Without this aim the richest differentiations of specialized study—the "privilege" of the adult—are mere quantitative acquisitions, bringing no intensification of life, no widening of its scope. Only a man equipped with the clarity of feeling and the sobriety of knowledge will be able to adjust himself to complicated requirements, and to master the whole of life. Working only from this basis can one find a plan of life which places the individual rightly within his community.

The Present System of Production

All educational systems are the results of economic structure. In the frenzied march of the industrial revolution, the industrialists set up specialized schools to produce quickly the badly-needed specialists. These schools favored the development of men's powers only in very few instances, and offered no opportunity to penetrate to the essential kernel of things and the individual himself. But—to tell the truth—no one concerned himself with this because no one could foresee its destructive results. Thus today neither education nor production springs from an inner urge, nor from an urge to make products which satisfy the requirements of one's self and those of society in a mutually complementary way.

Our modern system of production is imposed labor, mostly a mad pursuit, without plan in its social aspects, its motive is merely to squeeze out profits to their limit, in most cases a complete reversal of its original purpose.

Not only the working class finds itself in this position today; all those caught within the workings of the present economic system are basically just as badly off. At most there are slight degrees of difference. The chase after rewards in money and power influences the whole form of life today, even to the basic feelings of the individual. He thinks only of outward security, instead of concerning himself with his inner satisfaction. On top of all this, there is the penning up of city dwellers in treeless barracks, the extreme contraction of living space. This cramping of living space is not only physical: city life has brought with it herding into barren buildings, without adequate open space.

But How About Technical Progress?

It might easily be judged from the foregoing remarks that present-day industrial production, and especially our technical progress, is to be condemned. In fact there are numerous writers and politicians who suggest this. They mix the effect with the cause. In the nineteenth century some people tried to make a right diagnosis but suggested a wrong therapy. Gottfried Semper declared in the 1850's, for example, that if iron ever was to be used in building it would have to be used (because of the static nature of iron) in a fashion of transparent spiderweb. But, he continued, architecture must be "monumental," thus "we never shall have an iron-architecture."(!) A similar mistake was made by the Ruskin-Morris circle in the 1880's. They found that industrial mass production killed quality in craftsmanship. Their remedy was to kill the machine, go back to the handwork exclusively. They opposed machines so strongly that to deliver their hand-made products to London, they ran a horse coach parallel with the hated railway. In spite of this rebellion against the machine, technical progress is a factor of life which develops organically. It stands in reciprocal relation to the increase in the number of human beings. That is its real justification. Notwithstanding its manifold distortion by profit interests, the struggle for mere accumulation and the like, we can no longer think of life without such progress. It is an indispensable factor in raising the standard of life.

The possibilities of the machine—with its abundant production, its ingenious complexity on the one hand, its simplification on the other, has necessarily led to a mass production which has its own significance. The task of the machine—satisfaction of mass requirements—will in the future be held more and more singly and clearly in mind. The true source of conflict between life and technical progress lies at this point. Not only the present economic system, but the process of production as well, calls for improvement from the ground up. Invention and systematization, planning, and social responsibility must be applied in increased measure to this end.

The common error today is that usually questions of efficiency are viewed from the technical and profit standpoint, without regard to organic considerations. The Taylor system, the conveyor belt and the like, remain mistakes as long as they turn man into a machine, without taking into account his biological requirements for work, recreation, and leisure.

Biological Needs

Here the word "biological" stands generally for laws of life which guarantee an organic development. If the meaning of "biological" would be a conscious possession, it would prevent many people from activities of damaging influence. Children usually act in accordance with the biological laws. They refuse food when ill, they fall asleep when tired, they don't show courtesy when they are uninterested, etc. If today's civilization would allow more time to follow the biological rhythms, lives would be less hysterical and less often stranded.

In reality the basic biological needs are very simple. They may change and be deformed through social and technical processes. However, great care must be taken that their real significance should not be adulterated. This often happens through misunderstood luxury which may thwart the organic satisfaction of the biological needs. The oncoming generation has to create a culture which strengthens but the genuine biological functions.

Not Against Technical Progress, But With It

The solution lies accordingly not in working against technical advance, but in exploiting it for the benefit of all. Through technique man can be freed, if he finally realizes the purpose: a balanced life through free use of his liberated creative energies.

Only if it is clear to man that he has to crystallize his place as a productive unit in the community of mankind, will he come closer to a true understanding of the meaning of technical progress. For not the form, not the amazing technical process of production, should engage our real interest, but the sound planning of man's life. We are faced today with nothing less than the reconquest of the biological bases of human life. Only when we go back to these can we reach the maximum utilization of technical progress in the fields of physical culture, nutrition, housing and industry—a thoroughgoing rearrangement of our whole scheme of life. For even today it is currently believed that less importance than formerly needs to be attached to biological requirements, the motive power of life, thanks to our technically exact and calculable ways of dealing with them. It is thought that securing sleep by veronal and relieving pain by aspirin can keep pace with organic wear and tear. In this direction progress of civilization has brought along with it much beclouding of realities and grave danger. Apparent economies may easily deceive us. But technical progress should never be the goal, only the means.

Efforts Toward Reform

The creative human being knows, and suffers from the realization, that the deep values of life are being destroyed under pressure of moneymaking, competition, and trade mentality. He suffers from the purely material evaluation of his vitality, from the flattening out of his instincts, from the impairing of his biological balance.

And yet, although the present social structure is a thoroughly unsuitable medium for the balanced outlet of human capacities, in the private life of individuals some glimpses of a functional understanding have already appeared.

The intellectual advances in art, literature, the theater and the moving-picture in our time, and the various educational movements, have given important indications of this fact. Likewise the interest in physical culture and in recreation and leisure, and in systems of treatment by natural rather than chemical methods.

Such efforts, taken as a whole, portend a world which even today shows its initial stages at many points. But no small unit of this growth should be studied as an isolated fact. The relationship of the various members (science, art, economics, technical knowledge, educational methods) and their integration must be constantly clarified.

Not the Product, But Man, Is the End in View

Proceeding from such a basic readjustment, we may work out an individual plan of life with self-analysis as its background. Not the occupation, not the object to be manufactured, should be put in the foreground, but rather the recognition of man's organic functions. With this functional preparation, he can then pass on to action, to a life evolved from within. Thus we lay the organic basis for a system of production whose focal point is man, and not profit interests.

The Task for Education

Our educators have the task of co-ordinating the requirements of a normal development of human powers, laying the foundation for a balanced life even in the elementary school.

From Pestalozzi and Froebel up to the present time this problem has been in the foreground. The program extends from the kindergarten up to the university, from the single assignment up to the formation of the adult. We have sought to free the child's capacities in drawing and manual training, in language, in the plan of teaching as a whole. Czizek, Montessori, the Lichtwark school,

Wendekreis, Worpswede, Lietz in Ilsenburg, Wyneken in Wickersdorf, Heinrich Jacoby in Hellerau-Berlin, the Dalton system—country educational homes, work schools, experimental schools, etc., have in the last decade striven toward an organic structure of education for the child.

Nevertheless, the oncoming generation is even today turned over, for the most part, to the traditional branches of study, which supply information without clarifying its position in the environment and in society, nor its relationship to the material and content of its work.

The Bauhaus

The first Bauhaus, founded by Walter Gropius in 1919, attempted to meet this shortcoming, not placing "subjects" at the head of its curriculum, but man, in his readiness to grasp the whole of life.

Although for reasons of convenience a division into terms was retained, the old concept and content of "school" was discarded, and a community of work established. The powers latent in each individual were to be welded into a free collective body. Also the pattern of a community of students who learn "not for school, but for life" had to be worked out and converted into a cross-section of full, organic, and adaptable living. Such a society implies practice in actual living. Its individual members have to learn to master not only themselves and their own powers, but also the living and working conditions of the environment. The foundation of the educational program of the Bauhaus, or, more appropriately, its working program, rested upon the recognition of this fact.

The first year was directed toward the development and enrichment of feeling, sensation and thought—especially for those young people who, in consequence of the usual childhood education, brought with them a sterile hoard of textbook information. Only after this first year of development and enrichment did the period of occupational training begin, based on free selection within the Bauhaus shops. During the period of occupational training the ultimate end still was: man was a whole. Man, who, if he but works from his biological center, when faced with all the material things of life, can again take his position with instinctive sureness, who does not allow himself to be intimidated by industry, the rush-tempo, external evidences of an often misunderstood "machine-culture."

These are the principles behind the foundation of the Bauhaus in Dessau. We print below the curriculum of the New Bauhaus, as it worked in Chicago until a month ago.

Bauhaus Curriculum

The preliminary curriculum was divided into three parts:

1. The basic design shopwork.
2. Analytical and constructive drawing, modeling, photography.
3. Scientific subjects.

Basic Design Workshop. In the basic workshop the student learned the constructive handling of materials; wood, plywood, paper, plastics, rubber, cork, leather, textiles, metal, glass, clay, plasticine, plaster, and stone: their tactile values; structure; texture; surface effect and the use of their values in plane, in volume and in space. Henceforth the student became volume-, space- and kinetic-conscious.

In order to develop his auditory sense, he experimented with sound and built musical instruments.

He learned the subjective and objective qualities, the scientific testing of materials; the existence of the fourth dimension (time).

Drawing, Modeling, Photography. As he experimented he built, with small motors or other devices, toys, moving sculptures, spatial constructions, etc., and developed his sense for proportion, and penetrated his work with different and visual representation. He sketched by hand, and with photo-apparatus as well, in black and white and in color, and he worked in clay. Standard nature forms would be analyzed, and this analytical method led the student to the elementary forms, and later to the construction of these forms in relation to each other with the aim of free composition.

Scientific Subjects. The following scientific courses complemented shopwork and drawing:

1. Geometry ⎫
2. Physics   ⎪ Physical Sciences
3. Chemistry ⎬
4. Mathematics ⎭
5. Biology   ⎫
6. Physiology ⎬ Life Sciences
7. Anatomy   ⎭
8. Intellectual integration.

In addition to these, the curriculum included brief surveys of:

(*a*) Biotechnique—the system of conscious inventions (*e.g.* Edison).

(*b*) Psychotechnique (ability testing).

(*c*) Music.

(*d*) Guest lectures on other subjects.

(*e*) Lettering, writing (construction of letters, and printing types).

(*f*) Light (as an instrument of visual notes, using lights as a new medium of expression); photography, film.

(*g*) Visits to factories, newly constructed buildings, museums, exhibitions, theaters, etc.

(*h*) Exhibitions (some assembled by the students, some by the faculty or others).

After the first half-year of the preliminary course the first examination was held in the form of a students' trial exhibition. After the second half-year a similar exhibition was held as the final examination in the preliminary course.

After passing the examination in the preliminary courses the student entered one of the specialized workshops.

Second and third years:

1. Wood, metal.
2. Textiles (weaving, dyeing, and fashion).
3. Color (murals, decorating, wallpaper).
4. Light (photography, film, typography, commercial arts).
5. Glass, clay, stone, plastics (modeling).
6. Display (theater, exposition architecture, window display).

Workshop, tools and machines, book-keeping and estimating, drawing, scientific subjects and elementary lectures in architecture (construction and statics), with final examination for diploma.

Fourth and fifth years:

Architecture, landscape architecture, town-planning, and scientific subjects. Educational problems, kindergarten, grade, high schools and colleges. Social services, hospitals, recreation, leisure, and hobby organization with additional thesis for the Bauhaus degree in architecture.

A New Humanism   *Herbert Read*

Based on lectures which he gave at the Bauhaus between 1923 and 1928, [*The New Vision* by] Professor Moholy-Nagy was originally published in Germany several years ago. The present excellent translation by Miss Daphne Hoffmann appeared a year or two ago in New York, but no English publisher has yet had sufficient

From *The Architectural Review*, LXXVIII (October, 1935).

enterprise to issue an edition here. Since, however, the esteemed author has now taken up his residence among us, it is desirable that his book should become better known. For it is an extremely important book—one of the very few statements which are essential for an understanding of the modern movement in architecture and the plastic arts generally. It is a study of the basic relationships which subsist between man as a sensitive animal and the materials he uses in construction. More than once Professor Moholy-Nagy uses the word "biological," and it expresses the originality of his approach to these problems. The individual is for him not an abstraction, but an organism with five senses, all crying for development, and art will only be secure if it is a function of the whole organism. The present system of production destroys this wholeness by creating a monster with a specialized calling, a man with perhaps one beautiful muscle on an otherwise wretched body. The general health suffers. There is no integrity in the individual, and therefore no wholeness in art. For health, for beauty, we need the whole man, harmoniously developed. Here in the attitude of Moholy-Nagy we see the idealism, the almost moral fervor, with which Gropius inspired the whole Bauhaus movement. It is the most wrongful distortion of the facts to make out of this movement, the most fertile movement of modern times, a heartless and inhuman functionalism. Gropius, Moholy-Nagy, Breuer—these men are the prophets of a new humanism.

Germany has rejected this new humanism, and though the label "cultural bolshevism" is only justified if bolshevism implies a constructive and not a destructive movement, there is nevertheless no doubt that the program of the modern movement in art and architecture requires social changes inconsistent with the present structure of industry. It is merely childish to imagine that one can change the plastic features of our environment without at the same time changing the underlying structure. The disease is constitutional, and of long standing. Moholy-Nagy suggests that the injuries worked by a technical civilization can be combated on two fronts:

1. By the purposive observation and the rational safeguarding of the organic, biologically conditioned functions (science, education, politics).
2. By means of the *constructive* carrying forward of our over-scientific culture—since there is no turning backward.

Partial solutions cannot be commended; partial rebellion is only evidence of the monstrous pressure, a symptom. "Only the person who understands himself, and co-operates with others in a far-reaching program of common action, can make his efforts count.

Material motives may well provide the occasion for an uprising, for revolution, but they are never the deciding cause." This makes the moral basis of the Bauhaus attitude clear enough: *L'esprit d'abord!* "The revolutionist will always remain conscious that the class struggle is, in the last analysis, not about capital, nor the means of production, but it actually concerns the right of the individual to a satisfying occupation, work that meets the inner needs, a normal way of life and a real release of human powers."

The problem is primarily educational, and this is strictly a book about educational methods. But the outward conditions for the realization of the necessary reforms must be guaranteed. "At this point the educational problem merges into the political, and is perceptible as such in so far as man goes into actual life and must make his adjustment to the existing order." It was necessary to make so much very clear—necessary and courageous.

For the task of education we need:

1. Actual life examples of strong-minded people, leading others onward;
2. An integration of intellectual achievements in politics, science, art, in all the realms of human activity;
3. Centers of practical education.

All those needs the Bauhaus was providing, but its activities converged on the provision of practical education. Manual training was the key to the development of individual wholeness. But the manual training was directed to the requirements of the processes of production in our technical age, and in that way differentiated itself from the reactionary arts and crafts movement, which was right in spirit but wrong in method. Clarity, conciseness and precision were the qualities to be attained—the fusion of these into a single meaning. Such was the aim of the Bauhaus training and experiment, and "out of the welter of rejection and approval, of demand and intuition the principle implicit throughout our technical age slowly crystallized: *not the single piece of work, nor the individual highest attainment, shall be emphasized, but the creation of the commonly usable type, the development of the 'standard.' *" To attain this goal, scattered individual efforts proved insufficient; the Bauhaus was the co-operative solution.

The policy of the Bauhaus in general has been described by Professor Gropius himself in his recently published book,* reviewed in the August number of this magazine. The Bauhaus education, which is the subject of Moholy-Nagy's book, is only, of course, part of the complete curriculum. But it was a very important part,

---

* *The New Architecture and the Bauhaus.*

providing that basic sensory training which is the foundation of the new biological or humanistic attitude. The subject is divided into three stages: Material, Volume (sculpture), and Space (architecture), and these stages are progressive. It is perhaps unnecessary to remark that the author has the most lively awareness of the various developments of modern art, for he himself has made a vital contribution to them, and as painter, typographer, photographer, stage-designer and architect is one of the most creative intelligences of our time.

The author's treatment of the subject which more particularly concerns the readers of this journal may perhaps be best indicated by a few of his forceful aphorisms:

Architecture will be brought to its fullest realization only when the deepest knowledge of human life as a total phenomenon in the biological whole is available. One of its most important components is the ordering of man in space, making space comprehensible, and taking architecture as arrangement of universal space.

The root of architecture lies in the mastery of the problem of space, the practical development lies in the problem of construction.

Building material is only an auxiliary, insofar as it can be used as carrier of space-creating and space-dividing relationships. The principal means of creation is always the space alone, from whose laws the treatment has to proceed in all respects.

Declaration of Loyalty
Faculty of the New Bauhaus

We whose privilege it was to teach in The New Bauhaus during the first year of its existence wish to express our sense of the loss which education and the Chicago cultural community has sustained in the failure of The New Bauhaus to reopen this fall. The first year has convincingly shown the promise of the school under the leadership of L. Moholy-Nagy and we felt that the future development of the school was secure. It came as a great surprise to hear late in summer that there was even a question as to whether the school was to reopen.

The very lateness of the decision worked great hardships upon students, upon the existing faculty, and upon those who had given up positions to become new members of the faculty. Whatever the circumstances, the fact remains that the Association of Arts and Industries has failed in its side of the venture, whether the failure lay in starting the school at all upon an inadequate financial and organizational basis or in being unable to continue the school at the moment when a promising future seemed assured.

In its failure the Association of Arts and Industries has placed difficulties in the way of realizing a significant educational venture whose program is congenial to the best educational leadership and the deepest educational needs of this country. It is to be hoped that this administrative failure will not be interpreted as a failure of The New Bauhaus itself, and that L. Moholy-Nagy and the Bauhaus idea, fitted as this idea is to play an important part in the liberation of American creativity in the arts, will receive from some other quarters the support necessary to insure its success. (*1938*)

Signed:
Alexander Archipenko
Hin Bredendieck
David Dushkin
Carl Eckart
Ralph Gerard
George Kepes
Charles W. Morris
Andi Schiltz
H. H. Smith

The Bauhaus in Chicago: Moholy-Nagy Explains

To the Art Editor:

As a newcomer in this country I though it a matter of tact to be silent about my sad experience with the Association of Arts and Industries, the sponsor of the new Bauhaus in Chicago. Thus I avoided discussing in public the reasons for the closing of the new Bauhaus. Your article, however, about the Bauhaus exhibition in the Museum of Modern Art created a controversy in which the closing of the new Bauhaus is used as a negative argument. In the interest of the educational aims of the Bauhaus I am forced to state the facts:

On recommendation of Walter Gropius I was appointed last year by the Association of Arts and Industries as director of the new Bauhaus, American School of Design, with a five-year contract. We were assured that the association and the school project were backed by some of America's leading industrialists.

From *The New York Times,* January 1, 1939. © 1939 by The New York Times Company. Reprinted by permission.

49. *Nickel Construction,* 1921. Nickel-plated iron, welded, 14⅛″ high, including base. Collection The Museum of Modern Art, New York (Gift of Mrs. Sibyl Moholy-Nagy).

50, 51. Mobile, 1942. Wood and chrome. *Left:* At rest; *right:* In motion. Collection Busch-Reisinger Museum, Harvard University, Cambridge, Mass.

52, 53. Plexiglas sculpture mounted on stainless steel background, 1944 (destroyed). *Left:* Lighted frontally; *right:* Lighted laterally.

54. Plexiglas sculpture cut from one sheet, 1945. The Detroit Institute of Arts.

55. *Dual Form with Chromium Rods,* 1946. Plexiglas and chrome, *ca.* 26″ high. The Solomon R. Guggenheim Museum, New York.

56. *Loop,* 1946. Plexiglas, 14¼″ x 18″. Collection Raúl Villanueva, Caracas. Photo courtesy Museum of Contemporary Art, Chicago.

57. Sequence from *Light Display, Black
   and White and Gray,* 1930–32.
   The Solomon R. Guggenheim Museum,
   New York.

58. Gypsy dancing outside Berlin,
from *Zigeuner (Gypsies),* 1932.
The Solomon R. Guggenheim
Museum, New York.

59. Casting of lobster, from *Life of the Lobster,* 1936. The Solomon R. Guggenheim Museum, New York.

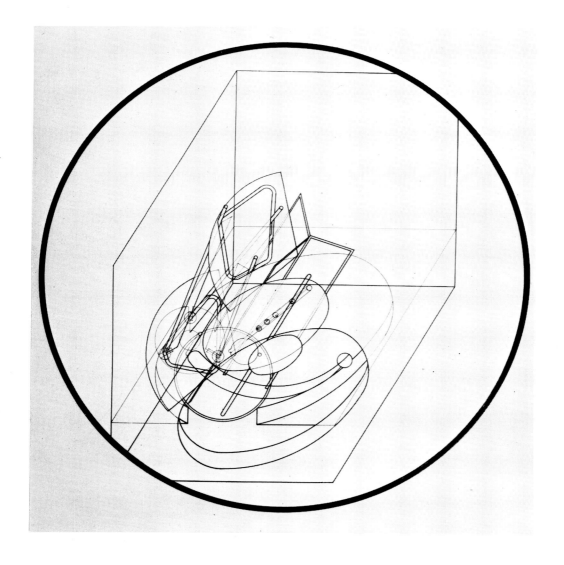

60, 61. *Light-Space Modulator,* 1921–30. Mobile construction with steel, plastic, and wood, 59½″ high, with base. *Left:* Diagram of movement scheme; *right:* Realization. Courtesy Busch-Reisinger Museum, Harvard University, Cambridge, Mass. (Gift of Mrs. Sibyl Moholy-Nagy).

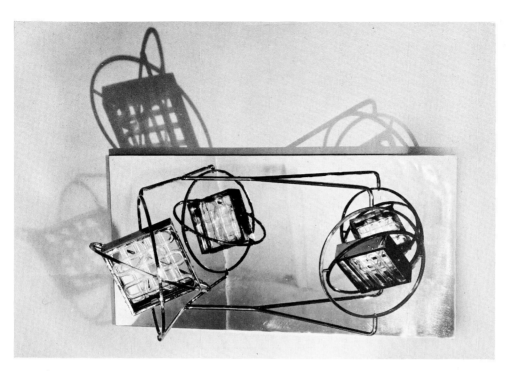

62, 63. *Kinetic Sculpture,* 1930–36. Glass rods filled with balls of quick-silver. *Above:* At rest. Collection George Eastman House, Rochester, N.Y.; *below:* In motion.

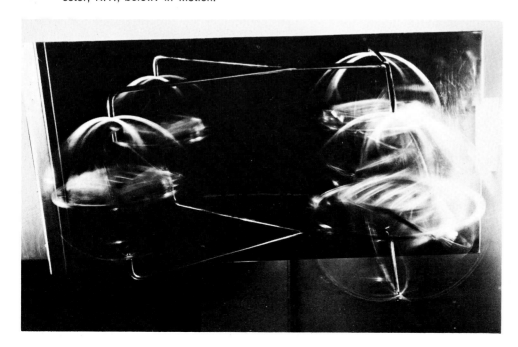

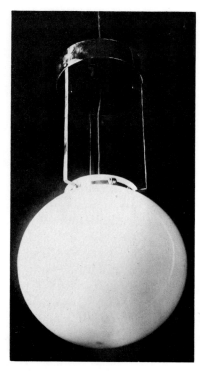

64. Lamps for mass production, designed by Moholy as prototypes for student use in the Bauhaus metal workshops, Dessau, 1924–26.

We know that art itself cannot be taught, only the way to it. We have in the past given the function of art a formal importance, which segregates it from our daily existence, whereas art is always present where healthy and unaffected people live. Our task is, therefore, to contrive a new system of education which, along with a specialized training in science and technique leads to a thorough awareness of fundamental human needs and a universal outlook. Thus, our concern is to develop a new type of designer, able to face all kinds of requirements, not because he is a prodigy but because he has the right method of approach. We wish to make him conscious of his own creative power, not afraid of new facts, working independently of recipes.

Upon this premise we have built our program.

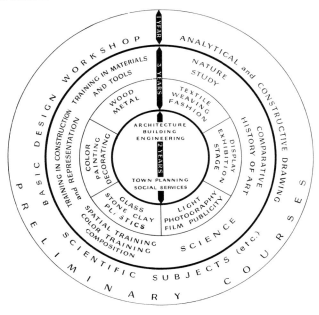

65. First program announcement, The New Bauhaus, Chicago, Fall, 1937.

EDUCATIONAL PROGRAM

AIMS The New Bauhaus requires first of all students of talent: the training is for creative designers for hand and machine made products; also for exposition, stage, display, commercial arts, typography and photography; for sculptors, painters, and architects.

ORGANIZATION The education of the student is carried on in theoretical and practical courses and in the workshops of the school. The school year is divided into two semesters, the first extending from the end of September to the middle of February and the second from the middle of February until the end of June. Each student must spend two semesters (a school year) in the preliminary courses and at least six semesters (three school years) in a special workshop. After the successful completion of this training he will obtain his Bauhaus diploma and he may, by continuing four semesters (two years) in the architectural department receive the architect's degree.

PRELIMINARY COURSE The preliminary curriculum offers a test of the student's abilities. It helps shorten the road to self-experience. It embodies briefly the essential components of the training given in the specialized workshops of the new bauhaus. It gives him ample opportunity to make a careful choice of his own field of specialization later.

The preliminary curriculum is divided into three parts:

(A) The basic design shopwork (tools, machines, building musical instruments).

(B) Analytical and constructive drawing, modeling, photography.

(C) Scientific subjects.

THE OBLIGATORY PRELIMINARY COURSE

(A) Basic Design Shopwork

In the basic workshop the student learns the constructive handling of materials; wood, plywood, paper, plastics, rubber, cork, leather, textiles, metal, glass, clay, plasticine, plaster, and stone;

(a) their tactile values;

(b) structure;

(c) texture;

(d) surface effect and the use of their values

(e) in plane,

(f) in volume,

(g) and in space. Henceforth the student becomes (1) volume- (2) space- and (3) kinetic-conscious.

(h) In order to develop his auditory sense, he experiments with sound and builds musical instruments.

(i) He learns: the subjective and objective qualities, the scientific testing of materials;

(j) existence of the fourth dimension (time).

(k) As he experiments he builds, with small motors or other devices, toys, moving sculptures, spatial constructions, etc.

(B) Drawing, Modeling, Photography

page **5**

(l) and develops his sense for proportion, and penetrates this work with the different

(m) visual representation. He sketches by hand and with photo apparatus as well in black and white and in color and he works in clay. Standard nature forms will be analyzed and this analytical method leads the student to the

(n) elementary forms, later to the construction of these forms in relationship to each other

(o) with the aim of free composition.

(C) Scientific Subjects

The following scientific courses complement shopwork and drawing:

1. Geometry ⎫
2. Physics ⎬ Physical Sciences
3. Chemistry ⎪
4. Mathematics ⎭
5. Biology ⎫
6. Physiology ⎬ Life Sciences
7. Anatomy ⎭
8. Intellectual Integration

In addition to these, the curriculum includes brief surveys of **Supplementary**

(a) Biotechnique—the system of conscious inventions (e.g. Edison)

(b) Psychotechnique (ability testing)

(c) Music

(d) Guest lectures on other subjects;

(e) Lettering, writing (construction of letters, and printing types);

(f) Light (as an instrument of visual notes, using light as a new medium of expression); photography, film;

(g) Visits to factories, newly constructed buildings, museums, exhibitions, theatres, etc.

(h) Exhibitions (some assembled by the students, some by the faculty or others).

66. Program and curriculum, The New Bauhaus, Chicago, Fall, 1937.

67. Walter Gropius and László Moholy-Nagy, School of Design, Chicago, 1943.

I had to build up the school from the very beginning and I found the most encouraging response from the American youth and from modern educators, especially Professors Eckart, Gerard and Morris, who gained from the president of the University of Chicago permission to teach sciences in the new Bauhaus. The first year (preliminary courses) showed very promising educational results and the association appointed for the second year four new professors—Herbert Bayer, Jean Hélion, G. F. Keck and Alexander Schawinsky—and planned to open five new workshops. The number of students was steadily increasing and we were looking forward to the second school year with justified hope for fruitful work.

Returning to Chicago from a Summer trip in the middle of August I was informed by letter of the president of the Association of Arts and Industries that, owing to financial difficulties, the school most probably would not open and the faculty was advised to look for other positions.

In a letter written on Aug. 30, 1938, by E. H. Powell, president of the Association of Arts and Industries, to Mr. Gropius, he states that "when the situation became very desperate I advised Moholy that I thought it is best to tell our instructors that they were released from any contracts they may have with us," and, further, he said: "None of us relish the idea of having our name connected with a school that is forced to close after one year of rather brilliant success due to the work of Moholy and his staff."

I hope this will be a help to stop unjustified rumors and misinterpretations. I would like to quote also a sentence from a declaration sent to the association at the end of October, 1938, by all nine faculty members of the first year (among them seven Americans): "In its failure the Association of Arts and Industries has placed difficulties in the way of realizing a significant educational venture whose program is congenial to the best educational leadership and the deepest educational needs of this country. It is to be hoped that this administrative failure will not be interpreted as a failure of the New Bauhaus itself and L. Moholy-Nagy."

In fact studying the early and recent progressive educational programs of this country I see in Gropius's art educational system a congenial approach to general educational problems which all the countries have had to face since the industrial revolution, and which have special significance for a country with so highly developed an industrial standard as the United States.

It would of course be too early after one year of work done in Chicago to prophesy about possible results of a Bauhaus education in this country. But I want to express my conviction that the continuation of our work and a re-establishing of the new Bauhaus with a solid and responsible backing would mean much more than an experiment. It would be a vital necessity. I am confident that this fact will be realized by farsighted people of this country and that by their support the American youth will be given a chance to develop their extraordinary gifts.

(Signed) L. Moholy-Nagy

Letter to Moholy-Nagy *Piet Mondrian*

Dear Moholy,

Many thanks for your letter. Certainly, you can bring my quotation that I sent you into your book; only, I promised Mr. Faber of "Circle" the copyright for two years. But this fragment does not matter, I think. Always you can ask him.

"New Vision" is a nice title. Really, we must have a "new vision," otherwise all effort is useless to future new life.

I am very glad you do like my statement that I published in "Circle." However, I think it will be good to explain to you my ideas more clearly. Perhaps this is superfluous, but I don't know if you see my relation to architecture and industry. I see by your letters that you are thinking that I could do good work at the Bauhaus in the future. But why did you not think of me firstly? I am, among the different artists, perhaps the most free from "art" and the most near to the "reality" and its esthetic construction; the most near to architecture and industry. I have studied the most consequently that what only create reality's true beauty, that is *pure relations of planes, lines and colors.*

Good relations comes first under discussion is it not?

Future life—more real, more pure—needs more real, more pure esthetic construction. This construction is the research for pure constructive elements and pure relations of them.

The research for good *forms* was the work in the past: the research for good *relations* is the gleam of the present. It is true, good forms create good relations, but *the way how to create them* is different. Relations must come first. This is very important in teaching. The difference is (in language teaching) like as between old school teaching and Berlitz school.

Nice architecture and nice objects must be created: not nice forms. Nice drawings are useless. That is why I see the usefulness of an artist at the Bauhaus only in this way that he is able to teach *how to make more perfect the material constructions.* A "painter"

Reprinted by permission of Harry Holtzman, Lyme, Conn.

and a "sculptor" are of no use at the Bauhaus: well their capability to teach all about forms, colors and their relations.

"Art" must be forgotten: beauty must be realized.

The material realizations: this is what is under discussion.

I think you have always well understood all this. But—at the old Bauhaus—Kandinsky and Klee . . . have teached in the way to maintain the separation of art and reality (architecture and industry) architecture and all what belongs to it, furniture, utilitarian objects, machines etc.. is what most occupy us. Pictures, sculptures decoration are of no use in new life and are an obstacle to realize it now in the present. Because I am sure that you feel most of this above as I do feel it, I do not understand that you have spoken to Mr. Sweeney, as he told me, not only about me, but also about Arp to have at the Bauhaus. Arp is a great artist, but nothing for our future environment. At that time you did not know perhaps his latest work.

Archipenko is a sculptor also, but Helion told me that he does not teach his "art" but develops the sense for good forms and composition of them. I think this is very good. And I am sure that Helion shall work for color and form in the same good way.

By this fact I have seen that you are creating a "new" Bauhaus.

I heard from Helion also that you intended to create a workshop for architecture and were looking for an architect. Why should you not go a new way and take an engineer with an esthetic collaborator. This latest must be an artist, but an artist *free from* "art."

But all this is perhaps not possible now. You know that better as I do. Best greetings to you and your wife, yours

(Signed) Piet Mondrian
(*1939*)

Letter to Robert Jay Wolff
L. Moholy-Nagy

June 7, 1942

My Dear Bob,*

Your letter arrived Friday morning when we had the greatest

* Written on stationery embossed "Braniff Airways, In Flight," to Robert Jay Wolff, formerly Dean of the Institute of Design and then taking his military service. Also a sculptor, Wolff has more recently been teaching at Brooklyn College.
Reprinted by permission of the recipient.

mess in history. We prepared the graduating exercises which we wanted to have impressive as possible. Charlie was in charge of an exhibition which became the best so far. He moved down everything in the big room—weaving and sculpture and camouflage in the big area. The first year work we put in the big drafting room, the art exhibition on the balcony. The childrens' show into the little lecture room. The exercises were held in the photo-studio and light workshop, and the crowd which we got filled the whole place. Everything went on perfectly; the speeches short. Five diplomas Bachelor of Design (Juliette, Charles, Nathan, Myron, Grace). There were shown three reels of color movie on the school, whereby your long fingers were admired and appreciated. I announced on this occasion the newest grant ($7500) which we received from the Rockefeller Foundation to develop our motion-picture dept. Everyone seemed to be satisfied, and the whole evening was booked as a success. We missed our Dean, and I hope you missed us too. Fred [Keck] is functioning now as Dean; he distributed the diplomas on parchment and gold seal. Yesterday we had our annual exhibition judgment and last night the celebration for the graduation. . . .

Concerning your plastic problems, here are some thoughts and answers to your questions:

1. Lumarith is a product of the Celluloid Corp. of America.
2. A cut-all will cut it easily, or bandsaw.
3. I would try to use transparent acetate cement—they must send with it one which is best for its cementing.

I do believe that no rough edge is needed as the acetate cement has the property to dissolve the top or edge of the sheet and unite with the cement.

I never worked with "L," so please ask your dealer.

One is sure, you must change in some way the joints so that they really stick. The bevelled edge seems to be a good idea as it enlarges the glueing (? how to spell?) surface. The whole process must be similar to the glueing of film shots together.

I do not know whether "L." can be heated or not. Celluloid is inflammable, so I would only try with hot water if bending is required.

Again, please ask your dealer. We could press in woodform (from Plexiglas) lens forms but not very deep.

We used wooden forms, male and female, turned on the lathe. These forms must be highly polished, as otherwise the transparency will suffer. Wood for short time easily withstands the heat 215° Fahrenheit that we used for Plexiglas heating.

By the way you can heat Plexiglas with 250 watt sealed reflector type Infra Red bulbs (General Electric or Westinghouse) without any oven. You have to make only experiments about time and placing the sheet under the light, because at bad timing the sheet may start to bubble which ruins the material. Also you could use a normal kitchen oven compartment which has a thermostat control (for Plexiglas of course). You could suggest Plexiglas for the curved parts and Lumarith for the other, if Lumarith can not be shaped so easily without heavy moulding presses.

For your purposes, to make a pressform I believe a vise or clamp would be perfect. But make male and female forms strong, so that they do not crack. You have to use a hardwood which finishes well, walnut for example.

Dear Bob, the plane gets bumpy and Wichita is coming. So best wishes and write!

Until June 20th

Texas State Women College
Art Dept. Denton Texas

Love to you both

(Signed) Yours, Moholy

Evening Classes
Chicago Institute of Design (1942–43)

1. Dress Design
Includes training in Dress Design and Cutting along with basic work in Color, Weaving and Fashion Illustration. Conducted by Marli Ehrman, Sydney Green, Robert Thompson.
2. Model Airplane Building
Prepares students in the Principles of Aeronautics, including experiments in plane design. Conducted by Carl Goldberg.
3. Soldering, Brazing and Welding
Preparatory work for War Industries and Industrial Design. Conducted by Eugene Bielawski.
4. The Principles of Camouflage
Research in natural camouflage; surface covering; mimicry; visual illusions; basic photography; investigation of camouflage techniques. Conducted by George Kepes.

5. Design in Plastics

Research into potentialities and use of thermo-setting and thermo-plastics. Conducted by Otis Reinicke.

6. Mechanical and Architectural Drawing

Training for the War Industries, offering opportunities especially for women. Conducted by Robert B. Tague.

7. Graphic Techniques

Silk Screen; Lithography; Typography, including Printing with Wood Blocks and Linoleum. Conducted by Myron Kozman.

8. Airbrush Technique

For beginning and advanced students. Conducted by J. Zellers Allen.

9. Mathematics and Physics

For beginning and advanced students. Conducted by A. Sayvetz.

10. Visual Fundamentals and Advertising Arts

For beginning and advanced students. Conducted by George Kepes.

11. Basic and Product Design

Conducted by L. Moholy-Nagy, assisted by Charles Niedringhaus and James Prestini.

12. Weaving

Textile design and execution. Conducted by Marli Ehrman.

13. Architectural and Interior Design

For beginning and advanced students. Conducted by George Fred Keck assisted by Robert B. Tague.

14. Photography

For beginning and advanced students. Conducted by James Brown, N. B. Lerner and Frank Levstik.

Through the generous grant of the Rockefeller Foundation the School is able to announce also a

15. Motion Picture Class

Offering fundamental training and opportunities for research. This grant helps the School to continue the avant-garde work which has been so essential in making the film a prominent part in our search for contemporary expression. Conducted by L. Moholy-Nagy with the assistance of Robert Lewis and Edward Rinker.

These classes, together with some day classes allow

Combination Schedules

whereby evening students will be allowed to attend day classes and day students to attend evening classes.

Official Directory
Chicago Institute of Design (*1946*)

Board of Directors
Walter P. Paepcke, Chairman
President, Container Corporation of America

Maurice H. Needham, Vice Chairman
President, Needham, Louis and Brorby, Inc.

Guy E. Reed, Vice Chairman
Vice President, Harris Trust & Savings Bank

E. P. Brooks
Vice President, Sears Roebuck & Company

Bertram J. Cahn
President, B. Kuppenheimer & Company, Inc.

Leverett S. Lyon
Chief Executive Officer, Chicago Association of Commerce

L. Moholy-Nagy
President, Institute of Design

William A. Patterson
President, United Airlines

J. V. Spachner
Vice President, Container Corporation of America

Officers
L. Moholy-Nagy, Director
Crombie Taylor, Secretary-Treasurer
Mollie Thwaites, Registrar

Faculty of the Institute of Design
Calvin Albert
Alexander Archipenko
George Barford
Robert Edmonds
Marli Ehrman
Robert Erikson
Joe Feher
Eugene Idaka
Myron Kozman
S. J. Taylor-Leavitt
Nathan Lerner

Frank Levstik
Robert Longini
L. Moholy-Nagy
Sibyl Moholy-Nagy
James Prestini
Ralph Rapson
Else Regensteiner
Nolan Rhodes
Edgar Richard
Arthur S. Siegel
Frank Sokolik
Robert Bruce Tague
Crombie Taylor
Hugo Weber
Ralph Weir
Marianne Willisch
Emerson Woelffer

Seen the worker unhappy "in strike of NJC" cos they are not educated in the spirit of the community. Worker sees no

Worker unhappy cos of routine work on machine. Cannot see he is contributing to the community but he should be able? Should be happy in his work? Constructively communicates to worker this spirit needed to transcend routine & see contribution to community

Constructivism and the
Proletariat *L. Moholy-Nagy*

Reality is the measure of human thinking. It is the means by which we orient ourselves in the Universe. The actuality of time—the reality of this century—determines what we can grasp and what we cannot understand.

And this reality of our century is *technology*—the invention, construction and maintenance of the machine. To be a user of machines is to be of the spirit of this century. It has replaced the transcendental spiritualism of past eras.

Before the machine, everyone is equal—I can use it, so can you —it can crush me and the same can happen to you. There is no tradition in technology, no consciousness of class or standing. Everybody can be the machine's master or its slave.

This is the root of socialism, the final liquidation of feudalism. It is the machine that woke up the proletariat. In serving technology the worker discovered a changed world. We have to eliminate the machine if we want to eliminate socialism. But we all know there is no such thing. This is our century—technology, machine, socialism. Make your peace with it. Shoulder its task.

Because it is our task to carry the revolution toward reformation, to fight for a new spirit to fill the forms stamped out by the monstrous machine. Material well-being does not depend on manufactured goods. Look around. The proletariat isn't happy today in spite of the machine.

Material well-being is caused by the spirit that is superior to the demand of routine work; it is a socialism of the mind, a dedication to the spirit of the group. Only a proletariat, educated to this grasp of essential community, can be satisfied.

Who will teach them? Words are heavy, obscure. Their meaning is evasive to the untrained mind. Past traditions hang on to their meaning. But there is art. Art expresses the spirit of the times; it is art that crystallizes the emotional drive of an age. The art of our century, its mirror and its voice, is *Constructivism*.

Constructivism is neither proletarian nor capitalist. Constructivism is primordial, without class and without ancestor. It expresses the pure form of nature, the direct color, the spatial element not distorted by utilitarian motifs.

The new world of the proletariat needs Constructivism; it needs fundamentals that are without deceit. Only the natural element, ac-

Excerpts from an article in the Hungarian magazine *MA* (May, 1922). Reprinted by permission of Mrs. Sibyl Moholy-Nagy.

cessible to all eyes, is revolutionary. It has never before been the property of civilized man.

In Constructivism form and substance are one. Not substance and tendency, which are always identified. Substance is essential, but tendency is intentional. Constructivism is pure substance—not the property of one artist alone who drags along under the yoke of individualism. Constructivism is not confined to the picture frame and the pedestal. It expands into industrial design, into houses, objects, forms. It is the socialism of vision—the common property of all men.

Only the today is important for the Constructivist. He cannot indulge in the luxurious speculations of either the Utopian Communist who dreams of a future world domination, or of the bourgeois artist who lives in splendid isolation. It cannot be either proletarian art or art of the precious salons. In Constructivism the process and the goal are one—the spiritual conquest of a century of technology.

Position Statement of the Group MA in Vienna to the First Congress of Progressive Artists in Düsseldorf, Germany (1921)

From the aims published in No. 4 of *Stijl* we have reached a conclusion about the fundamental contrasts in opinions and aims which exist between us and the organizers of this Congress. They keep insisting upon the special interests of the "individual artist," while we, on the other hand, can view life only from the social position of all men. We are conscious of the fact that man as an individual is merely an atom of society. Consequently whatever he does must at all times take a position and express the collective powers inherent in him. From this it becomes clear once more that we can relate to the ideas and decisions of the Congress primarily as human beings, and not as artists.

We therefore reject the formation of a Union, as announced. All our strength and our effort shall be directed toward a collaboration of all creative spirits, regardless, who believe in a future collective society as the only possible basis of a positive life. It will be our first task to point out that art as expression of subjective psychic experiences has lost all significance, and that art must fulfill the objective demands of this age. Art cannot shirk the task of solving the problems unsolved in its relationship to contemporary life. It must find ways to work with new means and practitioners on a collective, non-restrictive basis.

Directness of the Mind; Detours of Technology   *L. Moholy-Nagy*

Limited and infinite relationships are equally the result of cosmic determination. The chemical-physiological-transcendental influences of interacting relationships materialize in different ways, according to their innate laws—once into blue color, another time into an aggregate, and a third time into a sublimation of the mind. Thought—as functional result of cosmos-body interaction—is in its manifestations a constant emanation of human existence.

Under this determination of cosmically oriented relationships, it is not confusing to speak about an identity of all human thought at all times. Even formal variations of thought, so-called "mental attitudes" are recurrent at different epochs. Within this inevitable recurrence, all causal achievements are determined by the time-bound detours of technological conquest. This means that the brain works faster than the constructing hand. This can be characterized with the slogan: Directness of the Mind; Detours of Technology.

This directness of the mind is not a one-dimensional momentum toward economical or sublimated goals alone, but rather a cosmic expansion which knows how to take the shortest path toward every goal. Detours of technology means that in reality all paths for the achievement of a goal are longer and more complicated than seen by the mind. This means that everything could be done more effectively, because inspiration as origin of every action, the intuitive genius of centrifugal expansion, is nothing else but the primordial thought (*Urgedanke*) modified by temporal circumstances, including technology.

An example: man always desires to see more than is within the natural scope of his vision. The telescope reaches to the next village. The microscope splits cells. Television has already reached the Cape of Good Hope. The next station will be the moon! Detours of technology: current attempts to look at planets and stars through larger and larger lenses, instead of working on electromagnetic photographic impulses. Prediction: all observatories will become obsolete, because they are equipped with traditional technology.

To reduce this waste to a minimum: control individual work

Originally published in *Bauhaus,* I (1926). Reprinted by permission of Mrs. Sibyl Moholy-Nagy.

through a comprehension of the primordial thought (*Urgedanke*). A thesis, a basic premise, takes possession. It serves as justification of constellations of vast ramifications, till it turns the whole work into a fixed idea. It is impossible to protest against this power of ideas. Because no matter how coincidental the first impetus might have been, everything coincides toward a heightening of activity, a work-driven obsession which operates with logical-causal precision. This, frequently, is the genesis of a fruitful theory. The process is self-stimulating and self-controlling.

For some years, I was totally absorbed by the importance of the equation "production-reproduction." I tried to coordinate the totality of life under this aspect. It led me to an analysis of all reproduction tools and instruments, to knowledge and suggestions concerning mechanically produced music; and it supplied my basic insights into photography. A supplementary idea (probably more than supplementary because less mechanically oriented, broader in implications) led back to optical phenomena—there it is: directness of the mind, detours of technique.

Ever since I recognized the optical laws in the problem: painting-photography-film, have the byways of the ancient desire of chromatic light effects become clearer. The immanent mind seeks light—light! The detour of technology finds pigment—an intermediate state which only becomes real through the impact of light.

It has been the tragedy of human history that the emanations of the mind have been misused for false effects. Individual elasticity and ceaselessly advancing impetus must work against the human collective. The judgment of the sum total of individuals is, according to hallowed tradition, infallible in its decisions. Infallibility turns to honored custom and so justifies its own existence. This is what we experience as "the ties of tradition," spiritual mass-paralysis, time-bound circumambulation.

This too was the fate of the discovery of pigment. The earliest accidental use of pigment established the concept of color as a sort of light terminus, crassly material. Occidental painting is caught to this day in this technological detour. And this despite our knowledge, since the first *Laterna Magica,* that light is continuous creation, a DIRECT path to kinetic pigment: projected or reflected lightplays with liquid, waving, suspended, transparent, translucent colorfalls in luminescent swathes, vibrations of iridescent light-emulsion in space.

Detours of technology: from manual presentation to the photographic still; from still to cinematography; from planar to molded; from silent to talking; from opaque to translucent; from continuous to simultaneous; from pigment to light. As in a fever, mind and eye conquer the new dimensions of vision which today already are indicated by photo and film. Details can wait for tomorrow. Today the mind exercises a new vision.

—Translation from the German by Sibyl Moholy-Nagy

Analyzing the Situation   *L. Moholy-Nagy*

The Discrepancy

Since the industrial revolution our civilization has suffered from a growing discrepancy between ideological potentiality and actual realization.

The metamorphosis of the world through mass production, mass distribution, and mass communication forced man to think in economic terms and organize his business affairs on a global scale. But his life philosophy remained provincial. He absorbed the technological and economic aspects of the industrial revolution with surprising speed but without an understanding of their manifold implications, never realizing their dangerous antibiological and asocial dynamics if accepted without planning. The new technological trends developed rapidly but their social effects soon got out of control. In spite of exultant forecasts, the prodigious potentialities for healthy living, the fair participation in the benefits of mass produced goods, the persistent hopes to generate harmonious social relationships, have as yet not been fulfilled.

Man has invented pseudofundamentals to camouflage the ancient ailment of economic inequality and squalor. Only very slowly, if at all, have the manifold advantages of the amazing technical improvements seeped down to the bottom of the economic pyramid. (The last census revealed a staggering percentage of American homes without plumbing, electricity, cooking gas, or adequate heating installations.)

The great metamorphosis served mainly for the accumulation of individual profits; for a sharp increase in the destructiveness of competition decided by force; by a social ethics based on economic superiority rather than on the principles of justice. The result was an open fight between labor and management, and a half-hidden, smouldering class struggle between those who could afford the benefits of technological progress and those who could not. These ills, with their resultant monopolistic and fascist tendencies, finally led to repeated world wars which were cruel attempts to win capi-

From *Vision in Motion* (Chicago: Theobald, 1947), pp. 13–16. Reprinted by permission of Mrs. Sibyl Moholy-Nagy.

talistic competition, and to check the upward spiral of the social progress so vigorously undertaken by the American and French revolutions. Our generation must stop the recurrence of these wars by understanding the hazards of a planlessly expanding industry which, by the blind dynamics of competition and profit, automatically leads to conflicts on a world scale.

The social and economic chaos of the world and the intellectual, emotional, and spiritual misery of the individual are appalling. There is, however, no use blaming earlier generations or specific nations whose actions apparently laid the basis for the prevailing confusion. What they did and how they did it were the effects of short-term measures resulting either from lack of imagination or class-determined actions and social ignorance. It is the duty of our generation to point out this fact in order to counteract the assumption that a providential power is behind human shortcomings and an injurious economic and social machinery; that not we but our ancestors are responsible for our plight. We can hope for improvement only after we have surrendered metaphysical interpretations in favor of a scientific analysis of human history. Tradition is man-made and must be constantly reevaluated, adhered to, or discarded, depending upon fundamental, common needs, not upon delusions which only extenuate social guilt.

By concentrating insight, passion and stamina, we may recover the neglected fundamentals. Our generation must accept the challenge to reinvestigate the elements of healthy living so that these can be used as yardsticks to clarify conditions around us. By integrating this newly gained knowledge with the existing social dynamics, we could direct our steps toward a harmony of individual and social needs.

The Inalienable Rights

The industrial revolution started with an enthusiastic emphasis on human values. The American and French Revolutions were test fights. Although the change from handicraft and shop-manufactured goods of feudalist society to modern machine production was a technological shift, the accent was in the beginning not so much on economic aspects as on biological and social ones. This was even more strongly emphasized later when the individualistic nature of the crafts was superseded more by the social character of machine production in factories. The enthusiasm generated by the slogan "liberté, fraternité, égalité" quickly liquidated the paternalistic transgressions of the nobility; and the preamble to the American Declaration of Independence, written years before the French

Revolution, stated "that all men are created equal, that they are endowed by their Creator with certain inalienable rights: that among these are life, liberty and the pursuit of happiness: that to secure these rights Governments are instituted among men, deriving their just power from the consent of the governed: that whenever any form of Government becomes destructive of these ends, it is the right of the people to alter or abolish it and to institute new Government, laying its foundation on such principles, and organizing its powers in such forms, as shall seem most likely to effect their safety and happiness."

The creative bourgeois forces had the sincere intention of making these principles work. However, the task of building a new society was enormous, and the methods of realization were limited by the unconscious dependence upon the previous structure. The bourgeoisie concentrated all its power on the task of breaking the might of the nobility. In so doing it moved into the place and function of the feudal master. Where the prince had previously reigned, the merchant was now the ruler. But he was far from sharing his liberated life with the fourth class—the workers. The bourgeoisie fought against the discriminations of the class above it, but inherited the ancient ideology of superiority over those on the next lower level with whom it was not considered fit to share the responsibilities of government. In fact, in the later phases of capitalism, the nobility, otherwise purely vestigial, was permitted further existence in order to traditionalize that myth of superiority.

Specialists

Industry expanded quickly. The happily prospering businessman needed a vast number of mechanics, engineers, and supervisors to fulfill the profit requirements of an economic strategy which served exclusively the demands of mass-production prosperity. The common denominator was quick specialization, without any consideration of biological fundamentals. Vocational schools were founded for the required specialists. Fields of production were specialized and segregated from each other in the hope that the output would be greater if they were not distracted by manifold interests. Creative abilities, concentrated on limited problems, produced stunning results, expanding the boundaries of the capitalistic economy.

The wheels of industry turned fast and prompted a clear division of all labor, neglecting everything but these divided functions. All former responsibility and pride of the craftsman in the wholeness of a product was now eliminated. Participation in the mass-production process was limited to the execution of a small detail. As the laborer was deprived of the incentive and assurance of working for a creative result dependent upon his abilities for completion, the vital fluid which, as in a battery, carries the current from one unit to the other, evaporated. He became inanimate, working in the maze of tunnels and gangways of the specialized labyrinths.

With growing industrial opportunities the entire educational system attained a vocational aspect. Schools lost sight of their best potential quality: universality. They lost their sense of synthesis to the extent of a complete separation of the various types of experience. On the other hand "prosperity" increased, and with it the temptation to enlarge profits. Everyone seemed satisfied. Production figures and balance sheets "spoke for themselves," being sufficient justification of training for profit. High premiums were paid for labor-saving devices, automatic machines. The specialists, proud of their abilities which could be translated into dollars and cents, knew more and more about less and less. With the exception of a few, their complex biological capacities became inert, their vision narrowed.

Moral Obligations Diminish

The specialist had much detailed knowledge but their work floated in the air, missing both human and social direction. They were busy within their own territory of specialized tasks which had trained them to "mind their own business," neutralizing human sympathies, the natural social reflexes of a healthily developed individual.

This was the age of isolation, marked by fierce competition between specialists in the same field who at the same time maintained an attitude of *laissez faire* toward all others; consequently lessening the sense of obligation to cooperate, and fostering an unwillingness to share in the complex problems of society. The specialists worked to the best of their ability, aiming at an optimum performance of their given task. But their actions were determined by unrelated thinking, without the broad vista of social planning.

Early capitalists had accepted the basic premise of protestantism that man's greatest virtue is his conscience, responsible only to himself and God. They communicated personally with "providence" when a decision had to be made, and felt themselves—rightly or wrongly—as executors of God's will in the management of their merchant empires. Today no one feels even this responsibility, neither the abstract stockholder nor the usually inactive board of directors.

Irresponsibility prevails everywhere. An advertising artist, for instance, makes a layout for the sale of a product. He is responsible for nothing but his own art; that is, his professional standard. The merchant sells the product which is advertised. But he is not responsible for its possibly inferior contents, as it is already packed before it reaches him. The manufacturer is not responsible either, because he only finances the production; the formula comes from the hired staff of a research laboratory trained to produce results which will compete with products on the market. Altogether, responsibility has been subdivided to the evasiveness of the microscopic.

A Proposal   *L. Moholy-Nagy*

Youth Only?

"He who has the youth has the future." Preparations are made in all quarters to "have" the youth, often casting the adult generation aside. However, for a better world yielding more from its resources for the struggling millions, one should also make a blueprint for a comprehensive adult education. I would almost like to say "compulsory" adult education, or better, a cooperative *activity plan* or *active recreation*. This last is the more important since present technology (let alone the advances in the making) may cut down working hours and the new sciences may increase life expectancy. It would be a major tragedy to be unprepared for a creative, that is, active use of the coming leisure time.

Since pioneering days America has had its cooperative activities, such as the townhall meetings in New England, work sharing at crop time, barn raising and other parties, utopian colonies, community centers, freemasons, conventions of associations, labor unions, women's clubs, Y.M.C.A., Y.W.C.A., religious sects—an infinite number of opportunities to meet and discuss diverse matters. These are generally good pageantry and pastime but not always a humble apprenticeship toward a creative, erudite life.

Group activity of the future must be more consciously aware of the mechanics of its own operation as well as of its results. Though the ancient civic centers, the Greek agora and Roman forum, were rather good instruments for creating public opinion and group consciousness of communal issues, it is doubtful that the same type of civic instrument could be used for the same purpose in our time. It is most probable that we have to go through a period of trial and

From *Vision in Motion* (Chicago: Theobald, 1947), pp. 358–61. Reprinted by permission of Mrs. Sibyl Moholy-Nagy.

error—as in many other matters since the industrial revolution—before we can find the right framework for our own civic and "community centers." Some elements of a healthy approach existed in the now suspended Federal Art Project, in some art centers and settlement houses of this country, partly in the Swiss La Sarraz Group of Madame du Mandrot, partly in the English health center of Drs. Williamson and Pearse (Peckham). Also the village colleges initiated by Henry Morris (Cambridgeshire), which provided workshops, laboratories, play and health supervision for the urban and agricultural population of large areas, stimulated the participants not to "reception" but to creative expression.

The new activity "plan" must be more dimensional; an activity in relationships. It must bring about a complete integration of the technological and sociobiological values dormant in the industrial age. Instead of social climbing, charity or misplaced personal sacrifice, it should lead to a happy participation. Instead of the cocoon type of isolation, it should generate a mutual exchange. It should break down general prejudices by eliminating unchecked misprints of the mind, reverberations of superstitions and gossip. It should bring an abundant life as well as intellectual perseverance.

The new activity plan must be understood as part of activized social living in the most varied and productive forms of culture and health. Instead of a passive flood over the eyes and ears by radio, television, cinema and press, it must lead to an active participation in workshops and plays, symposiums and political discussions. This would create the stimuli for a rejuvenation of creative citizenship, spontaneity and an understanding of the needs of the community. But all this must have a preparation. There must be a natural demand for the forms of realization. Such a demand can be created best when integrated education—as outlined in this book—will be not an exception but the general rule.

Parliament of Social Design

Every civilization has to build up step by step its necessary working instruments. Young America achieved this mainly through the generosity of wealthy donors who erected scientific institutes, universities and colleges, museums, art institutes and foundations—giving special contributions for various research projects. Most of these institutions are working on specialized tasks according to the haphazard interest of the patrons. However, what neither America nor any other continent has built up yet are thriving agencies which strive for coordination of activities, for a synthesis. Such agencies should be cultural working centers, institutes of workers who, by mastering their own fields, could embody all specialized knowledge into an integrated system through cooperative action.

Such experts are already working in different parts of the world. If earnest efforts were made to relate their findings and if a suitable environment could be found for their work, a deeper insight into urgent problems would result. Regional groups, of the type proposed, would serve as catalysts for this process of integration.

It is astonishing how differentiated knowledge can be in spite of a generally similar educational and social background. By directing interest to commonly accepted tasks and problems, this varied knowledge of the experts could easily be united and synthetized into a coherent purposeful unity focused on sociobiological aims. By collaboration between these regional centers on the different topics "to restore the basic unity of all human experiences," a hundred facts of living, work, emotional outlets, sublimations, recreation and leisure could be worked out and translated into terms of common understanding.

As a first step for such a task, an international cultural working assembly could be established, composed of outstanding scientists, sociologists, artists, writers, musicians, technicians and craftsmen. They would work either for a long or a limited period *together,* in daily contact, in their studios and laboratories. They would investigate the roots of our intellectual and emotional heritage. They could deal with such problems as the individual and the group; town and country planning; production and dwelling; prefabrication and standards; nutrition with its old and new theories; recreation and leisure; opto-phonetics; psychological and physiological color values; functions of museums; music; theater; cinema; television; the eternal problem of general and higher education; industry and agriculture; village colleges; sociography of towns, cities, countries, continents; the social phenomena of working processes; folklore; crime and rehabilitation, economics and government, etc.

The assembly could then continuously publish its findings in reviews and books, motion pictures and broadcasts.

It could plan exhibitions, plays, symposiums and congresses; propose, demonstrate and indicate settlement of issues of fundamental importance.

Together with its possible branches the assembly could represent a center of the highest aspirations. As the nucleus of a world-government it could prepare new, collective forms of cultural and social life for a coming generation.

In accepting the responsibility of initiative and stimulus, it could serve as the intellectual trustee of a new age in finding a *new unity of purpose;* not a life of metaphysical haze but one based upon the

X criticism in retrospect

Moholy-Nagy *Sigfried Giedion*

The Position in 1935

More than a third of the present century lies behind us. A retrospective glance shows us that at approximately the same period in the preceding century all the problems which were destined to determine the evolution of art up to and beyond its close had already manifested themselves.

Notwithstanding that the conditions of today differ entirely from those of a hundred years ago, it is still possible to predict the general trend of future development. Such a prediction is based, not on mere guess-work, but on a critical estimation of the prognostic significance of the aims which have informed the technique of painters during the last three decades.

A Long Phase Is Ahead of Us

Although the various movements in art that are of prime importance for us today may differ in origin, they are nevertheless inspired by a common aim: to bridge the fatal rift between reality and sensibility which the nineteenth century had tolerated, and indeed encouraged. The urge behind all of them is the attempt to give an emotive content to the new sense of reality born of modern science and industry; and thereby restore the basic unity of all human experience. Neither temporary confusion nor momentary retrogression must blind us to the fact that we are witnessing the opening phase of what is bound to be a prolonged period in the evolution of art.

All these new tendencies in art have one thing in common: they seek to penetrate beyond its purely formal aspects. Each in its own way is striving to create emotive symbols proper to our new conception of life and thus hopes to regain the power of contributing to the task of reshaping the modern world we live in. In other words they are all bent on restoring that essential reciprocity between art and life. The methods by which this transformation of our visual perception could be attained were discovered in the decade 1909–23 (the war-years being naturally considered as inoperative, although developments were not entirely suspended during that interregnum).

In most intellectual centers new movements began to emerge, all of which recognized in their several ways that the old conceptions of the three-dimensionality of space (perspective) and the

Written 1935. Reprinted by permission of Mrs. Carola Giedion-Welcker.

naturalistic reproduction of objects that had held undisputed sway since the Renaissance were inadequate for our new projection of the visible world. This advance will in all probability prove as decisive for the future as did the revolution in art which bears that name for the epoch immediately preceding our own.

Berlin in 1920

Like most other large capitals, Berlin was a focus of artistic activity about the year 1920 for those imbued with the desire to enlarge the field of our optical perceptions. Most of the new movements in art were then coming to the fore there, although as a rule in relative obscurity; and many young artists who were unknown and without influence were beginning to reach maturity.

There were working in Berlin at that time, among others, the Dadaists Kurt Schwitters, George Grosz, Raoul Hausmann, Hannah Höch; the Swedish film-experimentalist Viking Eggeling, who laid the foundations of the abstract film; the Russian Constructivists Lissitzky and Gabo, and the Russian sculptor Archipenko; the Hungarians Moholy-Nagy and Péri; the Dutch architects Oud, van Eesteren, and Doesburg, the Italian painter Prampolini; the Danish architect Lönbergholm; and the editors of the American paper *Broom*. One of the most important studios in which these people were continually meeting, was that of Moholy-Nagy.

The emotive values latent in modern industry and in the realities of modern life in general were lost on the townsman in much the same way as the peasant of previous ages was irresponsive to the emotional appeal of the landscape. A steel bridge, an airplane-hangar, or the mechanical equipment of a modern factory is as a rule far more stirring to the imagination of those who do not see such things every day of their lives. It is not surprising, therefore, that most of the pioneers of the new vision hailed from agricultural countries with little industry of their own. Thus the Constructivists came from Russia or Hungary. That great innovator Picasso spent his youth remote from the big towns; and it was only after he moved to Paris that he was able to vitalize his consciousness of our age with the qualities he derived from the Moorish tradition of Spain. He it was who bridged the gulf between the last great cultural epoch that had found expression in abstract forms and modern civilization.

Coming from the outskirts of civilization, the Russian and Hungarian Constructivists similarly brought fresh energy to the problem of interpreting the realities of to-day.

The Hungarians occupy an intermediate position between the

volcanic energy and Slav fantasy of a Russian like Lissitzky and the purified tonal and plane harmonies of a Dutchman like Mondrian. Among them was László Moholy-Nagy. This young painter had begun his career as a contributor to the activist paper published in Budapest called *MA*, whose aims were resumed in *Das Buch neuer Künstler* (Vienna, 1922), which he wrote in collaboration with Kassák. In *MA* a small group of young Hungarians had succeeded in giving a far more precise and coherent expression to their consciousness of our age than the Berlin artistic circles of that day, which were still fettered by Expressionism. *MA* was, in fact, working on parallel lines to "l'esprit nouveau," in which Corbusier and Ozenfant had been revealing the interdependence of painting, sculpture and the technique of modern industry. After being wounded in the war, Moholy-Nagy came to Berlin in 1920. The paintings and sculpture he exhibited there so much impressed Walter Gropius that he appointed Moholy-Nagy to the staff of the Bauhaus in the spring of 1923. This appointment proved of cardinal importance for Moholy-Nagy's evolution, since it offered the fullest scope to his gifts as a teacher.

The lasting value of what the Bauhaus achieved was due to its success in evolving a new systematic method of art training based on recent discoveries in painting. All the most advanced artists in Germany were either attached to the Bauhaus or in close and regular contact with it.

After Itten left the Bauhaus, Moholy-Nagy was put in charge of the beginners' course there, where he had the responsibility of preparing young students for the training they were about to embark on; and (on the strength of his metal sculpture) of the metallurgical workshop as well. It was only natural that Moholy-Nagy's preoccupation with various problems connected with light should have led him to make practical experiments with various types of lamps. The manifold activities of the Bauhaus were coordinated by the comprehensive discipline of architecture; and architecture, no less than these more specialized branches of design, obviously called for direct contact with industry. Thus the short step from a purely educational investigation of the new concept of optics to active collaboration in the technical improvement of lamp-manufacture was only a logical sequence of events. Moholy-Nagy's book *Von Material zu Architektur,* which contains his lectures on the basic theories of the Bauhaus teaching during the period 1923–28 (Bauhausbücher No. 14, Munich, 1929; also published by Brewer & Warren, New York, under the title of *The New Vision*) explains the method he adopted. It was due to Moholy's influence that all new movements based on fresh advances in technique were thoroughly investigated and embodied in the curriculum, in order to open the student's eyes—for instance—to the entirely new effects in material that are implied in Picasso's *collages* and only waiting to be discerned. The close concatenation between the artistic evolution of our age and the occult forces of the *zeitgeist* which permeate our daily lives has rarely been so impressively demonstrated as in this book.

From his earliest articles in *MA* Moholy-Nagy's contribution has been characterized by a persistent endeavor to fathom the creative potentialities of light and color. All the same he has always been eager to apply his discoveries to the practical problems of life. There is hardly any field of artistic creation that Moholy-Nagy has not investigated. In many of them his influence has proved authoritative. His exhibitions, typographical work, publicity layouts, light-displays and stage-sets—*The Tales of Hoffmann* (1929), *Madame Butterfly* (1931), and Piscator's *Kaufmann von Berlin* (1930)—amply substantiate this claim.

Moholy-Nagy has exercised a decisive influence on photography, where he has systematized its potentialities and in some directions actually extended its scope. From the first he recognized that light in itself must be regarded as a medium of form. It is from this angle that his whole preoccupation with photography and the film should be judged. Moholy-Nagy saw that photography offered the possibility of expanding the existing limits of natural reproduction, and that in spite of its imperfections the camera was a means of increasing the range and precision of visual perception (i.e., in the arresting of movement, bird's-eye and worm's-eye views, etc.). I well remember how, during a holiday we spent together at Belle-Ile-en-Mer in 1925, Moholy-Nagy consistently ignored the usual perspectives and took all his snapshots upward or downward. A few years later the surprising artistic effects of foreshortening and of converging vertical lines had become part of the stock-in-trade of every up-to-date photographer. In *Painting, Photography, Film* Moholy-Nagy developed many stimulating suggestions, and defined the whole province of creative work in light-sensitive media, from ordinary to cameraless photography (which enables the concrete shapes of objects to be disintegrated into graduations of light and shade), and reflectional light-displays to photo-montage and the film *Dynamik der Großstadt* (1921), *Marseilles vieux Port* (1929), *Lichtspiel Schwarz-Weis-Grau* (1931), *Großstadtzigeuner* (1932), *Kongreß für Neues Bauen* (Athens, 1933).

Moholy-Nagy's painting is the vital thread linking all his manifold activities. There is no break in its development proceeding in a consistent line from his first publications up to the present day.

Nor is this all, for today he is feeling the need to resort more and more to this spontaneous fixation of artistic vision.

These pictures with their clear, optimistic attitude are the harbingers of that long-term development, for which a few hundred people dispersed throughout the modern world are today preparing the foundations.

A Great Teacher *Herbert Read*

In reviewing this posthumous book, *Vision in Motion,* which is a comprehensive account of Moholy-Nagy's philosophy and educational methods, I cannot refrain from referring in my turn to the vitality of the man himself, which made him one of the great teachers of our time. The principles which are formulated and illustrated in this volume are not exercises in *a priori* pedagogy: Moholy-Nagy was first and foremost a man of amazing energy, of warm sympathies, of creative deeds; and his teaching was the communication of his enthusiasms, of his inventions and discoveries. To see Moholy-Nagy in action as Director of the Institute of Design which he founded in Chicago was a demonstration of the fact that teaching, too, is an art—that the teacher is fundamentally an artist who works among a group of artists, a little ahead of his companions, setting the pace.

This substantial volume (376 pages, 440 illustrations, many in color) is a record based on more than twenty-five years experience, first at the Bauhaus in Germany, afterwards in Chicago. It is illustrated not only by typical examples of the work of leading modern painters, sculptors and architects, but also by the work of pupils, produced in the course of their education. This experimental material is the result of a method, and underlying the method is what one must call a philosophy of life. The method Moholy-Nagy called "Design for Life": for the philosophy he had no specific name—he said "the contemporary arts try to establish a new morality and a new ethics not hampered by metaphysical absolutes," but the keyword to describe his outlook is *organic*. In the foreword to this book he speaks of a *"biological* bill of rights, asserting the interrelatedness of man's fundamental qualities, of his intellectual and emotional requirements, of his psychological well-being and his physical health." The ills of modern society are a result of the conflict between new techniques and old ideologies. "We have to free the elements of existence from historic accretions, from the turgid

From *The Architectural Review,* CII, No. 221 (1947).

symbolism of past association, so that their function and effectiveness will be unimpaired." Integration implies a synthesis of the intellectual and the emotional, and this can only be achieved by "a well-balanced social organization and an appropriate education—an education for personal growth . . . a social organization in which everyone is utilized to his highest capacity."

Moholy-Nagy was not a sociologist, much less a politician. He concentrated on the educational problem, which he saw as a problem of *emotional* training. "At present the intellectual development of the individual is entirely his private affair, confined to a hit-or-miss approach. The consequence is emotional illiteracy, which means to be without compass, without assurance of feeling, in a complex, immensely expanded world."

The methods which Moholy-Nagy used to develop emotional literacy are too various to be summarized here; but essentially they consisted of an analysis of the physical properties of materials and of the laws of growth, and the experimental rearrangement of the elements thus defined. Parallel to this study of form is a study of function—not in the limited technological sense, but in the widest sociological application. Design from this point of view "is not a profession but an attitude."

> Design is a complex and intricate task. It is the integration of technological, social and economic requirements, biological necessities, and the psychophysical effects of materials, shape, color, volume, and space: thinking in relationships. The designer must see the periphery as well as the core, the immediate and the ultimate at least in the biological sense. He must anchor his special job in the complex whole. The designer must be trained not only in the use of materials and various skills, but also in appreciation of organic functions and planning. He must know that design is indivisible, that the internal and external characteristics of a dish, a chair, a table, a machine, painting, sculpture are not to be separated. The idea of design and the profession of designer has to be transformed from the notion of a specialist function into a generally valid attitude of resourcefulness and inventiveness which allows projects to be seen not in isolation but in relationship with the need of the individual and the community. One cannot simply lift out any subject matter from the complexity of life and try to handle it as an independent unit.

It must be admitted that the freedom gained by such a complete break with tradition is apt to produce an effect of *restless* experiment. Moholy-Nagy was fully aware of this possible criticism, and he was ready with an explanation. According to this, a "mutation" occurred in the historical development of art as a consequence of the experiments of the cubists.

> The abstract artists, the neo-plasticists, suprematists and constructivists discovered that in the efforts of the cubists not so much the representation of objects and the description of their motion was the most important feature but the visual force and emotional wealth of *relationships,* the constructive potential of the visual fundamentals. This development of the visual arts from fixed perspective to vision in motion is *vision in relationships.* The fixed viewpoint, the isolated handling of problems as a norm is rejected and replaced by a flexible approach, by seeing matters in a constantly changing, moving field of mutual relationships.

Moholy-Nagy believed that this new "vision" might inaugurate a new era in the history of mankind, that it is the clue to all the changes that are taking place in the sciences as well as in philosophy, including education and all other fields, in our whole civilization. But this is to assume that civilization and its esthetic modes of expression proceed—or can proceed—from changes in "vision" —literally from modes of seeing or perceiving the objective world. Anyone conscious of the profound changes which followed on the discovery of the laws of perspective in the fifteenth century will not be inclined to dismiss this opinion as absurd, but we must make a distinction between the general characteristics of a civilization and any specific features which are the end-products of that civilization, confined to an élite. The basis of a civilization is surely something broader than vision. It may be that there has been an evolutionary development in perception—we know that there are differences of perceptual organization between men and animals, between savages and civilized adults, between children and adults. But these differences are expressed in stylistic variations rather than in distinct types of civilization. Civilization as an evolutionary phenomenon is based on something at once deeper, more enduring, and more unifying. In the Middle Ages it was vision in another sense— religious vision, spiritual integrity. In the post-Renaissance world it has been a belief in the co-ordinating power of reason. A principle of this kind has not yet emerged in our contemporary world, and it is hopeless to expect it from scientific conceptions of space-time, or esthetic conceptions of "vision in motion." Such conceptions only serve to emphasize the separateness of the specialized functions named science and art; and as Margaret Mead says in the course of an admirable passage quoted by Moholy-Nagy, "by making art a specially precious part of life we have demoted it from being all of life, seen from one point of view. When this is done, everyone suffers—the 'artists' and all the people to whose lives significance might have been given." The very fact that he quotes this wise saying shows that Moholy-Nagy was aware of the difficulty; and he was anything but a separatist in his own life and work. No one participated more fully than he in the spirit of the age: it was the age that failed this visionary pioneer. We have a duty to insure that the lead he gave is not lost.

A Mine of Perceptions and Prophecies *Richard Kostelanetz*

> Ultimately all problems of design merge into one great problem: "design for life." In a healthy society this design for life will encourage every profession and vocation to play its part since the degree of relatedness in all their work gives to any civilization its quality. . . . It further implies that there is no hierarchy of the arts, painting, photography, music, poetry, sculpture, architecture, nor any other fields such as industrial design. They are equally valid departures toward the fusion of function and content in "design."—*Vision in Motion*

From his artistic beginnings, Moholy was an artist who also wrote, usually in clear and forceful prose; and it is as a writer most of all that he remains with us today. His theatrical ideas would probably have been forgotten long ago, had he not set them in print; and although his efforts in sculpture and photography have been memorialized by the critical historians of those fields, his own ideas and example, expounded in his lifetime by the Bauhaus books and such reviews as *i 10* in Amsterdam, now survive largely in his own prose. His much-reprinted essay on *The New Vision,* originally published in Germany in 1929, translated here in 1932, and subsequently reissued in 1947 in a considerably revised edition, with an autobiographical afterword entitled "Abstract of an Artist" (1944), remains in print and still stands as a fine critical introduction to Cubist-kinetic tendencies in modern art. Less a coherent polemic than a series of related polemical paragraphs, *The New Vision* is a compendium of concise statements (even the illustration captions are pithy), such as an itemized summary of Cubist innovations and wise generalizations about all contemporary art; for Moholy possessed the art historian's competence for discerning the character and drift of the whole. (On the other hand, the more philosophical passages on biological relevance, while ambitious and perhaps necessary to the argument, are less persuasive.) Moholy's writing marks him as perhaps the only major practitioner of modern art possessed of sufficiently broad experience and sympathy to write about more than his few most noted passions; in sheer bulk, he also published more critical prose than any other modern visual artist of note. Moreover, Moholy's writings are rich in such passing prophecies as a reference to film's "unexplored possibilities of projection, with color, plasticity and simultaneous displays, either by means of an increased number of projectors concentrated on a single screen, or in the form of simultaneous image sequences covering all the walls of the room."

The obvious paradox of Moholy's career is that as an adventurer in many arts he was the true master of none, which is to say that in no area except perhaps photography, book design, and kinetic light sculpture was he indisputably a seminal figure and that, though scarcely any of his signed works are outrageously bad, very few of them approach status as masterpieces of their form; the most likely candidates in media other than those noted above are the paintings on metallic and transparent surfaces, the films about Marseilles, and the light machine. The suspicion is that, unlike other artists of his stature, Moholy never really intended to be a "great painter," or a "great photographer," or master of any other specialty, though his intention to be nothing less than a great artist and his uncompromised aspirations to important work inform his endeavors in every medium. The more unusual paradox is that this artist's indisputably greatest work, to my mind, is his last book, *Vision in Motion,* the consummation of all his ideas and interests, which was written in English (in language sporadically peculiar and yet invariably clear), mostly in Chicago; and since hardbound publication, by definition, brings exploratory processes to a halt, it is perhaps appropriate that the book appeared just after Moholy's death. No other modern artist capped his career with a great book. Though considerably less known than it should be, selling only 40,000 copies in twenty years (mostly to art students) and seldom credited in print, *Vision in Motion* is indubitably among the half-dozen classic studies of modern art, as well as the best example I know, in Moholy's own phrase, of "text and illustration welded together." Indeed, I personally regard *Vision in Motion* as one of the most insightful guides available to contemporary art (much as his friend Giedion's *Space, Time and Architecture* [1941] remains the best on its subject), even though it was written twenty-four years ago (and regrettably neglects such issues as reductionism, inferential art, and post-modern dance); for instance, a recent book I did on "happenings," kinetic environments, and related endeavors, *The Theatre of Mixed Means* (1968) was intellectually more indebted to Moholy's masterpiece than to any other single text.

Compendious, discursive, conglomerate, *Vision in Motion* accomplishes several things. It is first of all a summary of Moholy's program at the Institute of Design, enhanced by many generous illustrations of his students' adventurous work (though very few of their names, curiously enough, are familiar to us today); here the theme is the nature and necessity of a truly multi-sensory education. Literacy, defined entirely by book-learning, is illiteracy in contemporary times, which require genuine polyliteracy. Second, *Vision in Motion* is an implicit record of both Moholy's artistic ambitions and his quest for a perceptual and creative sensibility distinctly appropriate to modern times, and it successfully ties together many strands of his multiple adventure. As a man of artistic and intellectual action, who instinctively translated his ideas into schemes and objects, Moholy frequently illustrated his own endeavors in painting, film, sculpture, photography, light machines, industrial design, and even poetry; this remains the most thorough guide to his own work. The book is finally an illuminating survey of recent achievements and ideas in various separate arts, and even points among and between, not only to define the multiple revolutions of modern art but also to outline a viable tradition behind further work.

While the academic art historian is predisposed to show how recent art draws upon aspects of the acknowledged tradition, Moholy, as a participant-observer, made his thesis the radically different style and opportunities of the modernist moment. He correctly identifies two pervasive tendencies peculiar to contemporary activity—kinesis and inter-media; and these crucial perceptions lead him to predict much that has since become important. The first revolutionary quality he traces back to Cubism and the resulting evolution from "fixed perspective to 'vision in motion,'" which is to say, the process of "seeing a constantly changing moving field of mutual relationship" that he finds exemplified in painting at least as "a new essay at two-dimensional rendering of related objects"; and Moholy concludes an extremely perspicacious analysis of Cubism's conventions by asserting, "From its inception, Cubism became a prime mover in the visual arts. All attempts at visual expression by the following generation have been directly or indirectly influenced by it." His commentary then draws upon the technical morphology of sculptural forms (from stasis to kinesis) elaborated in *The New Vision;* and as cinematic montage is regarded as an extension of Cubism, so film becomes, in Moholy's analysis, the climactic kinetic art. Thus, in all modern arts, Moholy finds "space-time" or "vision in motion," which he comprehensively defines as "a new dynamic and kinetic existence freed from the static, fixed framework of the past," and Moholy's critical remarks are as true for such contemporary painterly arts as music and post-ballet modern dance, since there are analogies between Cubist artistic space, with its simultaneously multiple perspective, and post-Schönberg serial music. "It is a tribute to Moholy's intellect and visionary powers," noted Jack W. Burnham in *Beyond Modern Sculpture,* "that the outlines of kinetic histories to date have pretty much followed his pattern."

On the second theme of inter-media, Moholy recognizes, for instance, that a light mobile of negligible weight, kinetic form, virtual and changing volume, moving parts, and, thus, "space-time relationships" is not sculpture in the traditional sense but something else; however, Moholy's criticism never quite takes the leap into inventing a new genre, as I would do, of sculptural (or artistic) machines to classify a mechanical entity built primarily for artistic (or useless) purposes. His imaginative remarks on theatrical possibilities suggest a hybrid between the old theater and spectacular display, and he tends to place the artistic use of light indefinitely between painting and something else. While Moholy would encourage the adventurous artist to explore unfamiliar terrains, he also insists that the integrity of each medium be respected—film cannot behave like sculpture or express essentially literary ideas, and vice versa.

His section on "Literature," amazingly enough, defines the avant-garde traditions as we currently know them, twenty-four years later —simultaneists, Futurists, Expressionists, Dadaists, Surrealists, and James Joyce. Back in the middle 1940's, Moholy ventured the increasingly persuasive opinion that *Finnegans Wake* was the extraordinary book of the age, and he typically risks a perceptive analysis of Joyce's language as the key to his multiplicitous theme, in addition to reproducing an intricate chart (by Leslie L. Lewis) that I have not seen in print anywhere else. As a critic who discriminately responded to radical originality, Moholy also knew that one possibility for language would be in the inter-medium of designed words; and he points up precursors of "concrete poetry" or "word-imagery" in Christian Morgenstern, Apollinaire, and Marinetti. "The ideograms of Apollinaire were a logical answer to their dull typography, to the levelling effects of the gray, inarticulate machine typesetting. . . . Already in Marinetti's Joffre poems, movement, space, time, visual and audible sensations were simultaneously expressed by the typography." As Moholy conceived it, the word-image art at its best would be not a design of letters and other verbal symbols, in the manner of orthodox "concretism" (most of which, particularly in anthological presentations, is trivial), or even the visualization of a single word, such as Robert Indiana's *Love* or the oil painting done of his own name (*Moholy*, 1921), but a field of words in various type-styles that would "create a quick, simultaneous communication of several messages"—a conception closer to, say, the Englishman John Furnival's work, if not certain posters full of words, than anything else. In addition, Moholy anticipates the recent interest in a poetry purely of spoken sounds, even establishing and quoting the tradition of Hugo Ball's "Verse Without Words," Kurt Schwitters' "Anne Blume" (but omitting E. E. Cummings' "ygUDuh"). Shrewdly again, he even looks into the writings of psychotics for alternative ways of structuring linguistic communication.

For his explanation of stylistic change in art, Moholy usually appropriates the theme of technological determinism. The end of Renaissance representational space, in which a scene is portrayed "from an *unchangeable,* fixed point following the rules of the vanishing point perspective," is attributed to "speeding on the roads and circling in the skies. . . . The man at the wheel sees persons and objects in quick succession, in permanent motion." He notes at the beginning that, "New tools and technologies cause social changes," adding elsewhere that "such a 'mechanical' thing as photography" had a similarly revolutionary effect upon the contemporary sensibility.

One has only to recall the romantic outlook of former generations upon the pictorial presentation of landscape and other objects, and compare it with the way they are perceived now, namely, "photographically." Many people may not realize it but the present standard of visual expression in any field, painting, sculpture, architecture and especially the advertising arts, is nourished by the visual food which the new photography provides.

(This echoes a striking statement in the very first book: "We have through a hundred years of photography and two decades of film been enormously enriched in this respect. We may say that we see the world with entirely different eyes.") And the concern with modulated shading in his own art Moholy also attributes to photography, which "revealed for the first time light and shadow in their interdependence." Needless to say, *Vision in Motion* also has some of the richest pages ever written on the possibilities of the photographic medium.

Technology is also regarded as crucially changing the sum of materials available to an art, so that the innovative design of even something as mundane as home chairs is indebted to "electricity, the gasoline and Diesel engines, the airplane, motion pictures, color photography, radio, metallurgy, new alloys, plastics, laminated materials." At another point, Moholy notes, with an appraisal more applicable right now than thirty years ago, "Today there are more technological sources for light painting than at any other period of human history," and a passing remark acknowledges the artistic potential, only recently realized, of the intermittent, "strobe" light that Harold Edgerton invented forty years ago. At times this bias toward technological determinism lapses off into a contrary Hegelianism; for instance, Moholy writes, "The best representatives of the arts whether in music, poetry, sculpture, or painting, even in their single works, always express the spiritual state of the age." However, this apparent contradiction can be explained by Moholy's establishing, at the beginning of the book, that technology is the primary force informing the spirit and produce of the era.

Vision in Motion is also a profoundly political book, not because Moholy was a politically active artist—publicized agitation was not his style—but because he regarded both the creation and comprehension of modern art as inherently political acts. Indeed, although he sometimes uses Marxian terms to explain certain historical cultural phenomena and favored a more or less socialist economy, Moholy broke with the orthodox Marxists, on one hand, over their resistances to both individual artistic integrity and non-representational modern art and with the artistic "humanists," on the other, over their resistances to technology. As a more organic revolutionary, Moholy favored radical changes in *both* art and life, and both technology *and* psychology, regarding transformations in each as feeding into the others, so that true political purpose for the artist lay not in portraying social injustice but in creating "powerful new relationships. He can do so either by developing tendencies or by opposing them. The gradual elimination of the still existing feudal residues, that is, obsolete economic theories, obsolete patterns of individual behavior, obsolete sexual and family relationships is not an automatic matter." Of a modest Christian Morgenstern ideogram, for instance, he argued, "Still it is an attempt to break the conventions of content and the customary form of typography, and with it, symbolically, the content and form of society which applied its great rules of the past only mechanically."

Innovative art is regarded as the anti-archaic force in contemporary culture, at its best an influence perhaps more powerful than politics. "Tyranny and dictatorship, manifestoes and decrees will not recast the mentality of the people. The unconscious but direct influence of art [plus, it would seem, technological change] represents a better means of persuasion for conditioning people to a new society." As technology ushers changes that make men emotionally behind-the-times, the task of art and education is to reclaim him for the present. In addition, Moholy regarded technological advance and the "satisfaction of mass requirements" as more of a blessing than a curse, though he viewed with dismay both capitalist exploitation and man's reluctance, or inability, to use all the machines available to him; and a parenthetical paragraph, set in a broad margin, connects truly functional design with "the revolutionary spirit of American democracy" and, by converse implication, pompously excessive ornamentation with "feudal, ornate forms of living." Moreover, it is by connecting change in art to social evolution that *Vision in Motion* profoundly comprehends, and advocates, the radical nature of the twentieth century.

Perhaps the key to Moholy's eclectically radical politics is his list of favored revolutionaries, grouped in a paragraph sub-headed "the avant-garde"; for along with Voltaire, "Proudhon, Marx, Bakunin, Kropotkin and Lenin," are included Pasteur, Einstein, Darwin, Stravinsky, Varese, "Whitman, Rimbaud, Dostoievsky, Tolstoy, Joyce," Le Corbusier, Gropius and, of course, Picasso, Malevitch, and Mondrian—all of whom envisioned radically different ways of practicing their respective arts. Along with his commitment to innovative revolution, Moholy recognized the importance of planning, or the implementation of vision; and just as the opening chapter of *Vision in Motion* calls for "a planned co-operative economy," so the conclusion indicatively proposes the establishment of a college of sophisticated planners, who would envision and then build a new world.

Moholy also differed from orthodox Marxists by assuming that mind change (and creations of the human mind, such as technology) precedes social change, and this induces a particularly revolutionary concern with education. Since the nature of the new age is defined by kinesis and inter-media, education should be redesigned to respect the new realities. On one hand, he favored training that involved not merely the transmission of information but also "hand and brain, intellect and emotion; the task is to give the student enough opportunity to use his brain together with his emotional potential; to provide for sensory experiences of eye, nose, tongue and fingers, and their transformation into controlled expression." Elsewhere in *Vision in Motion,* he describes the Institute of Design's program, which exposed students to basic materials and concepts of all the arts, as well as including a number of general exercises "mostly built upon sensory experiences through work with various materials. . . . In addition, there is work with sheet metal and wire, glass, mirrors, plastics, drawing and color, mechanical drawing, photography, group poetry, and music—a full range of potentialities." However, the final aim was not dilettante taste but organic integration of diversified competence—what Moholy defined as "seeing everything in relationship—artistic, scientific, technical as well as social." Most of this remains a persuasive and radical vision for future educational reform. As Mrs. Moholy-Nagy observed in a recent article, throughout his life her husband espoused the Constructivist thesis "that perception is the carrier of human emotion and that it is the subtlest awareness of this perception to all phenomena of life that saves men from stagnation and desperation."

As a richly polymathic discourse, *Vision in Motion* teems with miscellaneous aphorisms and genuinely good ideas, some of which are buried in long paragraphs or dropped off in captions; it is one of those rare critical books that yields fresh ideas with repeated reading. "The simpler [the artist's] medium and the less investment it involves, the easier it is to avoid possible censorship and to preserve the ways of genuinely free expression." "The finest solutions of functional design usually are found in new inventions." "Many achievements of the industrial revolution could be praised emphatically if people had not had to pay so dearly for them." "Art sensitizes man to the best that is immanent in him through an intensified expression involving many layers of experience." "The higher the window the better it solves its original function, which is to admit light deeply into the room." "The choice of medium is in the artist's hand; he must have the ability to summon artistic coherence out of the means he uses." "The illiterate of the future will be the person ignorant of the use of the camera as well as of the pen." "In 1927 in Zurich I suggested for cinema publicity . . . a gas curtain onto which motion pictures could be projected, through which the public could pass. This gaseous curtain could also, chameleon-like, change colors." "By analyzing the paintings of these various groups [of modern art], one soon finds a common denominator, the supremacy of color over 'story'; the directness of perceptional, sensorial values against the illusionistic rendering of nature; the emphasis on visual fundamentals to express a particular concept." "The intrinsic meaning of an abstract painting, as a peculiar form of visual articulation, lies mainly in the integration of the visual elements, in its *freedom from the imitation* of nature and the philosophy connected with it." Some of Moholy's most memorable comments sketch the interrelationship between technology and design. "The older the craft, the more restraining is its influence upon the imagination of the designer. It is easier to design a new product which is based upon the new sciences and technologies than, for example, to re-design the production-ways and shapes of pottery, one of the oldest handicrafts."

Vision in Motion fires ideas in so many directions that it has in-evitably become a mine for plagiarists and popularizers. Gyorgy Kepes, now of M.I.T.'s Center for Advanced Visual Studies, has cribbed freely from it for many of his recent books and anthologies, though he rarely credits Moholy, who not only supervised Kepes in London and Berlin but also brought his fellow Hungarian refugee to America to teach at the Institute of Design. Furthermore, it was Moholy, and not Marshall McLuhan, who noted, in 1947, that the contemporary newspaper, unlike its eighteenth-century predeces-sor, "tries to organize the many events of the day similarly as the Futurists; the reader should read all the news almost at once." McLuhan and Harley W. Parker note in their extremely interesting *Beyond the Vanishing Point* (1968) that, "Seurat, by divisionism, anticipates quadricolor reproduction and color TV," but this echoes Moholy's perception that "Seurat, for example, with his pointillist art, intuitively anticipates the science of color photography." At times Moholy even sounds like his intellectual successor McLuhan: "With the mass production of autos, the elevated lines became tech-nologically obsolete but were kept on as a cheap means of intercity travel." Although McLuhan is usually generous about acknowledg-ing his more modish sources, he rarely credits Moholy, who clearly stands behind many of the media-sleuth's ideas. (Indeed, it was McLuhan who first told *me* to read *Vision in Motion*.) All in all, though his name is scarcely known, Moholy's ideas still command considerable currency at the present time. He wrote on modern art a critical book that, more than two decades later, still has a con-temporary relevance, primarily for its genuine perceptions rather than its style (the customary virtue of enduring criticism); and for how many other books on any modern subject can this be said?

From *Theory and Design in the First Machine Age*   *Reyner Banham*

Born in 1895, László Moholy-Nagy was a clear decade younger than the pioneers in either architecture or the plastic arts, and grew up in a world in which Modern art existed already. His early

From *Theory and Design in the First Machine Age* (New York: Praeger; London: The Architectural Press, 1960), pp. 312–19.

imagination was colored by an agency that had come into the world at about the same time as himself, the illustrated magazines, to such an extent that he was overcome with disappointment on finding that Szeged, the nearest town of any size to his boyhood home in Hungary, had no skyscrapers. An injury received a few months after that which carried off Sant'Elia, and in the same battle zone though on the other side, kept him out of most of the later fighting in the war, and gave him time to investigate Modern art, although his formal training, like Marinetti's, was in law. By the time he arrived in Berlin, early in 1921, starving but a little ahead of other Abstractionists from Eastern Europe, he had undergone the education of a Modernist, revolutions and all, in compressed form.

Although he kept up his Hungarian connections, and represented the Hungarian, expatriate *MA-Gruppe* at the various congresses (Weimar, Düsseldorf, etc.) of the period, he was soon deeply involved in the turbulent artistic culture of Berlin. His authorship of the *Aufruf zur elementaren Kunst* has already been mentioned, and he was in touch with Lissitzky from the time of the latter's arrival, also with Gabo, Schwitters and Arp, with the *Stijl* and *Sturm* connections. But once a certain amount of Futurist rhetoric had been worked out of his system, his devotion was almost exclusively to the Russian connection, and from some point in 1921 onward, his work depends on Malevitch's Suprematist elements of circle, cross and square, at least for its point of departure, often for its entire formal repertoire. From a slightly earlier date he had begun to interest himself in "Modern" techniques like collage, and "Modern" materials like transparent plastics, not merely because they were new but because a consuming interest in light, as the ultimate *malerische Element,* felt by other young painters beside himself, could not be satisfied with traditional means.

However, his most spectacular excursion into Modern methods had quite another stimulus, and quite a different import, and must rank with Duchamp's *Bottlerack* as a major gesture toward a revision of the relationship between artist, subject, and public in a mechanized society. At his one man show at the *Sturm* gallery in 1922, Moholy exhibited a group of Elementarist compositions including three of identical design but differing size, of whose creation he gives the following account:* ". . . in 1922 I ordered by telephone from a sign factory five paintings in porcelain enamel. I had the factory's color chart before me and I sketched my paintings on graph-paper. At the other end of the telephone the factory su-

---

* This account of the telephone paintings is taken from the autobiographical fragment "Abstract of an Artist," which appeared as a supplement to the second American edition of *The New Vision* (New York, 1949).

pervisor had the same kind of paper divided into squares. He took down the dictated shapes in the correct position." This intrusion of a whole industrial organization and a telephone service into the accepted conventions of artistic creation has clearly the same kind of Dadaist significance as Duchamp's elimination of artist and painting from those conventions with the *Bottlerack*, though Moholy was, apparently, more conscious of the positive aspects of his action and the claims they made for the status of mechanical methods. And where Duchamp's apologists tended to explain his intentions in a platonic sense, Moholy was prepared to do this for himself—his esteem of the Phileban solids has been noted, and apropos the "telephone paintings" he later wrote, "But my belief is that mathematically harmonious shapes, executed precisely are filled with emotional quality, and they represent the perfect balance between feeling and intellect." If, as seems possible, he felt this way at the time that these paintings were executed, then they are not to be categorized with the tough-minded artifacts of the *G* connection—indeed, that party in Berlin seems to have regarded Moholy's *Vorkurs* at the Bauhaus as being just as deplorably "arty" as Itten's.

Nevertheless, it is noteworthy that the first task assigned to him when he joined the Bauhaus in 1923 was the reform of the metal-working shop, which suggests that he was regarded as particularly equipped for techniques and materials of that kind, and he only took over the *Vorkurs* later in the same year, in collaboration with Josef Albers, who had been allotted to the preliminary course a little earlier. Exactly how much of the *Vorkurs,* as it found its way into *Von Material zu Architektur,* is due to Albers and how much to Moholy is now difficult to assess, but it is clear that the latter soon became the dominant personality, and not only in the *Vorkurs,* for he seems to have risen rapidly to a position of eminence second only to that of Gropius as an exponent of Bauhaus ideas and a shaper of Bauhaus policy. Thus, although the editorship of the *Bauhausbücher* was ostensibly shared by himself and Gropius, the titles and authors represent so closely his own syncretic interests that one may suspect that they were largely his own choice—as if he wished all the Bauhaus public to have the same broad ground in the modern "isms" as himself.

Such a wish clearly underlies, in part, the organization of the subject matter of *Von Material zu Architektur.* Though Moholy disclaims that it is "lexikalisch" in its treatment of materials and methods, it is encyclopedic in its coverage of the Modern Movement, and illustrates, apart from Bauhaus products, works by Schwitters, Marinetti, Picasso, Brancusi, Archipenko, Barlach, Belling, Pevsner, Schlemmer, Vantongerloo, Servranckx, Rodin, Rodchenko, Cocteau, Gabo, Lipchitz, Le Corbusier, Stam, and Eiffel. It also discusses at less or greater length the following movements: Abstraction, Dadaism, Futurism, Constructivism, Tactilism, *merzbild,* Cubism, neo-Plasticism, Realism, Surrealism, Purism, Pointillism, and Impressionism, and the following extensions of the visual culture of educated Europeans: photography, microphotography, crystallography, kinetic sculpture, films, illuminated advertising, montage and primitive art.

This wide-ranging visual erudition and sharp appreciation of the environment of urban living are difficult to parallel, except possibly in the art and writings of Boccioni, but Moholy has the advantage over Boccioni in his ability to draw this mass of information and experience into a quite compact and orderly body of theory—the first orderly body of theory to be drawn out of, rather than put into, the Modern Movement. The first impression gained on reading the book is that for Moholy art started in 1900. There are a few references to the art of the past—the Pyramids and the Kaaba at Mecca to make a point about Phileban forms, a Leonardo and a Giambologna to make another point about sculpture—but his view does not really extend back beyond the Eiffel Tower. He harks back to neither the geometry of Greece nor the masonry of the Middle Ages, he is not interested in temples and cathedrals, his theories are to derive their authority from the present condition of culture, not from history.

The first part of the book is accordingly devoted to a discussion of the relationships between individuals, their mechanized environment, and the process of education. The line of argument was, by 1928, an established Bauhaus thesis, concerning the need to educate complete personalities, not narrow specialists, and the flavor of the discussion is adequately given by some of the paragraph headings:

The Future Needs the Whole Man
Not Against Technology, but with it
Man, not the Product, is the Aim
Everybody is Talented
The Responsibility for Putting This into Effect Lies with all of Us
Utopia?
Education has a Great Task to Fulfill Here

And this task of education is outlined thus:

We need Utopians of genius, a new Jules Verne; not to sketch in broad perspective an easily grasped technical utopia, but the very existence of future men whose basic laws of being respond to instinctive simplicity as well as the complicated relationships of life.

Our educators have the task of ordering development towards the healthy exercise of our powers, to lay the foundations of a balanced life even in the earliest stage of training.

He then pays tribute to the educational pioneers whose work preceded the Bauhaus—a register of names and movements that is a history in itself, and the concluding paragraphs of Section I seek to fix the place of the Bauhaus in this picture of society, culture and education—and to explain once more the reasons for handicraft training in a mechanized society.

Whatever the educational method outlined in the other three sections of *Von Material zu Architektur* may owe to the pioneers whom Moholy had listed in the first section, it has three very clear debts to sources nearer home: To Itten's original *Vorkurs,* to Klee and Kandinsky, and to Malevitch. The debt to Itten is clear and fundamental—the emphasis on learning by doing and on the nature of materials. Moholy's original contribution here is in changing over from the idea of an intuitive grasp of the "inner nature" of materials to an objective, physical assessment of their ascertainable properties of texture, strength, flexibility, transparency, workability, etc.

The debt to Klee and Kandinsky lies in the *von . . . zu* organization of the book. Both of their *Bauhausbücher* had started from a consideration of points, and proceeded from them to lines and thus to planes, at which level Kandinsky leaves off, though Klee goes on to volume and space. In Moholy's nondraughtsmanly view, point and line were simply aspects of planes, which he would call surfaces, but from that level onward he proceeds in step with Klee, albeit handling ideas in a manner that was utterly different in every way from that of the *Pädagogisches Skizzenbuch.* Malevitch is his predecessor in visual erudition, in close critical analyses of Cubist paintings, and in emphasis on such things as the views down from, and up to, airplanes.

The first point in which Moholy transcends all his predecessors is in his phenomenal command of the nonartistic visual experiences of his time. Words cannot convey the impact made on the eye by the original edition of this book, its emphatic typography, its businesslike layout, and the range of its illustrations, from neat diagrams and models of Bauhaus equipment, through reproductions of original works of art, and scientific documentary photographs, to extraordinary agency pictures of such things as dumps of old motor-tires, airships, sporting events, street-scenes, film sets, and a celebrated sequence, illustrating a point about texture, of a cat's fur in negative, an old man's skin and a mouldy apple. Brought up on illustrated magazines, Moholy communicates in this book something of the visual richness of a magazine-culture and brings it to bear upon the problem of visual education. For these images, however striking in their own right or in juxtaposition, are not, so to speak, a *musée imaginaire*,* they support and explain the educational system that is expounded in the three main sections of the book. Section II begins with the tactile qualities of materials, and illustrates the famous tactile-machines that were devised for their investigation at the Bauhaus and then goes on to consider the other aspects of the surfaces of materials that can be physically appreciated and physically manipulated, culminating in the use of surfaces as a screen for the projection of patterns of light. Section III also culminates in the use of light, as the ultimate means of creating sculptural volume, but the road that leads to it is interesting for the way in which it shows his methodical mind at work.

He begins with the "Block-like," a term which includes any unmodeled or unpierced solid of recognizable geometrical form. These recognizable forms are, as might be expected, the Phileban solids, but later in the section he produces an extended list of forms, in order to encompass also non-Phileban solids encountered in science and technology.

> Until a short time ago, geometrical elements, such as the sphere, cone, cylinder, cube, prism and pyramid, were taken as the foundation of sculpture. But biotechnical elements have now been added. . . .
>
> These biotechnical elements formerly entered more particularly into technology, where the functional approach called for maximum economy. Raoul Francé has distinguished seven biotechnical elements: crystal, sphere, cone, plate, strip, rod and spiral (screw); he says that these are the basic technical elements of the whole world. They suffice for all its processes and are sufficient to bring them to their optimum condition.†

However, these extensions to the repertoire of regular forms occur somewhat later in the argument, after he has proceeded from pure blocks to modeled blocks and thence to pierced blocks, from standing sculpture to balanced and kinetic sculpture or mobiles, and just before he tackles the problem of the creation of virtual volumes by the movement of lights in space (fireworks, illuminated advertising). By this point he is already entangled with the subject of Sec-

* Any more than are the illustrations—sometimes even more bizarre—in Amedée Ozenfant's almost exactly contemporary book *The Foundations of Modern Art*.

† Francé, whose ideas had been discussed earlier in the book, was not, it seems, an authority of standing in the field, but the author of works of popularization on scientific subjects.

tion IV, Space, but before tackling space he sets out, in a neat table, the *Formlehre* that has been covered so far:

A general systematization of the elements (of artistic creation) is based upon the relations of
1. Known forms, such as
    mathematical and geometrical shapes
    biotechnical elements
2. New forms, such as
    free shapes
The production of new forms may be based on
1. Relations of measurement (golden section and other proportions)
   Position (measurable in angles)
   Movement (speed, direction, thrust, intersection, telescoping interlocking, penetration, mutual interpenetration)
2. Differing aspects of material
   Structure
   Texture
   Surface treatment
   Massing
3. Light (color, optical illusions, reflected light, mirroring)
The relationships of forms may become effective as
1. Contrasts
2. Deviations
3. Variations
    shifting and dislocation ⎫
    repetition   ⎪
                              ⎬ and their combinations
    rotation   ⎪
    mirror images   ⎭

With this behind him, he turns to space, which for him is so much the stuff of architecture that the terms are interchangeable. He sees the play of space as the distinguishing characteristic of Modern architecture, so that the possibility of confusion in nomenclature as between large sculpture and small architecture which existed in older cultures when architecture too was only the manipulation of volume, no longer exists. The nature of this space is defined by him in various ways—at the beginning of Section IV he lists forty-four adjectives that have been used to describe aspects of space, and then cites a minimum definition: "Space is the relation between the position of bodies." This scientific definition he will accept only as a point of departure, and from it he approaches his subject on a number of lines. Firstly, as an aspect of functional organization: "The elements necessary to the fulfillment of the function of a building unite in a spatial creation that can become a spatial experience for us. The ordering of space in this case is no more than the most economical union of planning methods and human needs. The current program of life plays an important role in this, but does not entirely determine the type of space created." Visual justification of this concept of functional space is provided by a view up an airshaft, in which the stairs and landings are all pierced to promote better air-flow, and at the same time create quite accidentally the kind of play of space that would attract an Elementarist. Further explanation can be found in the caption to another illustration: "The concept 'façade' is already passing from architecture. No place remains in buildings for that which is not adapted to some function: to the development of the front (balconies, advertising) is added the exploitation of the roofs (garden terraces, landing grounds)." This last view of a building engaged functionally with the surrounding space on every side is clearly Futurist, and there are further descriptions of spatial manipulation which confirm that his attitude is both Elementarist and Futurist in approach. On the Elementarist side, "Out of cosmic space a 'piece of space' is cut by means of a, sometimes complicated-seeming, network of limiting and interpenetrating strips, wires and sheets of glazing, as if space were a divisible compact substance. Thus, modern architecture is founded on a full interpenetration with outer space." And on the Futurist side, "The organization of this space-creation will be accomplished thus: measurably, by the limits of physical bodies, immeasurably by dynamic fields of force, and space-creation will be the confluence of ever-fluid spatial existences." Though the last quotation is a very toned-down version of Boccioni's "field theory," most of the illustrations to this section thunder with Futurist rhetoric, even to the extent of being faked to heighten the effect, as where a flight of five Swedish seaplanes has been obviously collaged on to a view of a multi-level traffic intersection in San Diego, California.

No other document of the period gives so graphic or so encyclopaedic a view of what the architect can do with space, but it is emphasized that he does not work upon space as a private esthetic game: "The experience of space is not a privilege of the gifted few, but a biological function," and this brings in the most interesting aspect of Moholy's view of space: experienced space, and the linked concept of "biological":

We must acknowledge that in every respect, space is a reality of our sensory experience.

Man becomes conscious of space . . . first through the sense of sight.

The experience of the visual relations of bodies may be tested by movement, by changing one's position, and by the sense of touch.

Further possibilities for the experience of space lie in the acoustical and balancing organs.

Much of the importance of this view lies in the way in which it inverts earlier ideas on the subject. Just as he had inverted Itten's idea of the "inner nature" of materials and replaced it by an emphasis on their ascertainable physical properties, so Moholy replaces the idea of space entertained by say, Geoffrey Scott, as something affecting the inner nature of man by a symbolic *Einfühlung,* with the idea of space as something affecting the sense organs of men by direct physical *Erlebnis.* Scott would have taken the part played by the sense organs as a mere means to the greater end of esthetic experience, but for Moholy the mechanics are what matters, and is the esthetic experience itself.

Architecture—the ordering of space—is justified in Moholy's eyes in so far as it furthers the ascertainable biological needs of man, and where the book has a weakness in the eyes of a reader of today is in never coming to grips, in detail, with those needs. At the time at which it was written, they could probably be taken for granted since the subject was in the air, at least in the negative sense of minimum standards of sanitation, daylighting, floor-space, ventilation, etc. and anyone familiar with slums, such as those that were still being cleared at Frankfurt am Main, would know what Moholy had in mind when he quoted the *grausam wahren Spruch* of the low-life illustrator Heinrich Zille: "You can kill a man with a building just as easily as with an axe." Even so, the concept of "The Biological taken as the guide in everything" is clear in general outline, and it leads him to a restatement of a principle that tended to be overlooked in the twenties: "Today it is a question of nothing less than the reconquest of the biological fundamentals. Only then can the maximum use be made of technical advances in physical culture, nutritional science, dwelling design and the organization of work," summed up in the slogan already quoted: "Man, not the product, is the aim." His attitude emerges as a kind of non-Determinist Functionalism, based no longer on the bare logic of structural Rationalism, but upon the study of man as a variable organism. Though he probably accepted ideas like Le Corbusier's *besoins-type*—Giedion's use of the word *Existenzminimum* is another of the same family—his system was built on more liberal foundations than these, and was capable of interpretation and reinterpretation in a wider context than that of the International Style. For this reason, if for no other, it occupies the unexpected position of being at the same time the first book entirely derived from the Modern Movement, and also one of the first to point the way to the next steps forward.

bibliography

I.   Extended works by Moholy-Nagy

(In chronogical order)

Books:

Buch Neuer Künstler (with L. KASSÀK). Vienna: MA, 1922.

Die Bühne im Bauhaus (with OSKAR SCHLEMMER and FARKAS MOLNAR). Munich: A. Langen, 1925. (Facsimile edition: Mainz & Berlin: Florian Kupferberg, 1964. Trans. A. S. WENSINGER as *The Theater of the Bauhaus*. Middletown, Conn.: Wesleyan University Press, 1961.)

Malerei, Fotografie, Film. Munich: A. Langen, 1925. (Facsimile edition with a postscript by OTTO STELZER: Mainz & Berlin: Florian Kupferberg, 1967. Trans. JANET SELIGMAN as *Painting, Photography, Film*. London: Lund Humphreys, 1968. Cambridge: MIT, 1969.)

Von Material zu Architektur. Munich: A. Langen, 1929. (Facsimile edition with a postscript by OTTO STELZER: Mainz & Berlin: Florian Kupferberg, 1968. Trans. DAPHNE M. HOFFMAN as *The New Vision: From Material to Architecture*. New York: Brewer, Warren & Putnam, 1932. 2d ed. published as *The New Vision*. N.Y.: W. W. Norton, 1938. 3d and subsequent editions include "Abstract of an Artist." New York: George Wittenborn, 1946, 1947, 1964).

Vision in Motion. Chicago: Paul Theobald, 1947.

Graphic Portfolios:

6 Konstruktionen. Hanover, 1925.

Photographs:

Moholy-Nagy: 60 Fotos. Ed. FRANZ ROH. Berlin: Klinkhardt & Biermann, 1930.

The Street Market of London. Text by MARY BENEDETTA. London: John Miles, 1936.

Eton Portrait. Text by BERNARD FERGUSSON. London: John Miles, 1937. London: Muller, 1949.

An Oxford University Chest. Text by JOHN BETJEMAN. London: John Miles, 1939.

Films:

Berliner Stilleben (Berlin Still Life), 1926.

Marseille Vieux Port (The Old Port of Marseilles), 1929.

Lichtspiel schwarz-weiss-grau (Light Display: Black, White, Gray), 1930.

Tönendes ABC (Sound ABC), 1932.

Zigeuner (Gypsies), 1932.

Architekturkongress Athen, 1933.

Street Picture, Finland, 1933.

Life of the Lobster, 1935.

The New Architecture at the London Zoo, 1936.

Scenarios:

Dynamik der Großstadt (Dynamic of the Metropolis), originally written 1921–22. Reprinted in text form in ISTVAN NEMESKURTY, *A mozgokeptol a filmmuveszetig.* Budapest: Corvina, 1961. Trans. as *Word and Image.* London: Clematis Press, 1968. Reprinted in illustrated form in *Painting, Photography, Film* (1925; U.S. edition, 1969).

Once a Chicken, Always a Chicken, 1925–30. Published in *Telehor* (Brno, 1936). Reprinted in MYFAWNY EVANS, ed., *The Painter's Object.* London: Gerald Howe, 1937.

II.   Essays by Moholy-Nagy
(In chronological order)

"Aufruf zur elementaren Kunst," with RAOUL HAUSMANN, HANS ARP, *et al. De Stijl,* V/4 (October, 1921).

"Horizont monographie," *MA* (Vienna, 1921).

"Dynamo-Konstruktives Kräftesystem (Manifesto der kinetischen Plastik)," with A. KEMENY. Berlin: Galerie der Sturm, 1922.

"Konstruktivismus und das Proletariat," *MA* (Vienna, 1922).

"Light—A Medium of Plastic Expression," *Broom,* IV (1923). Reprinted in NATHAN LYONS, ed., *Photographers on Photography.* Prentice-Hall, 1966.

"Die Neue Typographie," *Staatliches Bauhaus in Weimar, 1919–23* (Munich, 1923).

"Die Arbeiten der Bauhaus—Werkstätten," *Thüringische Allgemeine Zeitung,* 288 (October 19, 1924).

"Das Bauhaus in Dessau," *Qualität,* 4–5 (May–June, 1925).

"Bauhaus und Typographie," *Anhaltische Rundschau* (September 14, 1925).

"Zeitgemässe Typographie—Ziele, Praxis, Kritik," *Gutenberg Festschrift.* Mainz: Gutenberg Gesellschaft, 1925.

"Fotoplastische Reklame," *Offset,* 7 (1926).

"Zeitgemässe Typographie." *Offset,* 7 (1926).

"Geradlinigkeit des Geistes—Umwege der Technik," *Bauhaus,* 1 (1926). Reprinted in *i 10 International Revue* I/1 (1927).

"Ismus oder Kunst (Isms or Art)," *Vivos Voco,* V/8–9 (Leipzig, 1926).

Editorial statement, *Offset-, Buch-, und Werkekunst.* Leipzig: Bauhaus Heft 7, 1926.

"Die Beispiellose Fotografie," *i 10 International Revue,* I/3 (Amsterdam,1927).

"Die Photographie in der Reklame," *Photographische Korrespondenzen,* LXIII/9 (September, 1927).

"Wie soll das Theater der Totalität verwirklicht werden?" *Bauhaus,* 3 (1927).

"Der Sprechende Film," *i 10 International Revue,* I/15 (1928).

"Filmkroniek," *i 10 International Revue,* I/17–18 (1928).

"Fotografie ist Lichtgestaltung," *Bauhaus,* II/1 (1928).

"Filmkroniek," *i 10 International Revue,* I/19 (1929).

"Confession," *The Little Review,* XII/2 (New York, May, 1929).

"Experimentale Fotografie," *Das neue Frankfurt,* III/3 (1929).

"La Photographie, ce qu'elle était, ce qu'elle devra être," *Cahiers d'Art,* IV/1 (Paris, 1929).

"The Future of the Photographic Process," *Transition,* 15 (Paris, February, 1929).

"Fotogramm und Grenzgebiete," *Die Form,* IV (1929).

"Lichtrequisit einer elektrischen Bühne," *Die Form,* V/11–12 (1930).

"An Open Letter," *Sight and Sound,* III/10 (London, 1932).

"Problèmes du nouveau film" (1928–30), *Cahiers d'Art,* VIII/6–7 (1932). Reprinted in English as "Problems of the Modern Film," *New Cinema,* 1 (1934) and *Telehor* (Brno, 1936).

"How Photography Revolutionizes Vision," *The Listener* (London, November 8, 1933). (Reprinted in *Telehor* [Brno, 1936].)

"Offener Brief an die Filmindustrie und an Alle, die Interesse an der Entwicklung des guten Films haben," *Ekran* I/1 (Brno, November 15, 1934).

"A New Instrument of Vision" (1932), *Telehor* (Brno, 1936).

Contribution to the symposium "Photography Today," *Modern Photography: 1935–6.* London: The Studio, 1936.

"From Pigment to Light" (1923–26), *Telehor* (Brno, 1936). Reprinted in NATHAN LYONS, ed., *Photographers on Photography.* Englewood Cliffs, N.J.: Prentice-Hall, 1966.

"Letter to Fra. Kalivoda" (1934), *Telehor* (Brno, 1936).

"Light Architecture," *Industrial Arts,* I/1 (London, Spring, 1936).

"Photography in a Flash," *Industrial Arts,* I/4 (London, Winter, 1936).

"Subject Without Art," *The Studio,* XII (London, November 4, 1936).

"Supplementary Remarks on Sound and Colour Film," *Telehor* (Brno, 1936).

Introduction to KATHERINE DREIER, *1 to 40 Variations.* Springfield, Mass.: 1937.

"Light Painting," in J. L. MARTIN, BEN NICHOLSON, N. GABO, eds., *Circle: International Survey of Constructive Art.* London: Faber & Faber, 1937.

"Modern Art and Architecture," *Journal of the Royal Institute of British Architects,* XXXXIV (London, January 9, 1937).

"Moholy-Nagy, Picture Hunter, Looks at the Paris Exposition," *Architectural Record,* 82 (New York, October, 1937).

"Richtlijnen voor een onbelemmerde kleurenfotografie," *Prisma der Kunsten* (Zeist, 1937).

"The New Bauhaus and Space Relationships," *American Architect and Architecture,* 151 (New York, December, 1937).

"Education and the Bauhaus," *Focus,* 2 (London, Winter, 1938).

"From Wine Jugs to Lighting Fixtures," in W. GROPIUS, H. BAYER, I. GROPIUS, eds. *Bauhaus 1919–1928.* New York: Museum of Modern Art, 1938. (Rev. ed., Boston: Branford, 1959.)

"New Approach to Fundamentals of Design," *More Business,* III/11 (Chicago, November, 1938).

"Why Bauhaus Education," *Shelter,* 3 (New York, March, 1938).

"Painting with Light—A New Medium of Expression," *The Penrose Annual,* 41 (London, 1939).

"The New Bauhaus: American School of Design, Chicago," *Design* (Columbus, Ohio, March, 1939).

"Light: A New Medium of Expression," *Architectural Forum,* 70 (Chicago, May, 1939).

"Make a Light Modulator," *Minicam,* III/7 (March, 1940).

"About the Elements of Motion Picture," *Design,* 42 (October, 1940).

"Objectives of a Designer Education," *Conference on the Expansion of Industrial Communities with Regard to Housing and City Planning.* Ann Arbor: University of Michigan College of Architecture and Design, 1940.

"Photography," in *A Pageant of Photography* (San Francisco, 1940).

"Design in Modern Theory and Practice," *California Arts and Architecture,* LVIII/21 (February, 1941).

"New Trends in Design," *Task,* 1 (New York, Summer, 1941). (Reprinted as "Design Potentialities' in *Plastics Progress* [Chicago, April, 1943].)

"Education in Various Arts and Media for the Designer," *Art in American Life and Education* (symposium). In National Society for the Study of Education. The Fortieth Yearbook. Bloomington, Ill.: Public School Publishing Co., 1941.

"Space-Time and the Photographer," *American Annual of Photography, 1943,* LVII (Boston, 1942).

"Better than Before," *The Technology Review,* XXXXIV/1 (Cambridge, Mass., November, 1943).

"New Trends in Design," *Interiors,* 102 (New York, April, 1943).

"Surrealism and the Photographer," *The Complete Photographer,* 52 (1943).

"Design Potentialities," in PAUL ZUCKER, ed., *New Architecture and City Planning: A Symposium.* New York: Philosophical Library, 1944.

"Photography in the Study of Design," *American Annual of Photography, 1945,* LIX (Boston, 1944).

"The Coming World of Photography," *Popular Photography,* XIV/2 (New York, February, 1944).

"On Art and the Photograph," *The Technology Review, XLVII,* 8 (June, 1945).

"In Defense of 'Abstract' Art," *Journal of Aesthetics and Art Criticism,* IV (Cleveland, 1945).

"Space-Time Problems in Art," in *The World of Abstract Art.* New York: American Abstract Artists, 1946.

"Photography," in DAGOBERT D. RUNES and HARRY G. SCHRICKEL, eds., *Encyclopedia of the Arts.* New York: Philosophical Library, 1946.

"Design Education," *The Architectural Review,* 99 (London, January, 1946).

"New Education—Organic Approach," *Art and Industry,* 40 (London, March, 1946).

"Industrial Design," *Parker Pen Shoptalker* (Janesville, Wis., June, 1946).

"Art in Industry," *Arts and Architecture,* LXIV/1 (Los Angeles, September, 1947); and LXIV/2 (October, 1947).

III. Selected Essays Primarily About Moholy-Nagy
(In alphabetical order)

BENSON, E. M. "The Chicago Bauhaus and Moholy-Nagy," *Magazine of Art* (February, 1938).

COOLIDGE, JOHN, ed. *Works of Art by Moholy-Nagy.* Cambridge, Mass: Fogg Art Museum, 1950.

CURJEL, HANS. "Moholy-Nagy und das Theater," *Du,* XXIV (Zürich, November, 1964).

DORNER, ALEXANDER. "In Memoriam Moholy-Nagy," *L. Moholy-Nagy,* Chicago: Art Institute, 1947. Reprinted as "László Moholy-Nagy," *Nueva Vision* (Buenos Aires, 1955).

ERFURTH, HUGO. "Moholy-Nagy," *Qualität. Zeitschrift für Ware und Werbung,* IX/1–2 (Dessau, 1931).

"From the Bauhaus: L. Moholy-Nagy," *Camera,* XLVI (April, 1967).

"Frontiers—The New Bauhaus," *Manas,* XXII/37 (Los Angeles, September 10, 1969).

FRY, E. MAXWELL. Introductory essay to *Moholy-Nagy.* London: New London Gallery, 1961.

GIEDION, SIGFRIED. "Foreword," *Telehor* (Brno, 1936). Reprinted as the introduction to *L. Moholy-Nagy.* London: New London Gallery, 1937.

————. "Laszlo Moholy-Nagy," *Metron,* 13 (Rome, 1946).

————. "Notes on the Life and Work of Laszlo Moholy-Nagy, Painter-Universalist," *Architects' Year Book,* 2 (London, 1949).

————. "The Work of László Moholy-Nagy," New York: Kleemann Galleries, 1957.

GROPIUS, WALTER. "László Moholy-Nagy, 1895–1946," *Collection of the Société Anonyme.* New Haven, Conn.: Yale University Art Gallery, 1950.

HESS, THOMAS B. "Memorial to a Many-Sided Non-Objectivist," *Art News,* XLVI (June, 1947).

"Hungarian Professor Directs New School in Chicago," *Newsweek* (September 20, 1937).

KALIVODA, FR. "Postscript," *Telehor* (Brno, 1936).

KÁLLAI, ERNST. "Ladislaus Moholy-Nagy," *Jahrbuch der Jungen Kunst,* (Leipzig, 1924).

KAUFMANN, EDGAR, JR. "Moholy," *Arts and Architecture,* LXIV (Los Angeles, March, 1947).

KEPES, GYORGY. "László Moholy-Nagy: The Bauhaus Tradition," *Print,* XXIII/1 (New York, January-February, 1969).

KOSTELANETZ, RICHARD. "Moholy-Nagy," *Artscanada,* 136–7 (Toronto, October, 1969).

————. "The Risk and Necessity of Artistic Adventurism," *Salmagundi,* 10–11 (Saratoga Springs, N.Y., Fall, 1969–Winter, 1970).

KOVACS, ISTVAN. "Totality through Light—The Work of László Moholy-Nagy," *Form,* 6 (Cambridge, England, December, 1967).

KUH, KATHERINE. "Moholy-Nagy in Chicago," *L. Moholy-Nagy.* Chicago: The Art Institute of Chicago, 1947.

MARTIN, J. L. "László Moholy-Nagy and the Chicago Institute of Design," *The Architectural Review,* CI (London, June, 1947).

MATYAS, PETER, ed. *Horizont 2.* Vienna: MA, 1921.

MELVILLE, ROBERT. "Paintings at the New London Gallery," *The Architectural Review,* CXXX (London, August, 1961).

"Message in a Bottle," *Time* (February 18, 1946).

"Moholy-Nagy: Experimentalist," *Art and Industry,* 22 (London, March, 1937).

MOHOLY-NAGY, SIBYL. "Documented Seeing," *Art and Photography* (Chicago, 1949).

———. "László Moholy-Nagy," *Art d'Aujourd'hui,* II/8 (Paris, October, 1951).

———. "The Making of a Constructivist," *Copy,* I/1 (San Francisco, January, 1950).

———. *Moholy-Nagy: Experiment in Totality.* New York: Harper's, 1950. 2d ed.; Cambridge, Mass., MIT, 1969.

———. "Moholy-Nagy und die Idee des Konstruktivismus," *Die Kunst und Das Schöne Heim,* LV/9 (Munich, June, 1959).

NEWHALL, BEAUMONT. "The Photography of Moholy-Nagy," *The Kenyon Review,* III/4 (Gambier, Ohio, Summer, 1941).

———. Review of *Vision in Motion, Photonotes* (March, 1948).

———, ed. *Moholy-Nagy: Photographs, Photograms, Photomontages.* New York: Da Capo, forthcoming.

PARKER, KENNETH. "L. Moholy-Nagy Dies," *Parker Pen Shoptalker* (Janesville, Wis., December, 1946).

PORTER, FAIRFIELD. "Reviews and Previews," *Art News,* LVI (October, 1957).

RANANICCHI, PIERO. "Le esperienze di Laszlo Moholy-Nagy," *Siprauno,* I (January-February, 1964).

READ, HERBERT. "A Great Teacher," *The Architectural Review,* CIII (London, 1947).

———. "A New Humanism," *The Architectural Review,* LXXVIII (London, October, 1935).

REBAY, HILLA. "Moholy-Nagy the Painter and Friend," *In Memoriam Laszlo Moholy-Nagy.* New York: Solomon R. Guggenheim Foundation, 1947.

REICHARDT, JASIA. "Moholy-Nagy and Light Art as an Art of the Future," *Studio International,* CLXXIV/894 (London, November, 1967).

———. "Moholy-Nagy at New London Gallery," *Apollo,* LXXIV (June, 1961).

"Reunion in Chicago," *Minicam* (New York, January, 1945).

ROH, FRANZ. Introduction to *60 Fotos*. Berlin: Klinkhardt & Bierman, 1930.

ROSENTHAL, GEORGE S. "Moholy-Nagy," *Minicam* (February, 1947).

ROTERS, EBERHARD. "Laszlo Moholy-Nagy," *Painters of the Bauhaus*. New York: Praeger, 1969.

SOUCEK, LUDVIK. "L. Moholy-Nagy," *Bratislava* (1965).

VERDONE, MARIO. "Laszlo Moholy-Nagy nella 'Bauhaus,' " *Bianco e Nero,* 11 (1962).

WEITEMEIER, HANNAH. "Vision in Motion," *Moholy-Nagy*. Eindhoven: Stedelijk van Abbemuseum, 1967.

WINKLER, HUGO. "Appreciation," *Qualität,* V/1–2 (Berlin, 1931).

WOODS, S. JOHN. "Moholy-Nagy," *Axis* I/6 (London, Summer, 1936).

YODER, R. N. "Are You Contemporary?" *Saturday Evening Post* (New York, July 3, 1943).

IV. Selected General Works Incorporating Discussions of Moholy-Nagy

(In alphabetical order)

BANHAM, REYNER. *Theory and Design in the First Machine Age*. London: Architectural Press, 1960. New York: Praeger, 1960. 2d ed.; New York: Praeger, 1967.

BLESH, RUDI, and HARRIET JANIS. *Collage*. Rev. ed.; Philadelphia: Chilton, 1968.

BREDENDIECK, HIN. "The Legacy of the Bauhaus," *Art Journal,* XXII/1 (New York, Fall, 1962).

BRION, MARCEL. *Art Abstrait*. Paris: A. Michel, 1956.

BURNHAM, JACK. *Beyond Modern Sculpture*. New York: Braziller, 1968.

COKE, VAN DEREN. *The Painter and the Photographer*. Albuquerque: University of New Mexico Press, 1964. 2d ed.; 1970.

EGBERT, DONALD DREW. *Socialism and American Art*. Rev. ed.; Princeton: Princeton University Press, 1967.

FENTON, TERRY. "Two Contributions to the Art and Science Muddle: I. Constructivism and Its Confusions," *Artforum,* VII/5 (January, 1969).

FERMI, LAURA. *Illustrious Immigrants*. Chicago: University of Chicago, 1968.

FROST, ROSAMUND. "Form and Function: A U.S. Bauhaus," *Art News,* XLIV (New York, August, 1945).

FUERST, WALTER RENÉ, and SAMUEL J. HUME. *Twentieth-Century Stage Decoration*. New York: Dover, 1967.

GERNSHEIM, HELMUT and ALISON. *A Concise History of Photography*. New York: Grosset & Dunlap, 1965.

GIEDION, SIGFRIED. *Walter Gropius: Work and Teamwork*. New York: Reinhold, 1954.

GIEDION-WELCKER, CAROLA. *Contemporary Sculpture: An Evolution in Volume and Space*. 3d ed.; New York: Wittenborn, 1960.

GROHMANN, WILL. "Art into Architecture: The Bauhaus Ethos," *Apollo*, LXXVI (London, March, 1962).

————. "L'art non-figuratif en Allemagne," *L'Amour de l'Art* (Paris, 1934).

————. "Introduction to *Painters of the Bauhaus*. London: Marlborough Fine Arts Gallery, 1962.

GROPIUS, WALTER. *Idee und Aufbau des Staatlichen Bauhauses Weimar*. Munich: A. Langen, 1923.

————. *The New Architecture and ·the Bauhaus*. Cambridge, Mass.: MIT, 1965.

———— *et al.*, eds. *Bauhaus 1919–1928*. New York: Museum of Modern Art, 1938. (Reprint; Boston: Branford, 1959).

GROTE, LUDWIG. "Les Peintres du 'Bauhaus,' " *Art d'Aujourdhui*, IV/4–5 (Paris, August, 1953).

HAFTMANN, WERNER. *Malerei im 20. Jahrhundert*. Munich: Prestel, 1954. Trans. as *Painting in the Twentieth Century*. New York: Praeger, 1965.

HILL, ANTHONY. "Constructivism—The European Phenomenon," *Studio International*, CLVII (London, April, 1966).

HITCHCOCK, HENRY-RUSSELL. *Painting Toward Architecture*. New York: Duell, Sloan & Pearce, 1948.

HULTÉN, K. G. PONTUS. *The Machine as Seen at the End of the Mechanical Age*. New York: Museum of Modern Art, 1968.

IRWIN, DAVID. "Motion and the Sorcerer's Apprentice," *Apollo*, LXXXIV (London, July, 1966).

JORDY, WILLIAM H. "The Aftermath of the Bauhaus in America," *Perspectives in American History*, II (Cambridge, Mass., 1968).

KÁLLAI, ERNST. *Neue Malerei in Ungarn*. Leipzig, 1925.

KIRBY, MICHAEL. *Happenings*. New York: E. P. Dutton, 1965.

KOSTELANETZ, RICHARD. *Metamorphosis in the Arts*. New York: Abrams, 1971.

————. *The Theatre of Mixed Means*. New York: Dial, 1968.

————, ed. *Social Speculations*. New York: Morrow, 1971.

KUHN, CHARLES C. "America and the Bauhaus," *American-German Review* (Philadelphia, December, 1948).

KULTERMANN, UDO. *The New Painting*. New York: Praeger, 1969.
————. *The New Sculpture*. New York: Praeger, 1968.

LISSITZKY-KÜPPERS, SOPHIE. *El Lissitzky: Life, Letters, Texts*. Greenwich, Conn.: New York Graphic, 1968.

MOHOLY-NAGY, SIBYL. "Constructivism from Malevitch to Moholy-Nagy," *Arts and Architecture,* LXXXIII/5 (Los Angeles, June, 1966).

MYERS, BERNARD. "The Bauhaus—Graphic Design," *Studio International,* CLXXVI (London, September, 1968).

NAYLOR, GILLIAN. *The Bauhaus*. London: Studio Vista, 1968. New York: Dutton, 1968.

NEMESKURTY, ISTVAN. *A mozgokeptol a filmmuveszetig*. Budapest: Corvina, 1961. Trans. as *Word and Image*. London: Clematis Press, 1968.

NEWHALL, BEAUMONT. *A History of Photography*. Rev. ed.; New York: Museum of Modern Art, 1964.

ORSO, MARTINO DELL. "A la recherche d'une synthèse de la forme et du mouvement," *Age Nouveau,* IX (1955).

PEARSON, RALPH M. "The School of Design: The American Bauhaus," In his *The New Art Education*. New York: Harper, 1941.

PIENE, NAN R. "Light Art," *Art in America,* LV/3 (New York, May-June, 1967).

POPPER, FRANK. *Origins and Development of Kinetic Art*. London: Studio Vista, 1968. Greenwich, Conn.: New York Graphic, 1969.

READ, HERBERT. "Abstract Art: A Note for the Uninitiated," *Axis,* 5 (London, Spring, 1936).
————. *A Concise History of Modern Sculpture*. New York: Praeger, 1964.

RICKEY, GEORGE. *Constructivism: Origins and Evolution*. New York: Braziller, 1967.
————. "Kinetic International," *Arts,* XXXV (September, 1961).
————. "The Morphology of Movement: A Study of Kinetic Art," *Art Journal* XXII (New York, Summer, 1963). Reprinted, in revised form, in GYORGY KEPES, ed., *The Nature and Art of Motion*. New York: Braziller, 1965.

RIPELLINO, ANGELO. *Maria. Mayakovskii e il theatro russo d'avantguardia*. Turin: Einaudi, 1959.

SCHEIDIG, WALTHER. *Crafts of the Weimar Bauhaus*. London: Studio Vista, 1967. New York: Reinhold, 1967.

SCHREYER, LOTHAR. *Erinnerungen an Sturm und Bauhaus: Was ist des Menschen Bild?* Munich: Langer-Müller, 1956.

Seuphor, Michel. *L'Art abstrait, ses origines, ses premiers maîtres.* Paris: Maeght, 1949.

———. "Art Construit," *XXe Siècle,* XXIV (Paris, June, 1962).

———. *Dictionnaire de la Peinture Abstraite.* Paris: Fernand Hazan, 1957.

———. *Sculpture of this Century.* London: A. Zwemmer, 1959; New York: Braziller, 1960.

Shand, P. Morton. "New Eyes for Old," *The Architectural Review,* LXXV (London, January, 1934).

Sharp, Willoughby. "Luminism and Kineticism," in Gregory Battcock, ed., *Minimal Art.* New York: Dutton, 1968; London: Studio Vista, 1969.

Spear, Athena Tacha. "Sculptured Light," *Art International,* XI/10 (Lugano, December, 1967).

Staber, Margit. "Bauhaus," *Artscanada,* 122–23 (Toronto, October-November, 1968).

Steinitz, Käte. *Kurt Schwitters.* Berkeley: University of California Press, 1968.

"The New Bauhaus," *Architectural Forum,* LXVII (October, 1937).

Vollmer, Hans (ed.). *Allgemeines Lexikon der Bildenden Künstler des XX. Jahrhunderts.* III. (Leipzig: E. A. Seeman, 1953–61).

Wingler, Hans Maria. *Das Bauhaus 1919–33: Weimar Dessau Berlin und die Nachfolge in Chicago seit 1937.* 2d ed.; Bramsche, Germany: Rasch & Co., & M. Dumont, 1968. Trans. as *The Bauhaus.* Cambridge, Mass.: MIT, 1969.

———. *Graphic Work from the Bauhaus.* London: Lund Humphries, 1969. Greenwich, Conn.: New York Graphic, 1969.

contributors

REYNER BANHAM, Reader in Architecture at University College, London, has been for many years an editor of *The Architectural Review* (London). His books include *Theory and Design in the First Machine Age* (1960) and *The Architecture of the Well-Tempered Environment* (1969).

JACK W. BURNHAM, a sculptor teaching at Northwestern University, has written a monograph on *Hans Haacke* (1968) and a brilliant critical study, *Beyond Modern Sculpture* (1968).

HANS CURJEL was manager of the Krolloper State Opera House in Berlin in the 1920's. He has since written numerous essays on avant-garde subjects, mostly for German and Swiss-German magazines.

SIGFRIED GIEDION, perhaps the most esteemed architectural historian of his time, wrote many books on ancient and contemporary art, the most famous of which is perhaps *Space, Time and Architecture* (1941). His friendship with Moholy-Nagy dated back to the mid-1920's.

ERNST KÁLLAI was an Hungarian artist closely associated with Moholy-Nagy and the MA group in Budapest, Vienna, and Berlin in the early 1920's.

ALFRED KEMENY, a fellow Hungarian, was the first editor of the journal *MA;* but his friendship with Moholy later turned to enmity.

SIBYL MOHOLY-NAGY, Moholy's widow, is an eminent architectural critic and historian who has recently been teaching at Pratt Institute and Columbia University. Her books include a history of urban environments entitled *Matrix of Man* (1968), *Native Genius in Anonymous Architecture* (1957), and *Moholy-Nagy: Experiment in Totality* (1950; 2d ed., 1969). Under her maiden name, S. D. Peech, she also wrote the novel *Children's Children* (1942).

PIET MONDRIAN was one of the great practitioners and theorists of modern art.

BEAUMONT NEWHALL, director of the George Eastman House in Rochester, has written many books and essays on photography, including *The History of Photography* (1964). He is currently completing a book of Moholy-Nagy's photographs, photograms, and photomontages.

KENNETH PARKER has been both president and board chairman of the Parker Pen Co., Janesville, Wisconsin.

HERBERT READ, the late English polymath, wrote many books about modern art, esthetics, and artistic education, in addition to fiction, poetry, autobiography, and much else. He also sponsored Moholy-Nagy's immigration into England.

FRANZ ROH was a renowned German art critic who was among the early champions of modernism in several artistic media.

index

Numbers in *italics* indicate that the indexed person is quoted on that page. All titles of works listed are by L. Moholy-Nagy unless otherwise noted. A page entry followed by an *n* indicates reference to a footnote on that page.